RECENT BOOKS
BY EDWARD WAGENKNECHT

Nathaniel Hawthorne, Man and Writer
Mark Twain, The Man and his Work
Washington Irving: Moderation Displayed
The Movies in the Age of Innocence
Edgar Allan Poe: The Man Behind the Legend
Chicago
Seven Daughters of the Theater
Harriet Beecher Stowe: The Known and the Unknown
Dickens and the Scandalmongers: Essays in Criticism
The Man Charles Dickens
Henry Wadsworth Longfellow: Portrait on an American Humanist
Merely Players
John Greenleaf Whittier: A Portrait in Paradox
The Personality of Chaucer
As Far as Yesterday
William Dean Howells: The Friendly Eye
The Personality of Milton
James Russell Lowell: Portrait of a Many-Sided Man
The Personality of Shakespeare
Ambassadors for Christ: Seven American Preachers
Ralph Waldo Emerson: Portrait of a Balanced Soul
The Letters of James Branch Cabell (editor)
The Films of D. W. Griffith (with Anthony Slide)
A Pictorial History of New England
Eve and Henry James: Portraits of Women and Girls in his Fiction
Fifty Great American Films, 1912–1920 (with Anthony Slide)

EDWARD WAGENKNECHT

Henry David Thoreau

WHAT MANNER OF MAN?

It is not of so much importance
to inquire of a man what actions he performed
at one and what at another period of his life,
as what manner of man he was at every period.

HDT, 1843

The University of Massachusetts Press
Amherst, 1981

Copyright © 1981 by
The University of Massachusetts Press
All rights reserved
Printed in the United States of America
Library of Congress Number 80–23542
ISBN 0–87023–136–7 (cloth), 0–87023–137–5 (paper)
Library of Congress Cataloging in Publication Data
appear on the last printed page of this book.

FOR LISA KELLEY CARLING

PREFATORY NOTE

THE AUTHOR'S INDEBTEDNESS to the researches of the dean of Thoreau scholars, Walter Harding, is perhaps sufficiently indicated by the free, but I hope not undiscriminating, use that has been made of them in the text. Actually, however, I owe Professor Harding more than his books. He has been the "onlie begetter" of this volume in the sense that he has more than once urged me to add a *Thoreau* to the list of books in which I have already tried to paint the portraits of a number of the Concordian's distinguished contemporaries. Moreover, he has given my manuscript a sympathetic, painstaking critical reading, and, though whatever shortcomings it may possess are mine alone, he must share in whatever virtues the reader may find in it.

I also wish to thank my friends and former pupils, Professors John and Priscilla Gibson Hicks, of the University of Massachusetts, for adding to many past favors by the interest they took in this book and for bringing it to the attention of my publishers.

E. W.

West Newton, Massachusetts

June 1, 1980

CONTENTS

HENRY DAVID THOREAU

END AND BEGINNING

WHEN HENRY DAVID THOREAU died in Concord, Massachusetts, in 1862, in his forty-fifth year, he had published only two books, of which the first—*A Week on the Concord and Merrimack Rivers* (1849)—had been a complete failure commercially and the second—*Walden; or, Life in the Woods* (1854)—at best a moderate success. Both were out of print. No wonder Emerson declared in his memorial address that "the country knows not yet, or in the least part, how great a son it has lost," nor that George William Curtis should write in *Harper's Magazine* that "the name of Henry Thoreau is known to very few persons beyond those who personally knew him." Hawthorne, to be sure, had included both *Walden* and the *Week* in the very brief list of good American books he sent to Lord Houghton, but Whittier was—for a man of his large charity—surprisingly ungenerous—

> Thoreau's *Walden* is capital reading, but very wicked and heathenish. The practical moral of it seems to be that if a man is willing to sink himself into a woodchuck he can live as cheaply as that quadruped, but after all, for me, I prefer walking on two legs.

—and Oliver Wendell Holmes was to be considerably worse as late as 1885, for though he granted Thoreau "many rare and admirable qualities," he described him as a "unique individual, half college-graduate and half-Algonquin, . . . who carried out a schoolboy whim to its full proportions" and a "nullifier of civilization, who insisted on nibbling his asparagus at the wrong end."

But the nineteenth-century writers who did most to undermine

Thoreau's early reputation were James Russell Lowell and Robert Louis Stevenson.[1] Lowell, who was pretty sour on transcendentalism in general (his brilliant take-off on its foibles at the beginning of his essay on Thoreau is by far the best thing in it), complained that Thoreau glorified the limitations of his own temperament and insisted upon our accepting all his own defects and weaknesses as virtues and powers. "He condemns a world, the hollowness of whose satisfactions he had never had the means of testing." Lowell considered "a great deal of the modern sentimentalism about Nature . . . a mark of disease" and thought it "a very shallow view that affirms trees and rocks to be healthy, and cannot see that men in communities are just as true to the laws of their organization and destiny." Unfortunately for the argument, Thoreau never entered any such claim.

Stevenson complained that Thoreau "had no waste lands nor kitchen-midden in his nature, but was all improved and sharpened to a point." Moreover, his point of view was "high and dry." He may have been a demi-god but he was not "one of us, for he was not touched with a feeling of our infirmities." He lacked pity, and he missed the real significance of the Christian religion. Stevenson indeed regarded Thoreau as a "skulker" and would only give him credit for being no ascetic but "an Epicurean of the nobler sort" who had only one great merit—that he succeeded in being happy.

Both *Walden* and the *Week* were back in print within a few weeks of Thoreau's death, and five posthumous volumes—*Excursions* (1863), *The Maine Woods* (1864), *Cape Cod* (1865), *Letters to Various Persons* (1865) and *A Yankee in Canada, with Anti-Slavery and Reform Papers* (1866)—followed hard upon. The "second edition" of the *Week*, however, was merely the remainder of the first edition, reissued by Ticknor and Fields with a new binding and title page. Between 1881 and 1892 H. G. O. Blake's four volumes of selections from the journal, named after the seasons, contributed much to Thoreau's reputation as a nature writer, at the same time unfortunately directing attention away from his other aspects. Thomas Wentworth Higginson tried to get the journal published in its entirety, but even Judge Hoar could not understand why he thought anybody would wish to read it. It remained in manuscript until 1906, when Houghton Mifflin brought out the bulk of it as the last fourteen volumes of the twenty-volume Manuscript and Walden editions of Thoreau's collected works and were astonished by the response. As recently as 1900, in his *Literary Friends and Acquaintance*, William Dean Howells had spoken of Thoreau as an author who had fallen into abeyance, then added, "I do not believe that Tolstoy himself has more clearly shown the hollowness, the hopelessness, the unworthiness of the life of the world," and the very next year, in a letter to Edward Garnett, published in *The North American Review*, the great Russian named Thoreau as one of "a bright constellation" of American writers, "who, I think, specially influenced me" and asked the American people why they did not pay more attention to "these voices" and less to those "of financial and industrial millionaires or successful generals."

How much direct influence Thoreau had upon the British labor movement in the 1890s has been disputed, but there can be no question that Robert Blatchford, Edward Carpenter, Henry S. Salt, and W. H. Hudson were all interested in him. Blatchford, whose *Merrie England* sold more than two million copies, slept with *Walden* under his pillow, and local units of the Labor Party were called Walden Clubs. Near the end of the century too Frederick Van Eeden used the name for the socialist colony he established near Amsterdam, in the same country where, many years later, Thoreau's name was to be invoked in the resistance to Hitler. As for Gandhi's work, first in South Africa and then in India, while it would be gross journalistic exaggeration to call Thoreau the man who toppled the British Empire, it may very well be true that he exercised, through Gandhi, a greater single influence than any other American writer has ever brought to bear upon world affairs. Gandhi's Satyagraha, which had its ultimate roots in earlier Hindu thinking, began on September 11, 1906, and Gandhi did not read "Civil Disobedience" until 1907, when he published it, first in his newspaper and later as a pamphlet. Thereafter, however, there can be no question of its importance for him. He himself said, "There is no doubt that Thoreau's ideas greatly influenced my movement in India," and he is reported to have told Roger Baldwin that the piece contained the essence of his political philosophy. It is interesting that when President Carter visited Prime Minister Desai in January 1978 he presented a set of Thoreau's *Journal* to the Indian leader who, the year before, had called Thoreau "perhaps even greater than Gandhi."

In his own country, Thoreau did not "make" the Hall of Fame until 1960; when he lost out to Stephen Foster in 1940, the *New York Times* called it "a victory for Sewanee River over Walden Pond," and even in 1960 there was sufficient nonsense uttered to cause Brooks Atkinson to suggest that Thoreau's nonconforming ghost must be doing its best to resist entry. Nevertheless, *Walden* now exists in nearly two hundred different editions and is reprinted more often than any other pre-Civil War American book, and when Walter Harding visited Tokyo, he found more editions of it on sale there than in New York.

According to Philip Van Doren Stern, the working manuscript of *Walden* in the Huntington Library is valued at more than $100,000, while that of the "lost" journal of 1840–41, which was sold for $160 in 1924, went to the Morgan Library for $12,700 in 1958. Harding's account of the founding of the Thoreau Society in 1940[2] is an amazing one, and this is only one chapter in the modern Thoreau success story. In 1945 more than a thousand people came to Cooper Union in wartime to observe the centenary of the Walden Pond experiment, and there were many exhibitions elsewhere; later, in 1962, the centenary of Thoreau's death was even more widely observed. Reference to the *Thoreau Society Bulletin*, which notes such things, will also show a rather astonishing number of references to Thoreau in contemporary news commentary and even in cartoons and advertising. Though one would not expect Thoreau to be a hero in Soviet Russia, he has not been entirely without admirers even there, and if a Czech edition of *Walden* was once impounded by the Soviets, perhaps we should remember that in the United States Emma Goldman, Upton Sinclair, and Norman Thomas were all arrested for reading from "Civil Disobedience" on the public platform, that in New York in 1936 an issue of an Italian newspaper was confiscated because it reprinted this same essay, and that Senator Joseph McCarthy later succeeded in getting it removed from USO libraries.

Michael Meyer, whose excellent book, *Several More Lives to Live*, deals with Thoreau's political reputation in America, gives Vernon Louis Parrington a pioneer's credit for calling the attention of Americans, in his *Main Currents in American Thought* (first volume published in 1927), to the fact that Thoreau was a social and political thinker and not merely a nature writer. This enormously influential work inaugurated a period during which not Thoreau alone but

American writers in general were to be interpreted primarily in terms of their sociological interests and outlook (in Parrington's vocabulary, *belles-lettristic* was a dirty word), and though Parrington was himself a Jeffersonian Democrat, such Marxian critics as V. F. Calverton, Granville Hicks, and Bernard Smith[3] found this line of approach completely congenial, and applied and interpreted it in their own way. The tide did not begin to turn until F. O. Matthiessen published *American Renaissance* in 1941. Though Matthiessen was himself a socialist, he never forgot that literature is an art as well as an instrument of persuasion, and after World War II Thoreau's critics began to find themselves increasingly preoccupied with form, symbolism, and other aesthetic considerations.

Without, however, relinquishing concern for social issues. In his First Inaugural Address in 1933 Franklin D. Roosevelt declared that "we have nothing to fear but fear itself." Whether this was a conscious or unconscious echo of Thoreau's "nothing is so much to be feared as fear" we cannot be sure, but we do know that it was not in the original draft, and Mrs. Roosevelt testified that her husband had been given a volume of Thoreau which contained the relevant quotation shortly before the inauguration and "that it was in his suite at the hotel" while the speech was being polished.[4] But it was not until the protest movements of the fifties and sixties got under way that either Thoreauvians or anti-Thoreauvians began to be fully aware of the dynamite packed into Thoreau's political writings, the result being of course that the cowboys mounted their trusty steeds and rode off furiously in every direction. In 1952 the *Christian Science Monitor* took high rank among the unconscious humorists by declaring that if Thoreau were alive, he would have no hesitation about paying taxes to support the war in Korea. In the late sixties, both Edwin N. Griswold (United States Solicitor General) and Eugene V. Rostow (Undersecretary of State) found Thoreau dangerous enough to be worth attacking, but in 1967 the post office issued a Thoreau stamp by Leonard Baskin so ugly that it pleased only the "hippies" who thought it made Thoreau look like one of themselves, though this did not keep Senator Byrd from protesting against honoring a man "who had a thoroughly anti-social personality."

The most important manifestation or application of that personality in the United States was of course that made by Martin Luther

King, Jr., who testified that it was when he read "Civil Disobedience" in college that he became fascinated with the idea of refusing
to cooperate with a wicked system. But if King's was the most spec-
tacular exemplification of Thoreau's civil disobedience principles, it
was far from being the only one. A. J. Muste and others, refusing to
pay taxes to support war, have sent copies of "Civil Disobedience"
to the IRS. Nuclear plants have been picketed in Thoreau's name,
and in Groton, Connecticut, a rowboat used in a demonstration
against nuclear submarines was called the *Henry David Thoreau*. In
1959 too the Reverend Willard Uphaus took a copy of the essay with
him when he went to jail for a year after having refused to give the
attorney general of New Hampshire the names of those who had
attended summer conferences at his World Fellowship Center.[5]

Among the many well-known persons who have been named as
admirers of Thoreau or who have acknowledged his influence in
their lives or works are Bernard Baruch, Sir Thomas Beecham,
Martin Buber, John Buchan, Bette Davis, Robert Frost, André Gide,
Jean Giono, Harry Golden, Ernest Hemingway, David Starr Jordan,
Gypsy Rose Lee, Lin Yutang, Benton MacKaye, Henry Miller, Lewis
Mumford, Margaret Naumberg, Gene Stratton Porter, J. D. Salin-
ger, Robert W. Service, Upton Sinclair, H. M. Tomlinson, Gene
Tunney, E. B. White, and N. C. and Andrew Wyeth, a list which
certainly shows the potentiality of his appeal to a wide variety of
human beings, even if it does nothing else. "Over the world," says
Carl Bode, "there are Thoreau addicts who read a few pages in the
Journal each night before retiring." The most important piece of art
inspired by him is undoubtedly Charles Ives' *Concord Sonata*. Leon
Edel has suggested that he may also have influenced *Finnegans
Wake*. Proust found *Walden* coming "from the depths of our intimate
experience," and Sinclair Lewis, who claimed Thoreau as a major
influence upon his own writing, called him the only man he would
trust with absolute power. In 1974 the English actor Eric Porter came
to Concord to make a Thoreau film, *One World at a Time*, for British
television. The photographer Ivan Massar read *Walden* while serv-
ing in the Navy at the age of eighteen. "The first act of my life that I
can attribute to Thoreau's influence," he writes, "is my going over
the hill. . . . Having been 'decorated' with six battle stars, I became a
pacifist. It was the first time I had dared to question anything that
was universally considered right."[6]

Henry David Thoreau, all but completely ignored during his lifetime, today ranks with Melville, James, and Mark Twain as the most completely "in" of the "classical" American writers, and surely no one of the others has exercised a comparable influence upon the conduct of his readers. If there ever was a writer who might have been justified in appropriating the motto of Mary Queen of Scots, *En ma fin est mon commencement,* it must be he. Surely it is natural to wonder what manner of man could thus function. That is the question which this book raises and tries to answer.

DAVID HENRY (later, by his own fiat, Henry David) Thoreau was born in Concord, Massachusetts, on July 12, 1817, and died there, of tuberculosis, on May 6, 1862. He was the only one of the important Concord writers who was born in the town. After his birth, the family moved to Chelmsford, to Boston, and then back to Concord, where they occupied a number of houses, including one that is now part of the Concord Inn. Unlike most of his neighbors, Thoreau was not a "WASP"; neither did his family belong to the local aristocracy, if there was one. His ancestry was French Huguenot on the father's side, Scottish on the mother's. The slight accent credited to him by some hearers might have come from either side, but, though Barrett Wendell assigned his individualism to Rousseau and his French heritage, New England Puritanism is a far more likely source closer home. The Thoreaus anglicized the pronunciation of their name, stressing the first syllable; Bronson Alcott in his journals spells it Thorow, Thoro, and Thorough.[1]

The first Thoreau in this country came to New Jersey after the revocation of the Edict of Nantes in 1685. Henry's grandfather, Jean, a privateer, was brought to Boston after having been shipwrecked in 1773. Briefly involved in the Revolution, he kept a shop on Long Wharf, came to Concord in 1800, and died there the next year, leaving an estate of some $37,000, much of which had disappeared by the time his widow, Jane Burns, who was of Scottish and Boston Quaker extraction, followed him in 1814. The maternal grandfather,

Asa Dunbar, born in Massachusetts in 1745, was first a clergyman, then a lawyer, and married the daughter of a wealthy Tory family; during the Revolution she helped her Tory brothers to escape from a Concord jail to Canada; after her husband's death, she first kept a tavern, then married Captain Jonas Minott and settled on a farm near Concord.

Henry's father, John Thoreau, was a quiet man, fond of books and music, who participated in a number of not very successful business ventures, until finally he became one of the pioneer American makers of lead pencils. We hear more about the mother, Cynthia Dunbar, whom some people heartily disliked, but, aside from her offending Mary Moody Emerson by wearing yellow ribbons on her hat, the only thing we really know against her is that she is supposed to have talked too much, and sometimes too tartly. She was efficient, conscientious, hospitable, socially sensitive, and capable of tenderness; it was she who helped persuade Emerson to write his stinging letter to President Van Buren, protesting the removal of the Cherokee Indians, and Isaac Hecker regarded her as a second mother. A committed abolitionist, she loved nature and was a great reader; she set a good table, and even when she had little to work with, served it with style. Mabel Loomis Todd has recorded that she would sometimes tell "stories of startling, terrifying or pathetic import," which sent Mabel to bed all a-tremble, to hide her head under the covers, and she adds that Cynthia's sister-in-law Jane was "a saintly character with a placid and lovely nature" and Jane's sister, Maria "a sharp and brilliant soul," who was "little, brisk, and energetic," with great confidence in her own opinions about everything. Henry had one brother, John, and two sisters—Helen, who died young, and Sophia, who survived him and became the devoted guardian of his fame.

Henry attended Miss Phoebe Wheeler's infant school, then public grammar school, where he learned by rote, largely from the Bible and English classics. At eleven he was enrolled in the Concord Academy, where he declaimed and debated, and, as he saw it, was "made unfit" for Harvard, which he entered in 1833. He was pretty scornful toward Harvard also, declaring that it taught all the branches of learning but none of the roots, and later praising John Brown because "he was not fed on the pap that is there furnished."

The burden of the Harvard curriculum at this time was carried by Latin, Greek, mathematics, and rhetoric, and there was heavy emphasis upon memory work and recitation, with a minute, intricate, and picayunish system of marking against which Thoreau and other students vainly protested. Henry took only one science course in college, but during his senior year he attended lectures on mineralogy, anatomy, and natural history. Edward Channing gave him good training in writing, and the tendency now is to regard the emphasis which some of Thoreau's earlier interpreters placed upon Channing's formalism as somewhat overdone. Like many other students, Henry dropped out for several months during his junior year to teach school in Canton; during this period he was associated with Orestes A. Brownson, and this contact is regarded by some scholars as educationally important. Though there is some evidence that the college authorities regarded Thoreau as rather overinclined to go his own way, we now know that he lived less aloof from his classmates than was formerly believed. We do not know whether he heard Emerson's oration on "The American Scholar," which was delivered the year of his graduation (1837), but he certainly did discover that writer's *Nature,* one of the major influences upon his work.[2]

After his graduation Thoreau taught very briefly at the town school in Concord, but walked out when he learned that he was required to flog his pupils. In 1838 he opened his own school in Concord, where Louisa May, Anna, and Beth Alcott were among those enrolled. This continued until 1841, when John Thoreau, now joined with him, became ill; after this Henry sent out numerous feelers toward securing a school elsewhere, but nothing came of it. In 1843 he tutored in the family of Emerson's brother William on Staten Island, but when, in 1856, Daniel Ricketson broached the subject of teaching elsewhere, he rejected it as a proposal that "would sap the very foundation of me." He was engaged to Concord and his way of life there, he wrote, by ten thousand ties which it would be suicidal to sever.

To Thoreau's way of thinking, "only the earnest and *free* man" can be said to be truly educated. He believed in a classical education, but he saw learning as "the bringing out, or development, of that which is in a man, by contact with the Not Me," and he did not believe that any one field should be cultivated to the neglect of others. Education as he conceived it was a governmental and community obligation, and as for teachers, "we should seek to be fellow students with the pupil, and we should learn of, as well as with him, if we would be most helpful to him."[3] At the Thoreau school, John taught English and mathematics, Henry Latin, Greek, science, and "natural philosophy." The brothers were careful to admit only pupils who were seriously interested and to give them a part in the daily routine of school operations. They made use of the project method and gave some attention to the study of mechanical processes. The curriculum also embraced local history, physical education, and the discussion of ideas. The customary ten-minute recess was extended to thirty in order that the rooms might be thoroughly ventilated during the interval. Nature study was important, for Thoreau believed that some of his own best learning had been acquired in the huckleberry patch. Though there was no corporal punishment, the discipline achieved has been called military. Possibly the adjective was ill-chosen (Emerson too said that Thoreau had "somewhat military in his nature"), but one of Henry's nicknames was "Trainer Thoreau," and though he got on well with his pupils, he was clearly less popular than his brother.

Thoreau's real business in the world, as he was well aware, was that of writing, and in addition to the two books he brought out during his lifetime, he published a good deal of material serially, in the transcendentalists' own organ, *The Dial,* and elsewhere. Outside of teaching, which he once rather crabbedly declared that he did not engage in for the benefit of his fellow-men, the only other occupation which came close to the main interests of his life was lecturing, which he began at the Concord Lyceum on April 11, 1838, and continued afterwards, at fairly long intervals, there and elsewhere. His notices, like Emerson's, were good, bad, and mixed. Sanborn thought his lectures less interesting than his conversation: "his presence on the platform was not inspiring." But when he was really roused, as in his address before the Anti-Slavery Convention at Framingham in 1854, he apparently could be very effective, and when he spoke for an hour and a half from Theodore Parker's pulpit in 1859, a Boston paper reported that he had "a fine voice, and a prompt, effective style of oratory that fixes the attention of the hearer." It seems clear that Thoreau could have been much more "successful" as a lecturer if he had not been quite so uncompromising in his attitude toward his audiences. He was sound enough in believing that a lecture depended for its success on a sympathetic interaction between lecturer and audience, but he resented being asked for his lighter lectures, and he would not agree to wear a muzzle unless he should become rabid. A lecturer who was in earnest, he thought, could "speak only to his like, and the adapting of himself to his audience is a mere compliment which he pays them. If you wish to know how I think, you must endeavor to put yourself in my place. If you wish me to speak as if I were you, that is another affair."[4]

These, however, were far from being his only occupations. In 1847, in response to an inquiry from the Harvard alumni, he replied, " I am a Schoolmaster—a Private Tutor, a Surveyor—a Gardener, a Farmer—a Painter, I mean a House-Painter, a Carpenter, a Mason, a Day-Laborer, a Pencil-Maker, a Glass-paper Maker, a Writer, and sometimes a Poetaster." He also tried white-washing, paper-hanging, wood-sawing, and agricultural pursuits, but he enjoyed more being "reporter to a Journal, of no very wide circulation" and "self-appointed inspector of snow storms and rain storms," and in 1848 he wrote Horace Greeley that for five years he had been maintaining himself entirely by manual labor, "not getting a cent from any other quarter or employment." Performing uncongenial work, he again and again compares himself to Apollo in the service of King Admetus, but no man was less the idler that many Concordians considered Henry. "I have never seen or heard of a more industrious resident," wrote Sanborn. "His tasks began before the earliest haymaker or woodchopper went to his work, and were continued after the latest evening seamstress had set her last stitch." But he knew that only that which is done for love is worth doing, and when his father thought he was being drawn away from his studies by his experiments in making maple sugar, which could be bought more cheaply at the store, he replied that this *was* his study and that he felt he had been to the university. It was hard for him to take money from a friend for services rendered, and the only instance of borrowing I have found is his accepting seventy-five dollars from Horace Greeley in 1852, which he paid back in less than a year.

Late in life, Thoreau came to be recognized as an authority on local natural history, and Bronson Alcott, as school superintendent, asked him to compile an atlas of Concord, but he did not live to do this. He did do an increasing amount of surveying and even advertised himself in this capacity.[5] Though he was interested in the commission he received to survey the depths of the Concord River and the dams and bridge abutments of the town, he spoke slightingly of surveying also, and apparently could be boorish on occasion to those who employed him. Yet Emerson thought he enjoyed his work as a surveyor, and he obviously did it well, for those who have checked his data have found nothing to criticize. But the one area in which he really might have made himself a capitalist (which is as startling a theme for a what-might-have-been speculation as Isaac Hecker's attempt to make a Catholic of him) came in connection with the family pencil and graphite business, for Concord and Salem were the pioneering centers in this field, and the Thoreaus got in on the ground floor. But all that need be said about this matter here is that Henry made important discoveries and achievements and took on increased responsibilities after his father's death.[6]

J. Brooks Atkinson wrote of Thoreau that he could "walk, skate, row, chop, build a boat, raise a house, plaster a chimney, repair a fence, and perform countless other manual labors with the pride in workmanship characteristic of the skilled artisan." There have been attempts to disparage his dexterity however. He admits that he was not a good farmer and decided not to plant beans a second year at Walden Pond even before harvesting the first crop. On the other hand, though he says he drove home every nail in his cabin there with a single blow of the hammer, many bent nails were found when the site was excavated, and it is amusing to learn that for years he had trouble keeping his shoestrings tied and then learned how to tie a square knot only by accident.

He seems to have given complete satisfaction to the Emersons when he lived with them as a kind of handyman and man of the house while Emerson was abroad, but Emerson himself, by his own testimony, had "imbecile hands" and was probably not hard to please.[7] Alcott was, if possible, even more inept, and when he and Thoreau attempted to build a summer house for Emerson, Alcott rejected all recourse to systematic planning and interested himself mainly in the addition of "gingerbread"—there had to be nine corner joists to honor the nine muses. Emerson's mother called the result "The Ruin," and it was never used. Hawthorne, however, testifies to Thoreau's skill in managing a boat, and Henry had an important share in building what the Thoreaus later called their "Texas house," perhaps because it was so far from the center of town.

In 1839 (August 31 to September 13) Thoreau made the water trip with his brother John which he described in *A Week on the Concord and Merrimack Rivers*. In November 1840 he proposed marriage to Ellen Sewall, who rejected him. The great sorrow of his life occurred in 1842, when John died, followed by their sister Helen in 1849 and their father ten years later. Between July 4, 1845, and September 6, 1847, Henry made his headquarters in the cabin he built at Walden Pond, and in the summer of 1846 he spent one night in Concord Jail because of his refusal to pay taxes to a government which supported slavery. The *Week* was published in 1849, *Walden* in 1854. In 1857 he met John Brown, whose execution, soon thereafter, inspired some of his most vivid and vitriolic writing. The only other events in his life were the various journeys which are mentioned elsewhere in this volume. He died, peacefully, after a fairly long illness, on May 6, 1862, and was buried in the New Burying Ground, whence, some time before 1874, his body was moved to Sleepy Hollow, where he now rests on Authors' Ridge, along with the other Concord literati.[8]

CHAPTER ONE

Himself

"I am simply what I am, or I begin to be that."
HDT, 1848

THE FULLEST DESCRIPTION we have of Thoreau's appearance comes from his friend Ellery Channing:

> In height, he was about the average [he himself says about five foot, seven inches]; in his build, spare, with limbs that were rather longer than usual, or of which he made a longer use. His face, once seen, could not be forgotten. The features were quite marked: the nose aquiline or very Roman, like one of the portraits of Caesar (more like a beak, as was said); large, overhanging brows over the deepest set blue eyes that could be seen, in certain lights, and in others gray,—eyes expressive of all shades of feeling, but never weak or nearsighted; the forehead not unusually broad or high, full of concentrated energy and purpose; the mouth with prominent lips, pursed up with meaning and thought when silent, and giving out when open a stream of the most varied and unusual and instructive sayings. His hair [which he parted on the left side] was a dark brown, exceedingly abundant, fine and soft. . . . His whole figure had an active earnestness, as if he had no moment to waste. The clenched hand betokened purpose. . . .

Others fill in details and add impressions. Though it has sometimes been reported that he sat or walked with his head bent down, George William Curtis says his posture was so erect that it seemed "impossible that he could ever lounge or slouch"; this was not essentially modified even during his final illness. According to Bronson Alcott, his arms were covered with thick, dark hair, "like a pelt," and there are references to feats of strength and endurance which must have imposed undue strain upon a physique predisposed to tuberculosis. Emerson says, "I have never seen a person with more sloping shoulders, and seldom a narrower chest," yet his son Edward calls Thoreau's type northern, with a suggestion of the seafarer about it, and Storrow Higginson was reminded of "some sturdy mountaineer or hardy lumberman, in whom a rugged life has left only yet sturdier strength, with finer traits awakened by a daily contemplation of stupendous mountains or primeval forests." Moncure D. Conway says that his eyes were "very large and bright, as if caught from the sky," and when the great Chicago preacher, Robert Collyer, met him on his westward journey, at the very end of Thoreau's life, he confronted a presence "which touched you with a feeling of perfect purity, as newly opened roses do. And it was a clear rose-tinted face he turned to you, delicate to look at as the face of a girl, and great gray eyes, the seer's eyes, full of quiet sunshine."

Naturally not all recorded impressions are either so favorable or so high-flown as these. To Hawthorne—himself, by all odds, the handsomest of the New England writers—Thoreau seemed "as ugly as sin, long-nosed, queer-mouthed, and with uncouth and some-what rustic, although courteous manners, corresponding very well to such an exterior. But," he immediately added, "his ugliness is of an honest and agreeable fashion, and becomes him much better than beauty." Later, Mrs. Hawthorne thought he had "risen above all his [earlier] arrogance of manner" and become "as gentle, simple, ruddy, and meek as all geniuses should be," with "great blue eyes" which "put into the shade" the long nose she had formerly believed "must make him uncomely forever." Her daugh-ter Rose seems to have been less impressed however, for she de-scribes Thoreau as flitting in and out of their house "with long, ungainly, Indian-like stride, and his piercing large orbs, staring, as it were in vacancy."

In his college days, Thoreau's classmate John Weiss found him smug and dull. "The lips were not firm; there was almost a look of satisfaction lurking round their corners." Though the eyes were "searching," the curve of his prominent nose "fell forward without firmness" over his upper lip, giving him the appearance of an Egyp-tian sculpture. Isaac Newton Goodhue too remembered him as "striding with duck-like legs across the common toward his weather-beaten home. He had a long body low to the ground. His face was a long oval and it wore an air of solemnity," and William Dean Howells' impression, when he called on him in the course of his own early pilgrimage to New England, is pretty much in harmony with this: "He came into the room a quaint, stump figure of a man, whose effect of long trunk and sharp limbs was heightened by his fashionless trousers being let down too low. He had a noble face, with tossed hair, a distraught eye, and a fine aquilinity of profile, which made me think at once of Don Quixote and of Cervantes, but his nose failed to add that foot to his stature which Lamb says a nose of that shape will always give a man." Even Daniel Ricketson, whose imagination had fondly pictured him, from their correspondence, as "stout and robust," was shocked by "the small and rather inferior-looking man" he confronted at their first meeting.[1] There are reports of people who did not know him mistaking him, upon first encounter, for a pedlar, tinker, deckhand, or tramp, and some even insisted upon relating him to the animal kingdom! Thus F. B. Sanborn, who thought the beard Thoreau grew toward the end of his life an improvement because it concealed his "weakest feature, a receding chin," compared him to "some retired philosophical woodchuck or magnanimous fox," and one woman was reminded of an owl.

He did not attempt to make up for any of his natural deficiencies through the use of clothes. "Honest traveling" he thought about as dirty work as could be done and one for which a man needed a pair of overalls. He went to Canada with "a thin palm-leaf hat without lining, that cost twenty-five cents, and over my coat one of those unspeakably cheap, as well as thin, brown linen sacks of the Oak Hall pattern," and his idea of luggage was a bundle of brown paper or a red bandana. He prided himself on going without overcoat, gloves, or underwear; in 1841 he continued this into February, when he came down with bronchitis. He thought he would as soon black his face as his boots, and his idea of a good hat was an "old, weather-beaten and indented affair" in which he could carry specimens. Above all he hated black clothes, but whether this was because he disliked the color or merely because they were fashionable I am not sure. "An honest, clay-colored" corduroy, such as the Irish laborers then wore, seemed just right to him; apparently it did not occur to him that this too was a conventional costume in its way.

Yet he philosophized about clothes, as he did about everything else, and his ideas were not unreasonable in themselves. He believed that people's clothes should express their individual characters, not merely the current fashion, and that a good tailor must measure more than the width of the shoulders. "I expect a time when, or rather an integrity by which a man will get his coat as honestly and as perfectly fitting as a tree its bark. Now our garments are typical of our conformity to the ways of the world, i.e. of the Devil, and to some extent react on us and poison us like the shirt which Hercules put on." On this basis, he is less out of character than he may seem when he complains of being made to wear handed down or made-over clothing during his childhood. "Our dress should be such as will hang conveniently about us, and fit equally well in good and in bad fortune; such as will approve itself of the right fashion and fabric, whether for the cotillion or the earthquake." Judged by this standard, he is quite correct when he finds that, properly speaking, man has not fully invented clothing yet.

II

Tuberculosis was endemic in the Thoreau family; the grandfather and Helen both died of it, and John had it. Henry seems to have suffered his first attack in 1836, when he withdrew temporarily from college, and it reappeared in 1841, in 1843, when he was miserably ill on Staten Island and described himself as "a diseased bundle of nerves," in 1855, and finally in 1860, when a cold beginning with exposure turned to bronchitis and opened old lesions in his lungs. After the 1855 attack, he seems never to have been really well again; it took him months to "begin to feel some stirrings of life in me," and he later wrote of his "two-year-old invalidity."

As to lesser matters, he was a poor sailor who had to pay "the usual tribute to the sea" even on the short trip to Nantucket, and he much disliked the idea of having his well-being dependent upon the condition of "such cheap pieces of Nature" as his lungs and stomach. When, in 1838, he lost a tooth, he was impressed by the fact that he was now but "a lame and halting piece of manhood," though conscious of no gap in his soul, but when, at thirty-four, he had all the rest of his teeth drawn, he liked his false teeth so well that he wished he had had them from the beginning! "If you have an inclination to travel, take the ether; you go beyond the furthest star."

Certainly there was never anything morbid about his attitude
toward illness. He believed that "the care of the body is the highest
exercise of prudence" and determined to "be liable to no accidents"
and that sickness should not be allowed to extend beyond the body
or touch the spirit within. So far from planning on a short life, he laid
out a scheme of work calculated to occupy him for many years. Nor
had he any use for "four-hour nights" but preferred a "fool's allowance" and told students that sleep might help them more than
study. Yet when the limitations of human strength irked him, he
wondered whether it might not have been better to put the soul into
the body of an antelope rather than a man.[2]

He was not always wise in the risks he took nor the exposure to
which he subjected himself, though probably neither he nor the
other members of his family realized how dangerous to their lungs
was the graphite dust which was permitted to sift through the house
from their pencil-making activities. Once, sleeping outdoors in the
mountains without a blanket, he covered himself with a board,
holding it in place with a stone. Certainly what the human spirit can
do, if not to conquer yet to refuse to be crushed by the weaknesses of
the body, was never better demonstrated than during his final illness when his equanimity was so firm and his spirits so equable that
visitors said they had never seen a man dying so peacefully and
pleasurably.

Certainly he was never in danger of digging his grave with his
teeth. Yet, though he was a fastidious eater, never far from being
repelled by the grosser aspects of feeding, even resenting the gap
breakfast made in the morning and the way supper "supersedes"
the sunset, he was still, in his own way, a connoisseur of food.[3] "I do
believe," he says, "that, if this process were rightly conducted, its
aspects and effects would be wholly changed."

He is often spoken of as a vegetarian. He was never consistently
that, though he did feel very strongly that flesh-eating was filthy
and barbarous ("our offense is rank, it smells to heaven"), and he
believed that it must be the ultimate destiny of the spiritual man to
give up meat. When at Provincetown he was offered a choice between hashed fish and beans, he chose beans, "though they never

were a favorite dish of mine," and the chapter on "Higher Laws" in *Walden* is certainly, though it essays no propaganda, one of the great philosophical and aesthetic considerations of vegetarianism. At Walden Pond his usual diet was rye and Indian meal, potatoes, rice, a very little salt pork, molasses, and salt ("it was fit that I should live on rice mainly, who loved so well the philosophy of India"), but he also tells of how he once killed and ate a woodchuck who was ravaging his beanfield, and when he was working himself up into an acceptance of the wilder aspects of nature, he could even admire a barbaric diet, "as if we lived on the marrow of koodoos devoured raw." In his account of his visit to Canada, where he tried in vain to buy pie or pudding, he says, probably playfully, "I am obliged to keep my savageness in check by a low diet."

Evidently meat was rather played down in the Thoreau kitchen, and coffee and tea too, though he did take strong, sugared tea with him on his tramping expeditions, finding it better than cocoa, coffee, or water. He ate bread, butter, and cheese, and was ecstatic over popcorn, every flake of which was "a perfect winter flower, hinting of anemones and houstonias," though once, in *Walden*, he oddly included both butter and milk among the foods he rejected. He liked watermelons, which contained "the richest wine in a convenient cask," muskmelons, strawberries, cranberries, and blueberries, and thought wild apples "more poetic" not only than pears but than almost any other fruits New Englanders could buy. What he really wanted was the berries people could gather themselves from the fields and eat fresh: " I trust I may not outlive the last of the huckleberries." In "Ktaadn" there is an appetizing description of a not wholly vegetarian Maine table: "There were piping hot wheatencakes, the flour having been brought up the river in batteaux,—no Indian bread, for the upper part of Maine, it will be remembered, is a wheat country,—and ham, eggs, and potatoes, and milk and cheese, the produce of the farm; and, also, shad and salmon, tea sweetened with molasses, and sweet cakes in contradistinction to the hot cakes not sweetened, the one white, the other yellow, to wind up with."

Temperance for Thoreau extended to everything that could be eaten or drunk. "Any excess—to have drunk too much water, even the day before—is fatal to the morning's clarity." The human body, he thought, "was to be treated as a musical instrument, and if any viol was to be made of sound timber," it was this one, "so that when the bow of events is drawn across," it might "vibrate and resound in perfect harmony." Still more amazing, however, is his connoisseur-like tippling of the drinks of nature, including, it would seem, some that not many had tried before him. "Wines of all kinds and qualities, of noblest vintage" seemed to him "bottled up in the skins of countless berries, for the taste of men and animals. To men they seemed offered not so much for food as for sociality, that they may picnic with Nature,—diet drinks, cordials, wines. We pluck and eat in remembrance of Her. It is a sacrament, a communion. . . . Slight and innocent savors, which relate us to Nature, make us her guests and entitle us to her regard and protection. It is a Saturnalia, and we quaff her wines at every turn." So he tapped maples and birches, tried hemlock tea, found yellow birch sap medicinal (black birch was less successful since it tasted swampy or sour), and even experimented with acorns and skunk cabbage. In winter walks he sometimes even stopped to "bruise between my thumb and finger, the dry whorls of the lycepus or water horehound, just rising above the snow, stripping them off" and using them as a smelling bottle or ointment.

Neither alcohol nor tobacco had any place in Thoreau's life. How could you disparage a barroom more effectively than by calling it "a place to spit," or a wine-bibber than by comparing his life to that of a fungus? "Fell in with a man whose breath smelled of spirit which he had drunk. How could I but feel that it was his own spirit that I smelt?" More seriously and more mythologically he speaks of New England rum as a demon "who comes in the guise of a friend or hired man, and then robs and murders the whole family."

The extent of his smoking was a few dried lily stems in boyhood. In his paper on Sir Walter Raleigh, he contented himself by mildly describing Raleigh's introduction of tobacco into England as a doubtful benefit, but elsewhere he was less moderate. Tobacco was a vile weed, sown by vile men. When he breakfasted with the Well-fleet oysterman on the Cape, the menu comprised eels, buttermilk, cake, bread, green beans, doughnuts, applesauce, and tea. He ate only the applesauce and the doughnuts, which he thought least likely to have been contaminated by the host's spitting tobacco juice into the fireplace. "I was glad to have got out of the towns," he wrote, "where I am wont to feel unspeakably mean and disgraced, —to have left behind me for a season the barrooms of Massachusetts, where the full-grown are not weaned from savage and filthy habits—still sucking a cigar." Once he went with the other New England literati to the Parker House but found it so hard to see through the cigar smoke that he never went again. And how could you dismiss politics more contemptuously than to describe it as "the cigar-smoke of a man"?

III

Certainly Thoreau had the temperament of a healthy and happy man. It was not that he was ever a cheerful idiot; his waking experience, he said, had been an alternate rough and smooth; he never closed his eyes to the sorrows and failures of life. He was considered quiet, solemn, and self-sufficient during his school days. When Mrs. Samuel Hoar invited him to play with her children, he declined, making no excuse except that he did not wish to, and when he was accused of having stolen a knife from a schoolmate, he merely denied the absurd accusation, disdaining to offer an alibi. In maturity there are expressions of discontent and dissatisfaction, sometimes connected with the thought of his own unworthiness. Churchyards were "grave" places to him, and he did not find it hard to understand why men living barren and worthless lives of quiet desperation should commit suicide or live on only by an effort of will.[4]

Nevertheless, take him all in all, Thoreau is certainly one of the great sons of joy. I cannot think of anyone more unlike him than the great French courtesan of the seventeenth century, Ninon de Lenclos, yet she surely spoke for him as much as for herself in her famous saying, "The joy of a soul is the measure of its force." He once carved upon a stump the letters HHH, meaning "Henry, Happy Heathen." "Surely joy is the condition of life," he cries. And again: "I love to live." "No run on my bank can drain it, for my wealth is not possession but enjoyment." "God could not be unkind to me if he should try." He quotes Sir Thomas Browne's "For the world, I count it not an inn, but an hospital, and a place, not to live in but to die in," only to add bluntly, "I hold the reverse," and the *Walden* title page itself boasts, "I do not propose to write an ode to dejection, but to brag as lustily as chanticleer in the morning, standing on his roost, if only to wake my neighbors up." He condemns greed because its effect is to cause men to postpone the enjoyment of life. At his Harvard commencement, he proposed one day a week of toil, with the other six dedicated to a "Sabbath of the affections and the soul," but even that was not enough for him, for he held that even work must be enjoyed. "Every man, and the woodchopper among the rest, should love his work as much as the poet does his."

It may be argued of course that what a man says is not always what he feels and that there is such a thing as whistling—or boasting —to keep one's courage up. And there are passages which suggest that Thoreau's happiness was bought with a price. Writing to Thomas Cholmondeley, he admits being "run down" but adds that this has not touched his spirits, which are "as indifferently tough, as sluggishly resilient, as a dried fungus." And to H. G. O. Blake in 1848 he declared his ignorance of acute sorrow on the ground that "my saddest and most genuine sorrows are apt to be but transient regrets. The place of sorrow is supplied, perchance, by a certain hard and proportionately barren indifference. I am of kin to the sod, and partake largely of its dull patience. . . . Methinks I am never quite committed, never wholly the creature of my moods, being always to some extent their critic. My only integral experience is in my vision. I see, perchance, with more integrity than I feel." But there was not much suggestion of the dried fungus about the man who confided to his journal that his "most sacred and memorable life" was "commonly on awaking in the morning. I frequently awake with an atmosphere about me as if my unremembered dreams had been divine, as if my spirit had journeyed to its native place, and, in the act of re-entering its native body, had diffused an elysian fragrance around." He once told an unhappy man that "the stones are happy, Concord River is happy, and I am happy too." The very grain and composition of walnut shell showed that it was made for happiness: "The most brutish and inanimate objects that are made suggest an everlasting and thorough satisfaction; they are the homes of content. Wood, earth, mould, etc., exist for joy. Do you think that Concord River would have continued to flow these millions of years by Clamshell Hill and round Hunt's Island, if it had not been happy—if it had been miserable in its channel, tired of existence, and cursing its maker and the hour that it sprang?"

Moreover Thoreau faced the future with hope and a reasonable degree of confidence. Morton Berkowitz has acutely pointed out[5] that his "exhorting men to be 'true to their natures' and to lead 'manly and independent lives,' . . . implies that the 'blind and unmanly love of wealth' to which he had earlier referred, is somehow not an essential part of human nature." "There is not necessarily any gross and ugly fact which may not be eradicated from the life of man," he says, and though he knows that civil government, with all the problems it creates, is a necessity now, he looks forward to a far-off time when men shall be capable of governing themselves.[6] "These may be but the spring months in the life of the race." "There is more day to dawn. The sun is but a morning star."

Nor was joy quenched during his final illness. He did not wish to die, for he had much to do in the world, yet his loving sister Sophia wrote that she felt "as if he were being translated, rather than dying in the ordinary way of mortals. It was not possible to be sad in his presence." Fearing nothing but strange dreams, he refused opiates, wrote Myron Benton that, though he did not believe he had many months to live, he was enjoying life as much as ever, and told Bronson Alcott that he was leaving the world without regret and that there was as much comfort in perfect disease as in perfect health.

Thus, though Thoreau was in many respects a Puritan, he had nothing of what has been described as the Puritan's inclination to go about the world as his Father's representative in an alien country. "Not by constraint or severity shall you have access to true wisdom, but by abandonment, and childlike mirthfulness. If you would know aught, be gay before it." Or, in verse,

> Build not on to-morrow
> But seize on today!
> From no future borrow
> The present to pay.

"There is nowhere any apology for despondency," he says. "Always there is life which, rightly lived, implies a divine satisfaction. . . . Disease and a rain-drop cannot coexist." Even seriousness must cut capers at times. "I exult in stark inanity, leering on nature and the soul." What wonder that Emerson called him "the boy"?

Some of the foregoing quotations are from the great epiphany at the close of *Walden*, the vision of regeneration which makes every spring resemble or re-enact the creation of Cosmos out of Chaos. "*Walden* is, in fact," as Stanley Edgar Hyman says, "a vast rebirth ritual, the purest and most complete in our literature." It "runs to symbols of graves and coffins, with consequent rising from them, to wombs and emergence from them, and ends on the fable of a live insect resurrected from an egg long buried in wood."[7] But, as Harding points out, this great passage does not stand alone. If the *Week*, "Civil Disobedience," and "Life Without Principle" do not achieve comparable stylistic grandeur, they do all end on the same upbeat note. Thoreau once misspelled buoyantly "boyantly." It was the right spelling for him.

Such a capacity for acceptance and affirmation implies something of an aggressive spirit, and, as we shall see, this was by no means lacking in Thoreau. "A man has not seen a thing," he says, "who has not felt it," and his own seeing was often ecstasy. He longed to live so that there should be no "desultory moment" in his life. "I thank you, God. I do not deserve anything, I am unworthy of the least regard; and yet I am made to rejoice. I am impure and worthless, and yet the world is strewn for my delight and holidays are prepared for me, and my path is strewn with flowers." "Ah, bless the Lord, O my soul! bless him for wildness, for crows that will not alight within gunshot! and bless him for hens, too, that croak and cackle in the yards!"

Unlike many who possess such appetence, Thoreau himself fully realized the more remote implications of his temperament. "I have the habit of attention," he says, "to such excess that my senses get no rest, but suffer from a constant strain." And again, "I wonder that I ever get five miles on my way, the walk is so crowded with events and phenomena."[8] Consider his excitement over the phosphorescent wood he found in Maine, having somehow overlooked it in Concord. "I was exceedingly interested by this phenomenon, and already felt paid for my journey. It could hardly have thrilled me more if it had taken the form of letters, or of the human face." Not infrequently he was thrilled by something commonplace that almost anybody else would have passed by; "I was in just the frame of mind to see something wonderful," he says. Nor was it only nature that exercised such power over his imagination. What he saw in Canada tied up with his reading, so that the names of the villages "affected me as if they had been those of the renowned cities of antiquity," and "the names of the mountains, and streams, and villages reel[ed], if I may so speak, with the intoxication of poetry," so that he "began to dream of Provence and the Troubadours, and of places and things which have no existence on earth." Sometimes, even, he could intoxicate himself with his own writing. "I trust that you realize what an exaggerator I am," he writes Blake, "that I lay myself out to exaggerate whenever I have an opportunity—pile Pelion upon Ossa, to reach heaven so."9

Such was Thoreau's intensity that if he could not have appetence without pain, he was ready to embrace that also. "It is never enough that our life is an easy one. We must live on the stretch; not be satisfied with a tame and undisturbed round of weeks and days, but retire to our rest like soldiers on the eve of a battle, looking forward with ardor to the strenuous sortie of the morrow. . . . As our bodies court physical encounters, and languish in the mild and even climate of the tropics, so our souls thrive best on unrest and discontent." When a speaker dwells on the sufferings of life, he advises going about one's business, "suggesting that no ecstasy was ever interrupted nor its fruit blasted. . . . We want no completeness but intensity of life." Sadness itself might be "fertile" and "positively joyful" because it saved life from being trivial. Even Mrs. Emerson must be told, when she was depressed, that "to hear you have sad hours is not sad to me. I rather rejoice at the richness of your experience."

Thoreau's independence in thought and action, encouraged by the transcendentalists' cult of self-reliance, shows in little things, like his reversing his given names and insisting upon teaching the Concord school in his own way or not at all, but it shows more impressively in the whole tenor of his life. Even God, he thought, could help a man only by strengthening him to help himself; if through trusting in God you lost your vigor, then you had better not trust Him at all. Whatever else he admired about the *Gita*, he did not accept its passivity. So Emerson thought that Thoreau himself had the capacity "for great enterprise and command" and attributed it to his lack of ambition that "instead of engineering for all America, he was the captain of a huckleberry-party."

In one of his most revealing phrases, Theodore Roosevelt speaks somewhere of "those who care intensely both for thought and for action." He himself was assuredly one of these men, and, in his own very different way, Thoreau was another. "Now I am Alexander," he says, "and then I am Homer." His way of life being what it was, the Alexandrian strain expressed itself in action only rarely, as when he physically collared two would-be seducers and turned them in. But we see the same man in his admiration for Sir Walter Raleigh in his youth and for John Brown at the end. Sir Walter Scott was never able to convince himself that writing about great deeds could match performing them, but Walter de la Mare says that a poem is a deed, and Joseph Conrad declared that "an artist is a man of action, whether he creates a personality, invents an expedient, or finds the issue of a complicated situation." For Thoreau not only writing but even reading "should be heroic, in an unknown tongue, a dialect always but imperfectly learned, through which we stammer line by line, catching but a glimmering of the sense, and still afterward admiring its unexhausted hieroglyphics, its untranslated columns," and he criticizes Gibbon for his love of fame, vanity, religious conformity out of prudential considerations, and the absence of "reckless and heroic action" in his life.

Lowell was never farther off the beam than when he declared bluntly that Thoreau had no humor, but he was not the only reader who failed to discern it. John Burroughs, for example, acknowledged that Thoreau had it, but thought that "it had worked a little— it was not quite sweet" and that "there was too much acid for the sugar."[10]

Thoreau himself lends some support to such writers. He considered humor incompatible with the loftiest literary genius and edited some of it out of his journals in later years: "I cannot bear the levity I find." He knew that the most serious things, even death, have their ludicrous aspects, but he found it pardonable to "spurn the proprieties, even the sanctities" only when one made them stepping-stones to something higher. His fullest commentary on humor is in his most extended piece of literary criticism, the essay on Carlyle, where he sees it as both an "indispensable pledge of sanity, without some leaven of which the abstruse thinker may justly be suspected of mysticism, fanaticism, or insanity," and an independent ingredient in fireside intercourse and at the same time discerns an element of sadness in it. Humor does not wear well, it "is apt to imply but a half satisfaction at best," and "a mere humorist . . . is a most unhappy man," a statement with which Mark Twain, for one, would have heartily agreed.

Yet he asks, "Do they not know that I can laugh?" He could, and loudly too, and he could "cut up" when he wanted to. "Everything that boy says makes merry with society," said Emerson, "though nothing can be graver than his meaning," and Channing says that "there was a lurking humor in almost all that he said, —a dry wit, often expressed. . . . No one more quickly entertained the apprehension of a jest; and his replies often came with a startling promptness." Thoreau teased Emerson himself by telling him that every time he reset his fence, he shoved it over a little further upon Sam Staples' property. When he heard the governor was coming to Concord for a muster, he went to the hardware store to buy a bolt for the front door, and when the clerk said the legislature was coming with him, he bought another for the back door. Walter Harding makes fun of those who read *Walden* as if it were the Bible, pointing out that Thoreau often wrote with his tongue far up in his cheek, using "just about every humorous literary device on record—puns, hyperbole, slapstick, mockery, parody, burlesque, and so on."[11]

To be sure, there are, or there have been, those who believed that Thoreau's later years were marked by discouragement and disillusionment and that he became bitter about mankind, to such an extent indeed that, as Willard Thorp expressed it, "his delight in Nature correspondingly dried." This view was advanced by Mark Van Doren, in his first published book, as early as 1916. It gained authority from Sherman Paul's imposing study, *The Shores of America*, in 1958, was accepted by Perry Miller, and has been most cogently and authoritatively opposed by J. Lyndon Shanley.[12] It should be noted, however, that though Paul allowed himself the use of such terms as "decay," "deepening despair," "quiet desperation," and "terrible spiritual struggle," he also entered many qualifications. If he speaks of *Walden* as "a form of self-therapy," he also says that

Thoreau continued to "affirm his faith" and that its marrow remained untouched. "The spring never failed to invigorate him," and "as he sauntered into the sunset he still believed—and beautifully expressed it in his last sentence—that 'an adventurous spirit turns everything into morning.' "

It is true that even in his mid-thirties Thoreau sometimes laments the passing of youth in almost Wordsworthian terms. There is a remarkable journal passage of 1851: "I think that no experience which I have to-day comes up to, or is comparable with, the experiences of my boyhood. . . . My life was ecstasy. . . . I wondered if a mortal had ever known what I knew. . . . I was daily intoxicated, and yet no man could call me intemperate." Eight years later he achieved what is almost a prose equivalent of the Immortality Ode. A young man, he says, is not yet an "assured inhabitant of the earth, and his compensation is that he is not quite earthy, there is something peculiarly tender and divine about him. . . . The young man is a demi-god; the grown man, alas! is commonly a mere mortal." Yet Ethel Seybold, who thought that such passages had received less attention than they deserved, admitted that they made up only a small part of his journal and that their force was weakened "by occasional expressions of hope" and matter-of-fact passages. What discouragement there was, she believed, centered on the early 1850s, but even then Henry was hoping for an Indian summer and by mid-July 1852 he thought he had achieved this. It should be remembered too that Hawthorne, meeting him again after coming back from Liverpool in 1860, found him "as simple and child-like as ever."

The basic difficulty with all such arguments is that they insist upon forcing an unearned consistency upon a man of whom Emerson said that "he lived for the day, not cumbered and mortified by his memory. If he brought you yesterday a new proposition, he would bring you today another not less revolutionary." In *Thoreau as a Romantic Naturalist*, James McIntosh, though admitting "a diminishing focus on the romantic notion of sympathy with a generous nature" in Thoreau's later work, sees this as "more a drift than a development" and points out that Thoreau worked on "Ktaadn," the *Week*, and *Walden*, all three, during his first stay at the pond: "But the style and temper of each work is radically different from the other two, and in each Thoreau develops his relation to nature differently. Thus, I infer, Thoreau was not committed in this period to one view of nature, but was capable of consciously entertaining different and even opposing views, and he felt compelled to present each view in a manner appropriate to it." In other words, he was a literary artist, not a Calvinistic, Freudian, or Marxian dogmatist. Though far from being an uncommitted man, he made his commitment to life and life experience, never supposing that he had settled everything once and for all so that he might thereafter confront the universe with a closed mind. He faced fundamental questions, including those to which humanity knows no final and absolute answers, to the last day of his life, and in different moods and connections he expressed differing attitudes toward them. He would, I believe, have understood perfectly what John Buchan wrote in 1909 in a story called "A Lucid Interval": "Every man has a creed, but in his soul he knows that that creed has another side, possibly not less logical, which it does not suit him to produce. Our most honest convictions are not the children of pure reason, but of temperament, environment, necessity, and interest. Most of us take sides in life and forget the one we reject."[13]

I V

But if Thoreau was by nature a writer and an artist, then obviously much of the time he spent with himself must have been devoted to the contemplation and consideration of works of literature and art. We know most of course about his reading, for though Perry Miller acutely suggested that "one immensely helpful way to deepen our appreciation of what Thoreau was seeking is to look closely at certain pictures of Thomas Cole . . . , Asher Durand, or Thomas Doughty,"[14] the writer lived in a milieu in which his opportunities to become familiar with either painting or sculpture were decidedly limited. He professed to hate museums as "the catacombs of nature"; whether he would have changed his mind if he had known them better is anybody's guess. One poem, "Guido's Aurora," was inspired by a painting. He seems to have admired the muscular figures of Michelangelo, and there is one reference to the Venus de Medici, but he declined to subscribe to a fund to erect a statue to Horace Mann because he thought a man ought not to take up room in the world after he was dead. "Henry," says Emerson, "when you talked of art, blotted a paper with ink, then doubled it over, and safely defied the artist to surpass the effect," which suggests both that he might have enjoyed some of the abstractions we are blessed with nowadays and that he would have had sense enough not to call them art. He praised Ruskin's *Modern Painters* as "singularly good and encouraging, though not without crudeness and bigotry," but *The Seven Lamps of Architecture* had "too much about art in it for me and the Hottentots." In his journal for 1854 he has a detailed commentary on Gilpin's *Essay on Picturesque Beauty* which has occasioned considerable discussion. [15]

Generally speaking, he seems to have felt that art could not compete with nature. "Let us have willows for spring, elms for summer, maples and walnuts and tupelos for autumn, evergreens for winter, and oaks for all seasons. What is a gallery in a house to a gallery in the streets!" The Christmas and New Year's treasures in Stacey's windows were nothing compared to the frosting on the panes, nor did the jewelers' shops contain anything to compare to the beauty of a snowflake or dewdrop. It was along this line that Norman Foerster argued that Thoreau looked at landscapes as art critics look at a painting: "he succeeded in some degree in acquiring the point of view of the plastic arts through training his eye for landscape." [16]

Thoreau's feeling that the architect should begin by considering first "how slight a shelter is absolutely necessary" makes it easy to underestimate his interest in architecture. He thought toadstools had better domes than Oriental temples and palaces, which were beautiful mainly through association, and that the character of a people expressed itself through poetry and "abstract thought" rather than through its buildings, and he took a dim view indeed of those who rambled about the world "to see that pile of stones which ambitious Mr. Cheops, an Egyptian booby, like some Lord Timothy Dexter, caused a hundred thousand poor devils to pile up for low wages, which contained for all treasure the thigh-bone of a cow."

But to stop there would be to pause upon the threshold. It is true that Thoreau's interest in architecture was largely confined to the domestic variety (he loved log houses, and in *Walden* he suggests that a large, one-room house, "a vast, rude, substantial primitive hall, without ceiling or plastering" is his ideal), and when he says that "the religion and civilization which are barbaric and heathenish build splendid temples but Christianity does not," he simply shows unbelievable ignorance of the Gothic cathedrals. His remarks about the Egyptian pyramids focus on social rather than aesthetic considerations; the "luxury of princes" held no appeal for him, and Charles R. Metzger underlines the simplistic elements in his approach when he remarks that "he failed to see that character is also recorded in architectures more complex than that of the rustic poor." Yet he was so far from being unsophisticated in his architectural convictions that he may be said to have anticipated the views of Louis Sullivan, Frank Lloyd Wright, and other "functionalists," though, oddly enough, he failed to perceive that he had an ally in this area in Horatio Greenough. He told Emerson that architecture should develop "out of the character and necessities of the indweller and builder, without even a thought for mere ornament, but an unconscious nobleness and truthfulness of character and life." In other words, the shell of the building should be determined by its inner life and the function should create the form. And all this was completely in harmony with Thoreau's whole philosophy and explains his objection that Ruskin approached nature through art rather than vice versa. "The need to fuse inner and outer space," says Theodore M. Brown, "stemmed primarily from Thoreau's cosmic view; he approached the design of his own house on both physical and metaphysical levels."[17]

One form of art he missed completely; toward the theater he seems almost as hostile as any Puritan. To his way of thinking, there was quite enough folly to be encountered in the world itself; it was not profitable to devote your evenings to seeing it reproduced upon the stage. Though he attended the opera at least once, I have found no record of his having ever witnessed a play, but he did have some slight contact with the fringes of the theater business. In 1838 he reports having seen "some illuminated pictures," probably magic lantern slides, and though he is caustic about the "poor simpletons" who "will go to a panorama by families, to see a Pilgrim's Progress, perchance" without ever having "made progress as far as the top of . . . a hill . . . at the dawn of a foggy morning," he himself saw panoramas of both the Rhine and the Mississippi and was quite carried away. The first was "like a dream of the Middle Ages. I floated down its historic stream in something more than imagination." The Mississippi was "a Rhine stream of a different kind; the foundations of castles were yet to be laid, and the famous bridges were yet to be thrown across the river; and I felt that *this was the heroic age itself*, though we know it not, for the hero is commonly the simplest and obscurest of men." In 1835 too he went to the circus, and though he smelled "a certain sourness in the air, suggesting trodden grass and cigar smoke," he found "the pagoda in perfection" in the shape of the tent and was impressed by "what graceful attitudes feats of strength and agility seem to require." There is a rather surprisingly sophisticated theatrical metaphor in the "Solitude" chapter of *Walden,* and Charles R. Anderson has suggested that the "doubleness" sometimes involved in Thoreau's attitude toward himself, as if the spectator were observing the actor, may have been influenced by a Hindu play, Kalidassa's *Sacontala.*[18]

Music was a very different story; indeed I cannot but wonder whether any other man who heard so little music as Thoreau did ever loved it so much. Certainly he came by this passion honestly, for it has been reported that the family went without tea, coffee, and sugar for years so that the girls might have a piano, and Helen gave music lessons.[19] In 1843 Richard Fuller gave Thoreau a music box, and when he went to Staten Island he lent it to Hawthorne. A music box was used at Helen's funeral and again in Thoreau's own sick room. He himself both sang and played the flute—at home, on the water, in Maine, and at his friends the Ricketsons', and there is one reference to his whistling at table. His favorite song was the lugubrious ballad "Tom Bowling," which he seems to have sung and danced with tremendous gusto.[20] Once he sang it during rain and thought the dampness kind to his voice! Sanborn thought the quality of the voice rather harsh and unmusical in both singing and speaking, but not all agreed. Robert Collyer, among others, was charmed by it, though it was "wasting away" when he heard it. "His voice is low, but still sweet in the tones and inflections," with the words as distinct and as clear as those of a great singer.

But what music did he hear? Once, in New York, with Horace Greeley, *I Puritani;*[21] the Tyrolean singers and similar groups;[22] "The Battle of Prague" and its ilk on the piano; the hand-organ and the accordion. Of a concert of instrumental music he records that "its sounds entered every cranny of the hall and lifted it to repletion with sweet liquid melody. . . . flowing in its own invisible and impalpable channels," and, being a good transcendentalist, he found in the harmony established by a group of singers or even a circus company the symbol of a much larger, more cosmic harmony. For one with so little experience of public entertainments, he felt rather surprisingly with the performer, realizing that before an audience even the simplest gesture became a conscious and deliberate deed. Even the intermission had its place, as affording an opportunity for the listener to detach himself from "the common pulse" of which he had been a part and achieve "self-recovery."

But he did not like the opera. Indeed he is nowhere more perverse than in the way he harps upon his dislike for it, upon the inadequate basis of a single encounter. "One will lose no music by not attending the oratorios and operas." "The wood thrush Mr. Barnum never hired nor can, though he could bribe Jenny Lind and put her into his cage." "Think of going abroad or out of one's self to hear music,—to Europe or Africa! Instead of so living as to be the lyre which the breath of the morning causes to vibrate with that melody which creates worlds—to sit up late and hear Jane [sic] Lind! Perhaps the opera in his time was too much associated with fashion and high living to command Thoreau's sympathies, to say nothing of the melodramatic excesses of its librettists, but why did he extend his animus to oratorios? What a pity it is that he never knew German *Lieder* or French *mélodies*, with which, one would think, he might easily have come to terms, and his interest in the music box suggests how much his life might have been enriched by the phonograph, had it been available in his time.

As to the ecstasy itself, however inspired, there can be no question. The aeolian harp brings tidings "of a vale which none hath seen." The thrumming of a guitar lifts Thoreau "above all the dust and mire of the universe." The sound of a "clarionet" seems to him "perhaps the most admirable accomplishment of man." Hearing passing travelers singing in the night helped him to understand "how unexhausted, how almost wholly unimproved, was man's capacity for a divine life," and the sound of a distant piano reminded him "of distant heroic ages; it suggests such ideas of human life and the field which the earth affords as the few noblest passages of poetry." In such moments, he no longer found himself standing upon the dull earth. "It is possible to live a grander life here; already the steed is stamping, the knights are prancing; already our thoughts bid a proud farewell to the so-called actual life and its humble glories." This is precisely the kind of thing which caused that most Thoreauvian of all composers, Charles Ives, to feel that

> Thoreau was a great musician, not because he played the flute but because he did not have to go to Boston to hear "the Symphony." The rhythm of his prose, were there nothing else, would determine his value as a composer. He was divinely conscious of the enthusiasm of Nature, the emotion of her rhythms, and the harmony of her solitude. In this consciousness he sang of the submission to Nature, the religion of contemplation, and the freedom of simplicity—a philosophy distinguishing between the complexity of Nature, which teaches freedom, and the complexity of materialism, which teaches slavery.[23]

There is one strange, very likely playful passage in *Walden* in which a strain of music coming through the woods makes Thoreau feel "as if I could spit a Mexican with a good relish,—for why should we always stand for trifles?—and looked round for a woodchuck or a skunk to exercise my chivalry upon." Once he wants to be "drunk, drunk, drunk, dead drunk to this world" with music, and again he wonders "that so few habitually intoxicate themselves with music; so many with alcohol." But the general emphasis is upon spiritual insight and nobility. Music "brings out what of heroic lurks anywhere." Through it "we put out our dormant feelers unto the limits of the universe," achieve "a wisdom that passeth understanding," and become invulnerable. After singing, all speech sounds profane. Falsehood and cowardice can only be spoken, not sung. Indeed "the prophane never hear music; the holy ever hear it. It is God's voice, the divine breath audible. Where it is heard, there is a sabbath."

Yet, when all is said and done, perhaps Thoreau was even more remarkable for his sensitivity to sound than for his love for what most people mean by music. He even inclined to think that those dependent upon "Paganini or Mozart" for their musical stimulation gave evidence of "debauched and worn-out senses," since those "not enervated by luxury, hear music in the wind and rain and running water." He pitied people who could not hear or heed the ring of the toads in spring. "The bell was ringing for town meeting, and every one heard it, but none heard this older and more universal bell, rung by more native Americans all the land over." He loved cow-bells as much as the cow's milk or beef, the swineherd's horn as much as bacon, the cackle of hens and the crowing of cocks as much as eggs, and the earth-song of the cricket, older than Christianity itself, cried "Health! health!" to the world; while its ambrosial sound endured, no crime could be committed. "All these sounds . . . are evidence of nature's health and *sound* state," and they did not need to be what we ordinarily call beautiful to exercise a beneficent effect: "if you had a discriminating ear," you might find "elements of concord" in the cat-owl's discord, as children like to make a noise "because of the music which their young ears detect in it." And here too he finds moral and spiritual meaning, for he thought he could hear the good music of nature "only when well employed, at any rate only when I have no reason to be ashamed of my employment."

But it is still more remarkable that Thoreau, who had so many reservations about science and technology, should not even have excluded this area as the source not only of pleasurable, ecstatic sound but even of revelation. None of his readers can have missed the many passages in which he responds enthusiastically to the sound of the telegraph wires "vibrating like a harp high overhead." He could not despair of a world "where you have only to stretch an ordinary wire from tree to tree to hear such strains drawn from it by New England breezes as to make Greece and all antiquity seem poor in melody." It was as if he had entered "into some world-famous cathedral, resounding to some vast organ." Orpheus was still alive, and the golden age was at hand. "This wire is my redeemer. It always brings a special and general message to me from the Highest."[24]

V

Since Thoreau was, after all, first and foremost a writer, his reading was more important than his adventures with any of the other arts. He was a very good linguist (the best in Concord, Sanborn thought), well-trained in both Latin and Greek, though his Latin was better than his Greek. At Harvard he took courses in French, Italian, Spanish, and German, where Longfellow gave him 99 points compared to Lowell's 132 in Italian, but 167 in German compared to Lowell's 153.[25] He also studied German with Orestes A. Brownson, but apparently never became so adept in it as he was in the Romance languages. He wrote letters to his sisters in Latin and made translations from Latin literature, and the Oriental books which Cholmondeley sent him from England were in English, French, Latin, Greek, and Sanskrit. Hebrew he seems to have left strictly alone; in the essay "Walking" he declares it too late in the day for that and judges it more important to understand contemporary slang!

Paraphrasing Pope, Thoreau thought an honest book the noblest work of man. His own library, at his death, contained some four hundred volumes, and his access to Emerson's made much more available to him. In a house in Maine, where he stopped on the 1846 excursion, he found "the Wandering Jew, cheap edition, and fine print, the Criminal Calendar, and Parish's Geography, and flash novels two or three. Under the pressure of circumstances," he says, "we read a little in these." Like other slaves to print, he evidently would read anything rather than nothing, but what he really relished were "books, not which afford us a cowering enjoyment, but in which each thought is of unusual daring; such as an idle man cannot read, and a timid one would not be entertained by, which even make us dangerous to existing institutions. . . ."

He knew that "the last and finest result," the "natural fruit" of "the loftiest written wisdom," was poetry, "the mysticism of mankind." It was in the same spirit that myth enthralled him, "the recorded wisdom of mankind, the ancient classics and Bibles" which he valued above all other literature. For though history was "central to all truth," he often found the distinction between fact and poetry vague. "To some extent, mythology is only the most ancient history and biography. So far from being false or fabulous in the common sense, it contains only enduring and essential truth"; indeed, as he sees it, "the most interesting and beautiful facts are so much the more poetry and that is their success." Consequently he even sets his own myth-making imagination to work upon native New England materials and upon his own life, rarely describing his experiences in literal, matter-of-fact fashion. Once, even, he longs to "take that walk, never yet taken by us in this actual world, which is perfectly symbolical of the path which we love to travel in the interior and the ideal world." At the same time, and perhaps not quite consistently, he sought in his reading a direct expression of the writer's personality, believing that the reader's interest is conditioned by "the depth and intensity of the life excited" and that "the real facts of a poet's life would be of more value to us than any work of his art." Thus he did not care for the *Decline and Fall* because Gibbon's personality did not attract him, and for some strange reason he classified Bancroft's with "the emasculated modern histories . . . cursed with a style." "Is not the poet bound to write his own biography?" he asks. "Is there any other work for him but a good journal? We do not wish to know how his imaginary hero, but how he, the actual hero, lived from day to day."[26]

The classicism generally credited to Thoreau is undercut by some critics, as by Clarence Gohdes, who declares that Thoreau was "a romanticist by nature and a classical scholar by mere force of circumstances," and Henry himself seems to support this when he says that "the Greeks had no transcendent geniuses like Milton and Shakespeare, whose merit only posterity could fully appreciate," even if we dismiss as merely frivolous his statement in *Cape Cod:* "I put in a little Greek now and then, partly because it sounds so much like the ocean." His classicism has been most carefully studied by Ethel Seybold and John Paul Pritchard, and though the former has been censured for seeing the Walden Pond sojourn as essentially a Homeric experiment, the general outlines of her study remain valuable. She traces three periods in Thoreau's classical reading. First, he re-read the authors he had been introduced to in college. Next, after *Walden,* he read the agricultural writers, the *Antigone* of Sophocles, and a little of Lucretius, whose materialism repelled him. Finally, in the late fifties, he turned to the early naturalists, and his last reading was in Herodotus and Strabo. Despite his theory, he did not do all his classical reading in the original languages, and the compactness and clarity of his own style were probably due basically to "his innumerable revisions," his Latinity revealing itself, if anywhere, "in the accuracy of his word usage and perhaps in his neat and precise pronoun references." The Orphic hymns appealed to his mysticism, Homer to his love of myth and nature, Plutarch and Aeschylus to his passion for the heroic. But he is not generally rated as an admirer of Plato, and he does not seem to have known Aristotle's *Poetics* at first hand.

Surely he must mentally have exempted Homer from his denial of transcendent genius to the Greeks, for he calls him the greatest of poets. It comforted him to have a copy of the *Iliad* in his cabin at Walden Pond, even though he found no time to read it, and *Walden* is full of Homeric echoes, most obviously of course in the account of the battle of the ants. He admired Latin verses for "the elegant terseness and conciseness of the language" and thought of the classics as a record of "the noblest recorded thoughts of man" and "the only oracles which are not decayed." "Two thousand summers have imparted to the monuments of Grecian literature, as to her marbles, only a maturer golden and autumnal tint." He read Pliny and talked of him during his final illness, and surely the *Antigone* is in harmony with "Civil Disobedience," whether it exercised any direct influence upon it or not. In the *Week* he wrote that "reading the classics or conversing with those old Greeks and Latins in their surviving works, is like walking amid the stars and constellations, a high and serene way to travel." But it lent dignity to his life also by delivering him from the tyranny of time: "I would read Virgil if only that I might be reminded of the dignity of human nature in all ages." Such things helped him to remember that he belonged to a "heroic race of men of whom there is a tradition." It was something to sit on the shore of your own Ithaca, "a fellow-wanderer and survivor of Ulysses."[27]

The fact that Thoreau shocked many of his contemporaries by seeming to rate the Oriental scriptures, then so little known in the West, as standing on a level of inspiration with the Bible has led some critics to exaggerate the importance of his Oriental reading upon his life and thought. Nevertheless it seems fair to say that the *Bhagavad-Gita* influenced Thoreau's thinking as importantly as Emerson's *Nature* had done, and we have his own word for it that his reading one night in *The Laws of Menu* so moved him that it woke him up next morning before cockcrow. He apparently read no Hindu books as an undergraduate, but when Thomas Cholmondeley sent him the magnificent gift of forty-four volumes in 1855, he wrote proudly to Daniel Ricketson: "I send you information of this as I might announce the birth of a child."

Here again there are the dissenters. Mark Van Doren thought

Thoreau took only "figures and sentences, not ideas, from his Oriental reading." "He cannot be said to have understood the true significance of the Oriental position, with its stern dualism, its difficult discipline . . . , its pessimism and its resignation." Wolf too thinks he valued mainly the atmosphere of his Oriental books (we do not know how many of them he actually read), and Thoreau himself reinforces this view when he says that, even "like some other preachers," he sometimes adds his Chinese and Hindu texts long after having written his discourse.

Nobody seems to feel that he was ever a good Confucian or that he ever accepted Oriental fatalism or "condoned the relinquishing of household duties and the dropping of the reins of state as commendable action at any stage in life." When Walter Harding was lecturing in Japan, he found it hard to make his hearers believe that Thoreau knew nothing of Zen Buddhism, to which he seemed to them to stand committed, yet no Zen was available in the West during his lifetime in any language that he could read. Thoreau himself gave his critics a cue for controversy when he wrote, "To some extent, and at rare intervals, even I am a yogi," but even those, like Arthur Christy and S. D. Stracner, who are most inclined to take this seriously are very careful to make it clear that he took what he wanted from yoga and ignored the rest, always carefully preserving his independence. "By occasional practice and experimentation," says Stracner, "he came to a better understanding of at least one Oriental way of life, but he by no means gave himself fully to it."[28]

He does not seem to have read extensively in Continental writers. Goethe is the one to whom he refers most. In the *Week* he says he is not much acquainted with Goethe's work and then proceeds to write about him, praising the realism of his record of his Italian journey and describing him as an artist rather than a poet: the difference between the two is that while the genius or poet may be, and often is, also an artist, his characteristic note is that he is "an originator, an inspired or demonic man, who produces a perfect work in obedience to laws yet unexplored," while the artist merely "detects and applies the law from observation of the works of Genius, whether of man or nature." J. Chesley Mathews has demonstrated Thoreau's familiarity with Dante, and there is at least one penetrating observation: "We *see* with Dante but we *feel* with Milton." He read Tasso in college, and there are possible echoes of Silvio Pellico in "Civil Disobedience." Norse mythology and Viking exploration interested him, and he also read such Scandinavian scientists as Kalm and Linnaeus.[29]

For one with his passion for early literature, Thoreau would seem to have made less than might have been expected of pre-Elizabethan literature in English. Though he has been credited with a knowledge of Anglo-Saxon, I have found no reference to *Beowulf;* indeed he speaks of "the meagre pastures of Saxon and ante-Chaucerian poetry," finding in it "less to remind the reader of the rudeness and vigor of youth, than of the feebleness of a declining age," which is penetrating at least to the extent of testifying to his realization, less common then than now, that the art of the Anglo-Saxon poet was not primitive but highly sophisticated. He seems to have relished the popular ballads, but he thought *Piers Plowman* an "obscure and interminable" allegory, and though he once planned an essay on Lydgate, Gower, and Skelton, his impression of the *Story of Thebes* was that "each line rings the knell of its brother, as if it were introduced but to dispose of him."

The early English writer he really cared for was Chaucer, but since he belonged to the generation that was taken in by the Ossianic poems, he ranked him below "Ossian." Yet when he calls Chaucer "in many respects the Homer of the English poets," he gives back with one hand what he has taken away with the other. Chaucer's humor was something of a stumbling block in his way, for he believed that the greatest writers were not humorists, and he felt a lack of heroic sentiment in him, but he certainly appreciated his serenity, innocence, humanity, and religion:

> Chaucer's remarkably trustful and affectionate character appears in his familiar, yet innocent and reverent, manner of speaking of his God. He comes into his thought without any false reverence, and with no more parade than a zephyr to his ear. If nature is our mother, then God is our father. There is less love and practical simple trust in Shakespeare and Milton. How rarely in our English tongue do we find expressed any affection for God. There is no sentiment so rare as the love of God. Herbert almost alone expresses it.

Yet, for some strange reason, he seems to have thought that *The Canterbury Tales* ended with a tale told by the Host.

Thoreau knew his Shakespeare well, but though he appreciated his humanity and his universalism, and even suggests that without him English literature would be tame, he seems rather less attuned to him than he was to Milton and the metaphysicals. In the *Week,* however, he extends a certain Shakespearean quality to the great dramatist's contemporaries. "All the distinguished writers of that period," he writes, "possess a greater vigor and naturalness than the modern. . . . It is as if a green bough were laid across the page, and we are refreshed as by the sight of fresh grass in midwinter or early spring." Though he rather neglects the eighteenth century, there is at least one interesting reference to *Gulliver's Travels;* his personal library included one volume each from Goldsmith, Sterne, and Cowper, and a two-volume anthology of English plays which included *The Rivals,* which it has been suggested that he drew upon for one passage in *Walden.*[30] He has sensible, sometimes penetrating comments upon many of the older, less "standard" English writers, some of whom at least he must have sampled in the twenty-one volumes of Alexander Chalmers' *Works of the English Poets from Chaucer to Cowper,* which he is supposed to have read through before entering Harvard and again later. Channing says he was fond of quoting from Daniel:

> Unless above himself he can
> Erect himself, how poor a thing is man.

In considering his references to Donne, we must remember how much less that poet was read in Thoreau's time than he is today. Thoreau quotes from Marvell twice in his John Brown papers, and he also relished Sir Thomas Browne. One would expect him to be excellent on Sir Walter Raleigh, who was one of his great early heroes, and his passion for books of travel would explain his interest in Purchas and Hakluyt, but his references to such dramatists as Dekker, Tourneur, and Davenant (*Gondibert*) are more surprising. In 1843 he became much interested in Quarles. "It is rare to find one who is so much of a poet and so little of an artist. He uses language sometimes as greatly as Shakespeare, and though there is not much straight grain in him, there is plenty of tough crooked timber. In an age when Herbert is revived, Quarles surely ought not to be forgotten." Wolf has suggested that he would have found much kinship also in Traherne, had that poet's work been available in his time.

Among the English writers of the nineteenth century, Thoreau gave most attention to Carlyle. In his own temperament and literary aims, he would seem to have had more in common with Wordsworth and, in some respects, with Burns, and, like the other transcendentalists, he felt some influence from Coleridge. He once quotes from *The Lay of the Last Minstrel,* he obviously had some interest in Landor, and Annie Russell Marble says he recommended Coventry Patmore's *The Angel in the House.* But what is most surprising in connection with Thoreau's comments on his contemporaries is less his comparative neglect of those we now consider the leading writers than his interest in such minor figures as Thomas Moore, Charles Wolfe, and Mrs. Hemans.[31]

As for the Americans, he read widely in New England history and travel and in colonial and Indian lore, but there is comparatively little to say about his reading of what we now think of as American literature. Whitman is the contemporary poet of whom he has most to say, though there is a college notebook of 1835 in which fourteen out of twenty-four pages are devoted to excerpts from Longfellow's prose. He seems to have read Melville's *Typee* and some of Irving, and there is one passage in which he paraphrases "Thanatopsis." Margaret Fuller's *Summer on the Lakes,* which he read in manuscript, has been believed by some to have influenced the form of the *Week,* though Thoreau said he did not like the book.

How Thoreau read and how he used his reading is quite as interesting as what he read. Though he was certainly capable of scholarship, he often showed a lofty indifference toward it. "Poetry cannot breathe," he says, "in the scholar's atmosphere," and he seems hostile to minute literary analysis. He thought of the writer's inspiration in imaginative and religious terms and he was as scornful and superior toward the work of historical societies as he was toward museums; thus he declares that "the historical societies have not recovered one fact from oblivion" and that "critical acumen is exerted in vain to uncover the past; the *past* cannot be *presented* [a characteristic Thoreauvian pun]; we cannot know what we are not," from which he goes on to declare somewhat irrelevantly that "one veil hangs over past, present, and future, and it is the province of the historian to find out, not what was, but what is." The Dark

Ages are dark "because we are so in the dark about them." On the other hand, "no era has been wholly dark, nor will we too hastily submit to the historian, and congratulate ourselves on a blaze of light. If we could pierce the obscurity of those remote years, we should find it light enough; only *there* is not our day." All this is an odd combination of penetration and willful blindness (as when he contemptuously dismisses ancient Egypt as of no interest to us), and on the whole Thoreau is much less keen in his perception of the relationship between fact and truth in history than he is in science, for while it is true that documents and excavations cannot alone re-vitalize the past for us, it is also true that unless our imaginations have established fact to build upon, we shall not achieve truth but only fantasy.[32] Thoreau's worst sins against scholarship, however, were his deliberate misquotations, for he took what he wanted from wherever he found it, altering and adapting it to suit his own mean-ing, regardless of the author's context. Emerson, Longfellow, and Samuel Daniel all suffered from this high-handedness, even if we are inclined to defend his unexplained application of *Julius Caesar* to *Paradise Lost:* "He is 'a plain blunt *devil*,' who 'only speaks right on— no orator as *Satan* is.' " Yet none of this is basically in conflict with the transcendentalist assumption that books have value only as powerhouses and that he uses them best who adapts them to his own needs.[33]

VI

The present chapter of this book has so far concerned itself with the man Thoreau as a solitary human creature—his appearance, his health and the means he employed or failed to employ to maintain it, his temperament and natural disposition, and his experience of and attitude toward the arts, including the one he himself practiced, literature. Except by implication, however, nothing has yet been said about Thoreau's own attitude toward either the self I have been attempting to describe or the expression of that self which he achieved in his writings. The first of these topics obviously calls for consideration here. But what of the second?

Since John Donne and Ernest Hemingway have long since joined forces to teach us that "no man is an island," the obvious shift of emphasis at the end of this chapter must be from *himself* to *others*. But where does that leave the writing? Surely no human being is capable of any lonelier or more personal activity than literary composition, and surely nothing else is more positively his own. But art is communication, and unless the writer under consideration is that lunatic creature who has been aptly described as "the poet talking to himself," his writing is social as well as personal and inevitably an attempt to establish contact with other human beings. Since this book is neither biography nor a piece of literary criticism but simply a study of Thoreau's character and personality, our concern with his writing here can only be as it serves to reveal him in these aspects. For this reason, the topic will be considered as a conclusion to this chapter, where it may, I hope, serve as a convenient bridge between the Me and the Not-Me.

Whether or not a person who possesses what Oliver Wendell Holmes describes as an intense interest in his own personality is necessarily more egotistical or more selfish than less introspective persons, it would be difficult—perhaps impossible—to say; but there can be no question that Thoreau was introspective in the extreme; he seems to have done nothing without at the same time standing off to watch himself doing it.[34] "I was not born to be forced," he says. "I will breathe after my own fashion." You can get along with another without respecting him very much, he believed, but not with yourself, and in one of his poems he asks for

no meaner pelf
Than that I may not disappoint myself.

He did not believe that you can conform outwardly and live rightly inside. This is "a greater strain than any soul can endure. When you get God to pulling one way, and the devil the other. . . . almost any timber will give way." He did not even believe that anybody could either give or receive "any very pertinent advice" in important matters. "Why should we ever go abroad, even across the way, to ask a neighbor's advice? There is a nearer neighbor within us incessantly telling us how we should behave." Imitation even of the wise and good was fatal; one must "preserve and increase" that nobility of nature which he himself possessed and follow it faithfully. "We hear and apprehend only what we already half know," and this holds true even in scientific discovery and experimentation. The classic expression of all this is of course the great word in *Walden*: "If a man does not keep pace with his companions, perhaps it is because he hears a different drummer. Let him step to the music which he hears, however measured and far away."[35]

Thoreau was certainly capable of self-assertion when it seemed called for; he could stand on his dignity like a duke when he met with rudeness or thought he had been taken advantage of. The most striking example is his stinging rebuke of Lowell over an unauthorized change in an *Atlantic* article, but he was equally firm, though less angry, with other editors. He also insisted upon choosing his own lecture topics—or remaining silent when he was not permitted to do this—and he stormed the Harvard College library, carrying his case before two presidents, invoking his privileges as an alumnus, insisting that the rules which governed the borrowing of books must bend to his will, and even virtually claiming the equivalent of benefit of clergy!

The most incredible incident in Thoreau's career was his accidentally setting fire to the Concord woods near Fair Haven in 1844. He says he burned a hundred acres, but the *Concord Freeman* reported it at the time as not less than three hundred. That this should have happened to so careful a woodsman and so devoted a conservationist is in itself sufficiently amazing, but that Thoreau should have taken up such a high-and-mighty attitude toward it is even more strange. It is said that Concord people called "burnt woods" and "damned rascal" after him for years, and if Edward Sherman Hoar had not been his companion (Squire Hoar may even have paid damages), the consequences might have been serious. "I had felt like a guilty person," so Thoreau confided in his journal in 1850, "—nothing but shame and regret. But now I settled the matter with myself shortly. I said to myself: 'Who are these men who are said to be the owners of these woods, and how am I related to them? I have set fire to the forest, but I have done no wrong therein.' . . . I settled it with myself and stood to watch the approaching flames. It was a glorious spectacle, and I was the only one there to enjoy it." Leon Edel's remark that this statement "expressed Thoreau's inner rage and his malaise" rests upon no known foundation but simply illustrates this critic's ineradicable predilection for preferring conjecture to established fact and stating it as such. For it is obvious that the "coolness" of Thoreau's statement reflects anything but an untroubled mind. The mere fact that the record waited six years after the event to get into the journal at all makes it abundantly clear that he is rationalizing long after the event in a continuing effort to make it easier for him to live with himself.

Thoreau clearly belonged to the Milton/Byron/Whitman/Mark Twain type of writer, who creates by dramatizing his own personality, rather than to the Shakespeare/Scott/Keats type, who uses his imagination to project himself into personalities essentially or apparently different from his own. Yet surely few even among the essential autobiographers can have gone quite so far as he did in deriving materials from their own lives or can have drawn the record out to such length, and one can well understand why Perry Miller should have felt that, beyond any other great writer's work, Thoreau's was a soliloquy, and why Norman Foerster should have declared that "he watched his mind as a cat watches a mouse hole" and that consequently he can "be enjoyed to the full only by readers who find his personality attractive."

Many readers have reproached Thoreau for this. James Russell Lowell's reaction has already been noted. To the elder Henry James he was "literally the most child-like, unconscious and unblushing egotist it has ever been my fortune to encounter in the ranks of manhood." And Virginia Woolf, who, of course, never saw him, but whose centenary essay about him shows remarkable penetration for its time, wrote: "Few people, it is safe to say, take such an interest in themselves as Thoreau took in himself; for if we are gifted with an intense egoism we do our best to suffocate it in order to live on decent terms with our neighbours."[36]

Individual passages in Thoreau's writing lend much support to such views. "None ever detained me, but I lagged after myself." "With regard to essentials, I have never had occasion to change my mind." And, most strikingly of all: "Genius is inspired by its own works; it is hermaphroditic."

Yet, on the whole, there is far more self-disparagement than self-approbation in Thoreau's thought of himself. If he longed to be able to worship his own body as "the worthiest temple of God," he did not often achieve this; even in his *Walden* days he feared he was growing more "coarse and indifferent" with the passage of the years, and when he seemed to himself, as he often did, more fortunately placed by the gods than others, he still found himself tingling in expectation of a reckoning to come. "I was never so rapid in my virtue but my vice kept up with me," and even when he sought redemption through looking upward "at an elevated angle," his life was still degraded. He knew he loved books more than his neighbors did, but he was not persuaded that this made him better than they were, nor did his knowledge that the world's way was that of death make him feel safe: "in my folly I am the world I condemn." When moments of depression came, like shadows flitting across the landscape of the soul, he wondered whether their origin must be sought "in sin," and there were times when even nature seemed to impose a handicap upon him by making him more obedient to it and less to spirit. If those who thought him vainglorious could only see him more clearly, he believed they would realize that he thought more meanly of himself than they could possibly think of him, his failures flowing as humbly as the gutters and his offenses as rank as ever assaulted the nostrils of heaven. In 1843 he wrote Lucy Brown that he was "an idle, inefficient, lingering . . . member of the great commonwealth" who stood most in need of his own charity and was as good a subject for his own satire as anybody else, and thirteen years later he assured Calvin Greene that he had all the best of him in his books and that out of his books he was only a "stuttering, blundering clodhopper" who was not worth seeing. Indeed the only real comfort he ever found in his degradation was in the thought of how blessed it would be to be purged of impurity and go to sleep "as expecting to arise to a new and more perfect day." When spring returned, it brought with it the desire "to do something in it worthy of it and me," to dare as he had never dared before, give all for his nobility, and purify himself anew "as with ice and water, soul and body." Surely this is even more touching than naive in a man of thirty-four, but, by the same token, it is far more suggestive of Thoreau's Puritan heritage than of the "self-reliance" of contemporary Unitarianism and transcendentalism.[37]

The situation, I believe, was much the same with Thoreau's writing. Nobody ever better understood the uniqueness of human personalities, or realized that if this failed of communication, something was lost forever. But he understood equally well that "a fact truly stated . . . acquires a mythologic or universal significance," and for this reason the communication at which he aimed was not wholly an individual, and certainly not wholly an egotistical, matter.[38] "I should not talk so much about myself," he says, "if there were anybody else whom I knew so well." Even Foerster and Miller felt this. "When he looked within," wrote Foerster, "it was to study spirit, soul, mind, the divinity in man." And Miller realized as clearly as anybody that Thoreau's self-revelation was never naked; even when he kept closest to his own experience, his was still the reserve of a self-conscious, perfectly possessed man. "The *Journal* is a sustained oratorio, varied with arias, trios, and with thematic recapitulations."[39]

Sherman Paul believes that Thoreau achieved in literature what he could not achieve in life, with *Walden* as an especially successful form of self-therapy. If this is true, it was not the way Thoreau wanted it, for he was as sure as Milton had been that "he who would write well hereafter in laudable things ought himself to be a true poem." And, as the same critic points out in another connection, "he believed that the artist and his work were one, that to be a hero-bard like Ossian or Homer one had to live like one." Great history could only be written by a great human being; the writer sees his subject in terms of his own personality; the best he writes is the best he is, and his character can be read in his book from the title page to the end.

> My life hath been the poem I would have writ,
> But I could not both live and live to utter it.

In this emphasis Foerster long ago found a suggestion of the "Puritanical distrust of all art," and Thoreau's own feeling—that, though "an honest book's the noblest work of man," writing was dangerous because "I feel as if my life had grown more outward when I can express it"—lends force to the suggestion. As a matter of fact, he felt the same thing about reading: "What I began by reading, I must finish by acting," for the greatest book soon requires you to "lay it down and commence living on its hint," which was a conviction he shared with both William James and Theodore Roosevelt. This was not primarily a matter of Puritanism however, or, at least, it was something larger than that. Thoreau was a writer predestined, and none ever devoted himself more diligently to the disciplines of his trade, but he always grasped and held firmly the great truth so many artists miss, that you must give yourself up to your art completely, at the same time sitting lightly upon it; otherwise you will find yourself writing *writing*, and not functioning as the "man writing" that both Emerson and Thoreau aspired to be, and your life outside of art will be so empty that the art itself must at last wither away. Consciously or unconsciously echoing Gray's "Elegy," Thoreau declares that Massachusetts has produced "greater men than Homer, or Chaucer, or Shakespeare, only they never got time to say so; they never took to the way of writing." "To be a philosopher," he says, "is not merely to have subtle thoughts, nor even to found a school, but so to love wisdom as to live, according to its dictates, a life of simplicity, independence, magnanimity, and trust." When he was at his best he could feel in himself "a fullness of life" even when it did not "find any channels to flow into."

When Thoreau speaks of the poet, he is generally thinking not specifically of verse-making but of literature of quality, whatever form it may take and however one may think of the "inspiration" which produced it. To him the poet was "no tender slip of fairy stock . . . but the toughest son of earth and of Heaven. . . . It is the worshippers of beauty, after all, who have done the real pioneer work of the world." He realized the natural, indeed inevitable, tendency of writing which rose above a certain level of intensity to assume what is generally thought of as poetic form, and he rejected the idea that poetry belongs only to youth. "In that fervid and excitable season we only get the impulse which is to carry us onward in our future career. . . . The mere vision is little compared with the steady corresponding endeavor thitherward." Yet he could also feel that "great prose, of equal elevation, commands our respect more than great verse, since it implies a more permanent and level height, a life more pervaded with the grandeur of the thought." "The poet often only makes an irruption, like a Parthian, and is off again, shooting while he retreats, but the prose writer has conquered like a Roman, and settled colonies."[40]

In 1932 Raymond Adams chose 1840 as the year Thoreau decided to become a writer, and saw him consciously at work creating a literary style in the spring of 1841, but Emerson thought Thoreau had always looked forward to authorship as his work in life. Date his consecration where you will, there can be no doubt as to his zeal. John Burroughs, never very sympathetic to Thoreau, thought him a slave to his journal—"he lived for that Journal, he read for it, he walked for it; it was like a hungry, omnivorous monster that constantly called for more"—and even thought he "went to Walden for subject-matter for his pen; and the remarkable thing about it all is that he was always keyed up to the writing pitch."[41]

He did not disdain practical considerations: thus the writer should "write on many subjects" and "try many themes," avoid "spurious and artificial" words and those "which drag a dead tail after them," and never use "for the sake of emphasis," words "which really add nothing" to the force of his sentences. Nor was he above being interested in the response he awakened in his readers. "I am encouraged to know that, so far as you are concerned," he wrote one correspondent in 1862, "I have not written my books in vain." I doubt his wisdom when he writes, "let thy report be colorless as respects the hue of the reporter's mind; only let it have the color of the thing reported." Certainly this was not in harmony with either his practice or his conviction that all seeing was necessarily subjective. Quite as doubtful is his idea that the man who works with his hands is more likely to write directly and forcefully than one who does not: "We are often struck by the force and precision of style to which hard-working men, unpracticed in early writing, easily attained when required to make the effort. . . . The sentences written by such rude hands are nervous and tough, like hardened things, the sinews of the deer, or the roots of the pine." This sounds logical enough, and one might support it by reference to General Grant and perhaps also Lincoln and John Brown, but it can hardly be a rule, and even Thoreau adds that the man must not work too much.[42]

In his journal in 1854 Thoreau set down what he himself considered his weaknesses as a writer:

My faults are:
Paradoxes,—saying just the opposite,—a style which may be imitated. Ingenious.
Playing with words,—getting the laugh,—not always simple, strong, and broad.
Using current phrases and maxims, when I should speak for myself.

Not always earnest.
"In short," "in fact," "alas!" etc.
Want of conciseness.

He has other faults which he does not mention here. Despite the clarity and concreteness he often achieves, he can be obscure and contradictory, and he sometimes uses "proud words" and takes off on flights which are comprehensible only on the transcendental level. He does not specifically mention his punning in the list he makes of his faults, though he probably had it in mind under "play-ing with words." Brooks Atkinson thought his "bastard humor" in this aspect "elephantine" and out of place in "so reserved and aus-tere" a writer, but both Emerson and Burroughs assigned it to his contrariety, and the latter comes close to meeting him on his own ground when he writes that "he is too religious to go to church, too patriotic to pay his taxes, too fervent a humanist to interest himself in the social welfare of his neighborhood." As for the exaggeration with which he is often charged, he feared only that he might not "wander far enough beyond the narrow limits of our ordinary in-sight and faith, so as to be adequate to the truth of which I have been convinced." He apparently distinguished this kind of exaggeration from the "harsh, extravagant, and cynical expressions concerning mankind and individuals" to which his "companion" (I suppose Channing) often tempted him. "I find it difficult to make a suffici-ently moderate statement. I think it is because I have not his sym-pathy in my sober and constant view. He asks for a paradox, an eccentric statement, and too often I give it to him." Incidentally this suggests that Thoreau was less resistant to pressure from compan-ions and surroundings than is commonly supposed.[43]

He wished to write of "homely every-day phenomena and adven-tures" and to describe them in what Mencken was afterwards to call the American language, free from "the weak and flowing periods of the politician and scholar." Even the *Farmer's Almanac* was better than that, and "the strong and hearty but reckless, hit-or-miss style" of such early New England writers as Josselyn and William Wood was better still, for they wrote "with a relish, smacking their lips like a coach-whip, caring more to speak heartily" than to be sci-entifically accurate, and using "a strong, coarse, homely speech which cannot be found in the dictionary, nor sometimes heard in polite society, but which brings you very near to the thing itself described." As a good linguist he rarely overlooked the etymologies of his words, and many of the puns and figures with which his books abound derive from this.

Describing, or trying to describe, how he wrote, he tells us: "From all the points of the compass, from the earth beneath and the heavens above, have come these inspirations and been entered duly in the order of their arrival in the journal. Thereafter, when the time arrived, they were winnowed into lectures and again, in due time, from lectures into essays." But complicated as this sounds, it unduly simplified his process, for many journal entries were themselves not only revised but re-revised. It is evident that he used his journal to try things out, seizing upon the first glow of inspiration with a view to polishing afterwards and, as Perry Miller says, depositing "a vastly larger capital than he ever withdrew."[44] He was equally diligent in revising what he had designed as the published text, "so constant and insistent," says Sanborn, "that some of his manuscripts are from correction practically illegible." "A piece of writing need not be long," says Thoreau, "but it will take a long while to make it short," which is very close to Pascal's "Please excuse the length of my letter. I had no time to write a short one." He turned out bad copy along with good and did not expect to be able to tell the difference between them until after a lapse of time. "Nothing goes by luck in composition. . . . Every sentence is the result of a long probation. The author's character is read from title page to end. Of this he never corrects the proofs."

In 1939 Henry Seidel Canby placed Thoreau with Bacon, Shakespeare, Pope, Dr. Johnson, Franklin, and the translators of the King James Bible among the "great makers of the English sentence" and declared that "as a story-teller, he recalls the effective simplicity of Defoe," but at that time there was still far too much tendency to underrate his mastery of structure and to classify his work, along with Emerson's, as mere accumulations of brilliant sentences. Both Channing and Foerster had realized that this was inadequate, but the real pioneer in perceiving that *Walden* was a highly integrated work of art was F. O. Matthiessen in his *American Renaissance* in 1941, and the really heroic job of minute analysis was done by J. Lyndon Shanley in *The Making of Walden* in 1957. The truth is that, here and elsewhere, Thoreau's organization of his materials is so subtle and delicate that it has taken scholars a hundred years to achieve anything like a full appreciation of it. Since they have not all discerned the same things, they cannot all possibly be right, but even when all allowances have been made Odell Shepard's 1920 judgment—that Thoreau never learned to write but only to exclaim—now seems utterly fantastic. [45]

The change has involved a new definition of Thoreau's purpose in *Walden* and a new understanding of the nature of his work as a whole. *Walden* can no longer be regarded as an autobiography or even, in the narrower sense, as a truthful or accurate record of his experiences at the pond. It is instead a fable, a work of art in which the raw material derived from those experiences has been re-created into art forms which are real but not actual because, as they come to us, they existed only in the artist's creative imagination.

The real Walden Pond is oblong, but Thoreau makes it round to harmonize with the circular imagery he plans to employ. He lived there a little over two years, but he draws his materials into the compass of a single year, not only ignoring the differences between the two but even drawing other materials in. Philip Van Doren Stern questions even the figures he gives us about his expenses. Leo Marx, more radically, is not even sure that the pond of the book is in Massachusetts, preferring to see it as "another embodiment of the American moral geography—a native blend of myth and reality. The hut beside the pond stands at the center of a symbolic landscape in which the village of Concord appears on one side and a vast stretch of unmodified nature on the other." Lawrence Buell goes further still when he calls *Walden* "the closest the Transcendentalists came to creating a major work of prose fiction." And if the pond is "a mythical world," then "I" must be a persona who serves as both the narrator and the subject of the book, and so Charles R. Anderson can compare its "dramatic scenes and ambiguous symbols" with those of *The Scarlet Letter*, *Moby-Dick* and Wordsworth's *Prelude*. Harding counted more than fifty different types of figures of speech in *Walden*, with rebirth and renewal predominating. It opens in spring, runs through the cycle of the seasons and ends with the rebirth of nature the following spring. But the cyclic movement of the day is described, as well as that of the year; individual chapters are alternated between actualities and reflections; and chapters and paragraphs are also carefully balanced within themselves. In all this, it should not be necessary to say, there was no attempt to deceive. Thoreau described his own aims and methods as a writer, in *Walden* and elsewhere, when he confided to his journal: "I, too, would fain set down something besides facts. Facts should only be as the frame to my pictures; they should be material to the mythology which I am writing; . . . facts to tell who I am, and where I have been or what I have thought. . . . My facts shall be falsehoods to the common sense. I would so state facts that they shall be significant, shall be myths or mythologic. Facts which the mind perceived, thoughts which the body thought,—with these I deal."[46]

Of late years Thoreau's other works have been approached in much the same spirit as *Walden*. The *Week*, with its many essay-like digressions breaking into the story of the journey, was long considered formless, and some still tend to accept this view. At the other extreme, Buell regards the book as "the most ambitious literary work—in scope if not in accomplishment—that the Transcendentalist movement produced" and an attempt "to encompass the whole of Thoreau's intellectual and spiritual development," while Robert F. Sayre tentatively advances the idea that it is a history "in abbreviated visionary form of savage-civilized relations in America." If this seems extravagant, let us at least remember that Paul and McIntire have also defended the unity of the book pretty convincingly, while Kenneth Lynn, who declared that "the use of a drifting rhythm as the matrix for the thought and action of a book would not be exploited as successfully again by an author until *Huckleberry Finn*," also argued that "the subjects which Thoreau discusses enroute are not fortuitous, but organically related to the unfolding panorama of the journey and the particular day of the week."[47] Lesser works have been scrutinized in a similar spirit: thus the Cape Cod book combines three journeys into one. Harding finds Thoreau the virtual creator of the nature essay ("he was the first to realize that in writing about nature he could do more than simply report on natural phenomena, that he could weave and polish his findings into a truly belletristic form"), and Frederick Garber has found both unity and diversity in "Walking," hitherto considered as unorganized as anything Thoreau ever wrote.[48]

Thoreau knew from the beginning that sincerity is the great requirement in writing and that one must always write about what is important to one's self. Above all, one must never write "down"; the way to please others is to please oneself. One cannot choose a theme, but must be chosen by it. Having found it, the writer concentrates on the thought, and if he really has anything to say, it will drop from him as simply and directly as a stone falls to the ground, though, to be sure, "whatever has been produced on the spur of the moment will need to be reconsidered and reformed with phlegm."

Perhaps some of the things Thoreau says about writing require a reader who has at least a touch of transcendentalism himself. Once at least, in the poem called "Inspiration," which, despite its technical imperfections, gives us as good evidence as we have anywhere of his capacity for mystical experience, he distinctly suggests Emily Brontë:

> If with light head erect I sing,
>   Though all the Muses lend their force,
> From my poor love of anything,
>   The verse is weak and shallow as its source.
>
> But if with bended neck I grope,
>   Listening behind me for my wit,
> With faith superior to none,
>   More anxious to keep back than forward it,
>
> Making my soul accomplice there
>   Unto the flame my heart hath lit,
> Then will the verse forever wear;
>   Time cannot bend the line which God hath writ.
>
> Always the general show of things
>   Floats in review before my mind,
> And such true love and reverence brings,
>   That sometimes I forget that I am blind.
>
> But now there comes, unsought, unseen,
>   Some clear, divine electuary,
> And I, who had but sensual been,
>   Grow sensible,—and as God is, wary.
>
> I hearing get, who had but ears,
>   And sight, who had but eyes before;

I moments live, who lived but years,
    And truth discern, who knew but learning's lore.

I hear beyond the range of sound,
    I see beyond the range of sight,
New earths and skies and seas around,
    And in my day the sun doth pale his light.

A clear and ancient harmony
    Pierces my soul through all its din,
As through its utmost melody,—
    Farther behind than they,—farther within.

More swift its bolt than lightning is,
    Its voice than thunder is more loud;
It doth expand my privacies
    To all, and leave me single in the crowd.

It speaks with such authority,
    With so serene and lofty tone,
That idle Time runs gadding by,
    And leaves me with Eternity alone.

More often, however, he expresses it better in prose, and in physical and psychological rather than religious terms:

1851: We cannot write well or truly but what we write with gusto. The body, the senses, must conspire with the mind. Expression is the act of the whole man, that our speech may be vascular. The intellect is powerless to express thought without the aid of the heart and liver and of every member.

1852: Do nothing out of good resolutions. Discipline yourself only to yield to love; suffer yourself to be attracted. It is in vain to write on chosen themes. We must wait till they have kindled a flame in our minds. There must be the copulating and generating force of love behind every effort destined to be successful. . . . The poet's relation to his theme is the relation of lovers.

1859: We exaggerate the importance and exclusiveness of the headquarters. . . . The poet's words are, "You would almost say the body thought!" I quite say it.

And, most suggestively and most cryptically of all:

1851: Sentences which suggest more than they say, which have an atmosphere about them, which do not merely report the old, but make a new impression; sentences which suggest as many things and are as durable as a Roman Aqueduct; to frame these, that is the *art* of writing. Sentences which are expensive, towards which so many volumes, so much life, went; which lie like boulders on the page, up and down, or across; which contain the seed of other sentences, not mere repetition, but creation; which a man might sell his grounds and castles to build. If De Quincey had suggested each of his pages in a sentence and passed on, it would have been far more excellent writing. His style is nowhere kinked and knotted up into something hard and significant, which you could swallow like a diamond, without digesting.

CHAPTER TWO

Others

Man is not at once born into society,—hardly into the world.
The world that he is hides for a time the world that he inhabits.

HDT, 1838

THROUGH HIS WRITINGS and his lectures, then, Thoreau communicated with the world, but how did he communicate with the individuals in it? He often disparages sociality. He would "rather keep bachelor's hall in hell than go to board in heaven," and he would prefer to sit on a pumpkin and have it all to himself "than to be crowded on a velvet cushion." Nor was it only as he confronted such "communities" as Fruitlands and Brook Farm that he felt thus; one meeting of Alcott's Town and Country Club was enough for him. "By myself I can live and thrive," he says, "but in the society of incompatible friends I starve." "If I have had a companion only one day in a week, unless it were one or two I could name, I find that the value of the week to me has been seriously affected. It dissipates my days, and often it takes me another week to get over it." "Woe to him who wants a companion, for he is unfit to be the companion even of himself." He admits that he missed company at Walden Pond, but he finds this slightly insane, and even when acknowledging the refreshment he derived from his visits to town, he cannot get further than to suggest that men and boys may be as interesting "in homoeopathic doses" as birds, squirrels, frogs, and the rustle of leaves. He is grateful for "the simple, reserved countrymen among his neighbors" who mind their own business and leave him alone, and he even boasts that he has no need of newspapers or the post office, though we know he made good use of both. "I have enjoyed very much my visits to you and my rides in your neighborhood," he writes Daniel Ricketson, "and am sorry I cannot enjoy such things oftener; but life is short, and there are other things also to be done."

It can hardly be claimed, then, that Thoreau was "popular" in Concord; doubtless it would have been too much to expect the average villager or farmer to feel quite at home with a man who preferred spending his time watching frogs and squirrels to devoting himself to some "useful" occupation. His "signing off" from the First Parish and refusing to pay his poll tax can hardly have helped his reputation either, and many never forgave him for his carelessness in setting the woods afire in 1846. Emerson speaks of his finding it easier to say no than yes, "a habit . . . a little chilling to the social affections," and Emerson's son says that when Thoreau was in a perverse mood, it was like having Pan at a dinner party. When young Howells visited Thoreau, he found himself placed "not quite so far off as Ohio," but still "across the whole room, for he sat against one wall, and I against the other," and even Sanborn, though insisting that Henry was "at heart profoundly unselfish and courteous," admits that "he was on the surface brusque and pugnacious; and at times, in spite of his distinction, a little too plebeian in his nature."

His speech, we are told, was "deliberate and positive," easy and interesting, "but it was of the kind that proceeds by a succession of short paragraphs, deliberately constructed, lecturewise, rather than by suggestive sentences and phrases neatly and sympathetically adjusted to what is said by others."[1] Channing says he seldom replied directly to a question. Apparently he often talked about what he had been reading, and Emerson says that he would say what he had to say "in a lump" and depart without waiting for or regarding any comment. He reminded one hostess "of an eagle ready to soar to great heights or to sweep down on anything he considered evil."

Clearly this is not the whole story, however, nor do either Thoreau or his friends leave it there. He himself says that he loved to talk. He knew how to laugh and make merry too (once we hear of his jumping over the table), and when his mother and sister heard of his dancing at the Ricketsons', "Sophia said they had often seen Henry cut up in such a manner." He can tell us, on the one hand, that "the mass never comes up to the standard of its best member," but he can also assert that "it is the charm and greatness of all society, from friendship to the drawing-room, that it takes place on a level slightly higher than the actual characters of the parties would warrant; it is an expression of faith." E. Harlow Russell, who thought Henry "talked rather like one who was accustomed to be listened to than to listen," yet adds that, "he gave you a chance to talk, attended to what you said, and then made his reply," though he "did not come to very close quarters with you or help you out with your thought after the manner of skilled and practiced conversers," and one Concordian says that "he was always straight in his ways and was very particular to be agreeable. . . . When I saw him crossing my field I always wanted to go out and have a talk with him. . . . He liked to talk as long as you did, and what he said was new." We hear too that he could "talk a fellow dumb" if the other had any information in him that Thoreau wanted, and he seems to have had no difficulty in approaching strangers on his travels, or in living and sleeping in close quarters with others on camping trips; neither was he easily repelled or quick to take offense. In Canada he sometimes had difficulty making himself understood by those who spoke only French, yet he writes of one such occasion that "we had a long and merry chat with the family this Sunday evening in their spacious kitchen." He would have liked to move among men as naturally and as easily as he moved through the woods, and there were times when it seemed to him that he had done this. Whatever his fellow Concordians may have thought of him earlier, the attentions they paid him and the gifts they sent him during his final illness would certainly seem to indicate that he was held in high regard then. "I should be ashamed to stay in the world after so much had been done for me," he said. "I could never repay my friends."

To be sure, he was not equally successful with all types of people, but who is? He did not enjoy those who neither asked what he thought nor minded what he said, nor could he walk or sail happily with somebody who used up all his energy in talk and argument. "They do not consider that the wood-path and the boat are my studio, where I maintain a sacred solitude and cannot admit promiscuous company." Even such good friends as Alcott and Hawthorne could fail him here, for Alcott always wanted to rest on the nearest stump, and when they reached a perfectly enchanting swamp, Hawthorne would always want to get out of "this dreadful hole."

Yet his heart was full of longing for the companion with whom he could achieve a true meeting of minds; he knocked on the earth for such a person, and looked for him at every turn, and even when he relished solitude, he knew that solitude was not the end. "You think I am impoverishing myself by withdrawing from men, but in my solitude I have woven for myself a silken web or *chrysalis*, and nymph-like, shall ere long burst forth a more perfect creature, fitted to a higher society." He contributed to the Concord Athenaeum and Lyceum and used them; he was hospitable at Walden Pond to even half-witted or highly eccentric visitors, and though he chafed at those who wasted his time, it is clear that, like the rest of us, he did sometimes allow himself to be imposed upon. Often he showed more toleration toward the idiosyncrasies of others than they accorded his own.[2]

Paradox does not disappear from the record when we turn from Thoreau's attitude toward sociality in general to his attitude toward humanity. Conventional, stereotyped forms of politeness meant little to him, he was suspicious of professional philanthropists, and he can call a "sickly preaching of love" a kind of "dyspepsia of the soul." He disclaims any interest in doing good, being, he says, in no more of a hurry to help men than God is. He could also be unresponsive to complaints over ailments, thinking that invalids should not be encouraged to coddle themselves, and when Channing begged off from a hike because of a headache, he replied coldly that there were people who had a headache every morning but went about their business nevertheless. Life as most men lived it, apparently chose to live it, seemed to him to make it a trivial farce. There is a bitterly resentful passage on the farmer Flint, who refused to allow him to build a cabin at Sandy Point, but one may hope that his outburst against the two girls who borrowed a dipper from him at Walden Pond, and failed to return it, was written with tongue in cheek: "They were a disgrace to their sex and to humanity. Pariahs of the moral world. Evil spirits that thirsted not for water but threw the dipper into the lake. Such as Dante saw. What the lake to them but liquid fire and brimstone? They will never know peace till they have returned the dipper. In all the worlds this is decreed."

Yet his ideal for humanity was high. That, of course, was just the trouble, and that was why it hurt him so much when people fell

short. "Man is the crowning fact, the God we know." "Who shall
say that there is no God if there is a *just* man?" "There is the same
ground for faith now that there ever was. It needs only a little love in
you who complain so to ground it on." He is sure that human beings
have faculties they have never yet discovered nor cultivated, and
summons them to enter consciously upon a new stage in development, yet even so, "in this strange, outlandish world," it is wonderful to think that "so divine a creature as man does actually live."

Certainly he was capable of putting himself to considerable inconvenience to serve his friends when the occasion warranted. He
looked out a house for the Ellery Channings in Concord and super-
vised the repairs thereon. He helped the Alcotts settle in Orchard
House and served as a pallbearer at Beth's funeral. He took care of
the proofs of Emerson's *English Traits,* brought his retarded brother
Bulkeley to their mother's funeral, and later himself made the ar-
rangements for Bulkeley's burying. He went to Fire Island to search
for Margaret Fuller's remains after she and her family had been
shipwrecked there, and I think we should not be chilled by his remark anent this experience, "that actual events . . . are far less real
than the creations of my imagination," for I take this as a sensitive
man's attempt to save himself from being hurt too much. "I perceive
that we partially die ourselves, through sympathy," he wrote, "at
the death of each of our friends or near relatives," and he himself
was crushed not only by the death of his brother but also by that of
his friend, Stearns Wheeler.

Sometimes it seemed easier for him to find the vestiges of divinity
that he knew existed in mankind in those at the bottom rather than
at the top of the social pyramid, and there may have been an element
of inverted snobbery in this. He even thought he would rather talk
with or lecture to such people than to more cultivated ladies and
gentlemen whose personalities were swallowed up by their manners and who took care never to say anything that might provoke
disagreement. Young Goethe, he thought, "was defrauded of much
which the savage boy enjoys." He "had no intercourse with the
lowest class of his towns-boys. The child should have the advantage
of ignorance as well as of knowledge, and is fortunate if he gets his
share of neglect and exposure." "It is a pleasant fact that you will
know no man long, however low in the social scale, however poor,

miserable, intemperate and worthless he may appear to be, a mere burden to society, but you will find at last that there is something which he understands and can do better than any other."[3]

One of Thoreau's very earliest pieces of writing, an obituary notice for an aged Concord woman, breathes an attractive spirit of reverence and sympathy.[4] We hear too of his patient, persistent services "to an elderly woman, a dependent and complaining person," and how he once took a child from a tired mother trying to catch a train, sprinted ahead, and succeeded in delaying the train's departure until she could reach it. There is at least one example of a generous response on his part to an offender who had acknowledged and repented his fault,[5] but he lapses into an unaccustomed sentimentality in his admiration for the derelict Bill Wheeler simply because he had gone his own way, and even more in what he writes of the drunken Dutchman whom he encountered on an oyster boat, "snoring and rolling in the vomit produced by his debauch" and blurting forth "some happy repartee like an illuminated swine. It was the earthiest, slimiest wit I ever heard," and it made him "one of the few remarkable men I have ever met. I have been impressed by one or two men in their cups. There was really a divinity stirred within them, so that in their case, I have reverenced the drunken, as savages the insane, man." Perhaps a little of this charity might better have been reserved for Alek Therien who, when he visited Thoreau in his cups, was advised to go home and cut his throat and do it quickly.[6]

In Thoreau's time and milieu three classes—the Indians, the blacks, and the Irish—provided special tests for his humanity. His attitude toward the first two of these is considered elsewhere in these pages, but it should at least be stated here that though the determined non-joiner Thoreau never joined an abolition society, he was up to his neck in the Underground Railroad activities of his family, and that Moncure D. Conway recorded a touching account of his tenderness toward one fugitive whom Conway happened to find in his care. "He must be fed, his swollen feet bathed, and he must think of nothing but rest. Again and again the coolest and calmest of men drew near to the trembling negro, and bade him feel at home, and have no fear that any power should again wrong him." His comments on the Irish immigrants, whom he encountered in

Concord as laborers on the railroad, are by no means all admiring (he never blinks their dirt, shiftlessness, or drunkenness),[7] but he defended them heartily against Yankee prejudice, performing many personal services for them, and in one instance circularized his neighbors for funds to reimburse an Irishman for the money his employer had unjustly withheld from him. Above all, he loved little five-year-old Johnny Riordan and saw to it that he was adequately clothed to go to school in the cold Concord winter. "Oh, I should rather hear that America's first-born were all slain than that his little fingers and toes should feel cold while I am warm."

Sentimental though this may be, it was not uncharacteristic, for Thoreau seems to have been at his best as a social being with children. To be sure he could declare that "children appear to me as raw as the fresh fungi on a fence rail," and there was nothing of what we now call "permissiveness" in his treatment of them, but he seems to have been equally successful as mentor and entertainer. A woman who knew him when she was a child has recorded how he played juggler's tricks for children, swallowed his knife and produced it from their ears and noses, made willow whistles and trumpets from the stems of squash and onion leaves, and popped corn so that when the lid was lifted, they would be covered with a beautiful white fountain. "I do not remember a check of reproof from him, no matter how noisy we were." He also sang and played the flute for the children and told them stories out of Scandinavian mythology and his own childhood. In later years children often came to see him to report their discoveries in fauna and flora, and he longed to see them even during his final illness. "Why don't they come to see me? I love them as if they were my own." When he died, the Concord schools were closed so that the children might attend his funeral and place flowers on his grave.

With the Emerson children, the Alcotts, and others he had special relations. In looking after the little Emersons while their father was in Europe, he was so successful that Edward asked him if he would not be his father! Moncure D. Conway tells of the tact, humanity, and understanding he displayed one day when Edward was distressed and unhappy over having spilled the basket of huckleberries he had picked. "Thoreau came, put his arms around the troubled child, and explained to him that if the crop of huckleberries was to continue it was necessary that some should be scattered. Nature had provided that little boys should now and then stumble and sow the berries. We shall have a grand lot of bushes and berries in this spot, and we shall owe them to you." Nor did he ever lose interest in the boy, giving him good and helpful advice even as late as when he was preparing for Harvard. He shared Margaret Fuller's and the Emersons' own impressions of Waldo as being almost too spiritual a being for this world, and there is a charming letter to Ellen Emerson and, comparatively recently recovered, a poem to Edith.[8]

I I

But whatever his attitude toward humanity at large may be, a man lives his life with individual people—the members of the family into which he is born, the friends he makes, and those whom he loves. Thoreau lived virtually all his life with his family, which embraced, at various times, not only his parents, two sisters, and a brother, but aunts, an uncle, and a number of boarders and even transients. After his father's death in 1859, he became the head of both the family and the family business.

Naturally this proximity involved strain at times, and it would be evasive to pretend that Thoreau never felt it. We do not know just what he had in mind when he wrote that "the fathers and the mothers of the town . . . don't want any prophets born into their families—damn them!" but we do have the 1854 journal entry in which he complains that conditions in his attic chamber had compelled him "to sit below with the family at evening for a month. I feel the necessity of deepening the stream of my life; I must cultivate privacy. It is very dissipating to be with people too much." Long before this he had lamented to his sister Helen that often when they had been closest bodily, they had been spiritually most removed. "Our tongues were the witty foils with which we fenced each other off." But perhaps the sharpest expression comes in the next year 1841: "No true and brave person will be content to live on such a footing with his fellows and himself as the laws of every household now require. The house is the very lair and haunt of our vice. I am impatient to withdraw myself from under its roof as an unclean spot. There is no circulation there; it is full of stagnant and mephitic vapors." And the very next day he adds that "it leavens the rest of our hours" to be able "to retire to our chamber and be completely true to ourselves" for a few moments, but for a rather odd and perverse reason. "In that moment I will be as nakedly vicious as I am; this false life of mine shall have a being at length."

The Freudian critics, notably Raymond D. Gozzi and Richard Lebeaux, have naturally made the most of such utterances, though their methods would seem peculiarly inappropriate to a man with Thoreau's antagonism to preformulations. J. G. Taylor quotes George Eliot's saying—"that the mysterious complexity of our life is not to be embraced by maxims, and that to lace ourselves up in formulas . . . is to repress all the divine promptings and inspirations that spring from growing insight and sympathy"—and we may be sure Thoreau would agree. Indeed Gozzi himself admits, with a frankness, tentativeness, and humility rare in psychoanalytically conditioned writers, that a "satisfying comprehension" of Thoreau "eludes" him.[9]

Lebeaux is considerably less reckless than many writers of his persuasion and certainly much more coherent. He has no difficulty in showing that there were tensions at times in the Thoreau family, but since there never has been nor ever will be a family of which this is not true, the demonstration is not in itself a great achievement. Inevitably too anybody who guesses as often as he does must sometimes, by the law of averages, guess right. But when he seeks to impose a Freudian/Eriksonian frame of reference upon his findings, he frequently creates the impression not of a biography but a work of fiction. Actually only the novelist is ever able to create a completely explicable character, for only the novelist possesses a Godlike omniscient knowledge of his characters. When the biographer aspires to the novelistic type of knowledge, and becomes a writer of fiction without either realizing or admitting it, one is reminded of Thoreau's own words to the "slimy" reformer who proposed to "dive" into his "inmost depths." "I trust," said Henry, "you will not strike your head against the bottom." The biographer who is willing to honor and observe the differences between fact and fiction must be content with partial understanding and explication, which is all we can ever achieve even of ourselves. It is all a little like the difference between solving mysteries which you yourself have set up, as the writer of detective stories does, an art which manifests only an ability to devise elaborate puzzles, and investigating actual, real life mysteries concerning which nobody is in possession of all the facts.

Nevertheless we do have abundant evidence to support the view that the Thoreaus lived a close and affectionate family life. It is true that when inviting Daniel Ricketson to Concord in 1855 Thoreau went out of his way to prepare him for "our awful unsocial ways, —keeping in our dens a good part of the day, sucking our claws perhaps—but then we make a religion of it, and that you cannot but respect." Others, however, describe their reading, singing, and playing games together, their tea parties, walks, and evening visits, and Thoreau's own cheerfulness and courtesy in all these connections.[10] The children hung up their stockings for Santa Claus every Christmas until disillusioned by a schoolmate, and there is the well-known story of Henry bursting into tears when his mother suggested his going out to seek his fortune and being consoled by his sister Helen, who assured him that he should stay at home and be loved by them. Certainly there can be no doubt that he was desperately homesick when tutoring in William Emerson's family on Staten Island. We know too that during his final illness he came to the table for his meals as long as possible because "it was more sociable" and also that he enjoyed and encouraged callers.[11]

Perhaps enough has been said of the father and mother in the biographical section of this volume. Thoreau's sister Sophia outlived Henry and became the guardian of his fame, and Perry Miller prints what seems an almost hysterical panegyric to Helen, written after her death in 1849.[12] But the closest personal relationship was undoubtedly that with his brother John, the shock of whose sudden and horrible death from lockjaw on January 11, 1842, when he was only twenty-seven, was the greatest agony Henry ever experienced. After John's death, Henry himself came down with all the symptoms of lockjaw and became so sick that his life was despaired of, when suddenly, inexplicably, he began to recover. He himself clearly recognized what we should now call the psychosomatic character of this illness,[13] but his grief did not end with his recovery. For five weeks after his brother's death, he could make no entry in his journal, and though he thought grief for the death of an individual selfish and partial except as "a paean to the departed soul," he wrote that years had been crowded into a month and that a man could attend only one funeral during his lifetime. It is true that, being what he was, Henry had to transcendentalize even this experience ("I do not wish to see John ever again,—I mean him who is dead,—but that other, whom only he would have wished to see, or to be, of whom he was the imperfect representative"), yet it is said that he involuntarily clenched his hands when he spoke of his brother and that at least once he turned pale and had to go to the door for air. His poem, "Brother Where Dost Thou Dwell," is aesthetically inconsequential compared to Emerson's "Threnody," the notable lament for the loss of his son Waldo, which so closely followed and in whose agony Thoreau shared, [14] but in their spirit the two pieces are closely allied:

> Brother where dost thou dwell?
>   What sun shines for thee now?
> Dost thou still haunt the brink
>   Of yonder river's tide?
> And may I ever think
>   That thou art at my side?

III

The perfervid transcendental cult of friendship almost wiped out the line of demarcation between friendship and love and consequently carried all the agonies of one relationship over into the other. [15] Thoreau's most extended consideration of the subject is in the long essay on friendship in the Wednesday section of the *Week*, [16] but the same attitudes expressed there run all through his journals.

"A man cannot be said to succeed in this life," he says, "who does not satisfy one friend," and he thought that "to attain a true relation to one human creature is enough to make a year memorable." In theory, to be sure, he yearned for a sense of union with all men, as he puts it in the not necessarily literal poem, "I Knew a Man by Sight," in which he speaks of the possibility of acquaintance with one he had often seen but not spoken to, and which ends with the hope that all

> Both great and small
> That ever lived on earth,
> Early or late their birth,
> Stranger and foe, one day each other know.

But he knew this was only an ideal, for though even his Harvard classmates had their place in his heart ("but that is too sacred a matter even for a classbook") and though when any human being showed an "implicit faith" in him, even in trivial matters, he felt "addressed and probed even to the remote parts of my being," he was well aware that the laws of consanguinity were difficult or impossible to pin down. "I love that one with whom I sympathize, be she 'beautiful' or otherwise, of excellent mind or not." He might long for one to whom he could be "transparent," revealing all his thoughts, but in his heart he knew that even this much was impossible. "The lover learns at last that there is no person quite transparent and trustworthy, but that every one has a devil in him that is capable of any crime in the long run." And though he did not always believe that, he never forgot that no friendship can be a static relationship, but rather "a miracle which requires constant proofs" and tending. Nevertheless, the death of a near friend or relation robs one of "vital force. It becomes a source of wonder that they who have lost many friends still live." Watch around the deathbed of a friend and you must "partially give up the ghost with him."

There were other difficulties. As Thoreau saw it, a true friendship "takes place on a level higher than the actual character of the parties would seem to warrant." Estranged persons are "two friends explaining," for where true friendship exists, "there is no veil and there can be no obstacle." Nor could he apologize, for he rested always under "an awful necessity to be what I am."

This would seem, then, to rule out any toleration for faults, for friendship is so delicate a plant that "the least unworthiness, even if it be unknown to one's self, vitiates it." If your friend sees wrong as right, he robs you of your eyes, darkens the day for you, and becomes your enemy, and when Henry hears of a friend having spoken of him coldly or indifferently, it seems "the sum of all crimes against humanity." So exclusively is he the friend of his friend's virtue that he is "compelled to be silent for the most part because his vice is present." Friendship thus becomes a kind of communion of saints, who meet "religiously," so as not to "prophane one another." Our friend's is "as holy a shrine as any God's, to be approached with sacred love and awe," and we can feel shame there more readily than elsewhere. "Our hour is a sabbath, our abode a temple, our gifts peace offerings, our conversation a communion, our silence a prayer. In prophanity we are absent, in holiness near, in sin estranged, in innocence reconciled."

At times it is hard to avoid the conclusion that the idea of friendship attracted Thoreau more than the fact, and that he loved his own idea of his friend more than the actual person. "When I see only the roof of a house above the woods and do not know whose it is, I presume that one of the worthies of the world dwells beneath it, and for a season I am exhilarated by the thought. . . . But commonly, if I see or know the occupant, I am affected as by the sight of the almshouse or hospital." "I love my friends very much," he says, "but I find it is no use to go to see them. I hate them commonly when I am near them." And again: "When I am withdrawn and alone, I forget the actual person and remember only my ideal." He believed it possible for friends to "know of each other through sympathy merely, without any of the ordinary information," and was capable of experiencing unspeakable joy when thinking of those to whom he was "truly related" though "hardly on speaking terms"; sometimes, even, the death of a friend might have the odd effect of bringing him closer.

Obviously this is a view of friendship which can hardly be achieved in this life, and one need not be surprised to encounter in the journal from time to time lamentations over the ending of "one more" unidentified relationship. It is clear that such things caused him real anguish. "I could better have the earth taken away from under my feet, than the thought of you from my mind." "What if we feel a yearning to which no breast answers? I walk alone. My heart is full. Feelings impede the current of my thoughts—I knock on the earth for my friend." "If the teeth ache, they can be pulled. If the heart aches, what then?" Moreover the decaying of a friendship can be as painful as a break. "Morning, noon, and night, I suffer a physical pain, an aching of the breast which unfits me for my tasks."

Did it ever occur to him that the fault in such cases might be his own? Clearly it did. "If I have not succeeded in my friendships, it was because I demanded more of them and did not put up with what I could get; and I got no more partly because I gave so little." And, much later: "I do not know what has made my friend doubt me, but I know that in love there is no mistake, and that every estrangement is full founded." Though his letters do not in general seem cold to me, he declares that "I am of the nature of stone. It takes the summer's sun to warm it" and that he rarely rises above a mere patient or wholesome good will in his relations with men. And it is certainly true that he began his letters "Mr. Ricketson" and "Mr. Blake" until Ricketson protested, after which he warmed up but not to the boiling point with "Friend Ricketson," who himself signed one letter, protestingly and satirically, "Yours exceeding, 'Mr. Ricketson.' "

Thoreau was neither the first man nor the last to perceive that love and hate lie closer together in the emotional spectrum than either inclines toward indifference, but he certainly makes more of a point of it than many have made. "Those whom we love, we can hate; to others we are indifferent." The most striking expressions are in the poems:

> Let such pure hate still underprop
> Our love, that we may be
> Each other's conscience,
> And have our sympathy
> Mainly from thence.

And again:

> Indeed, indeed, I cannot tell
> Though I ponder on it well,
> Which were easier to state,
> All my love or all my hate.
> Surely, surely, thou wilt trust me
> When I say thou dost disgust me.
> O, I hate thee with a hate
> That would fain annihilate;
> Yet sometimes against my will,
> My dear friend, I love thee still,
> It were treason to our love,
> And a sin to God above,
> One iota to abate
> Of a pure impartial hate.

It would not be correct to say that these verses convey the same kind of chill as Christ's words about the necessity to hate father and mother in order to be worthy of him. But they certainly stand quite as clearly among the "hard sayings."[17]

I V

Emerson, Hawthorne, Alcott, and Ellery Channing were perhaps Thoreau's best friends. His friendship with Emerson was the most important and, in a way, the saddest, and that with Channing probably the closest and most surprising. But it may well be that his intercourse with Alcott and Hawthorne was the least troubled.

Though Alcott's notorious impracticality annoyed Thoreau at times, as when they tried to build Emerson's summer house together, he called him a "King of Men," who diffused sunshine wherever he came. "The divine in man has had no more easy, methodically distinct expression." Perhaps it was because of Alcott's uncommittedness that there were never any obstacles between them. "He is not pledged to any institution. The sanest man I ever knew; the fewest crotchets, after all, has he." And Alcott seems to have appreciated Henry, on the whole, and accepted him more fully and warmly than Emerson did, for though he thought him "a little over-confident and somewhat stiffly individual, perhaps— dropping society clean out of his theory," he still found his company "tonic . . . like ice-water in the dog days to the parched citizen pent in chambers and under brazen ceilings." "Thoreau has the profoundest passion for the aboriginal in Nature of any man I have known; and had the sentiment of humanity been equally strong and tender he might have written pastorals that Virgil and Theocritus would have envied him the authorship of. As it is, he has come nearer the primitive simplicity of the antique than any of our poets, and touches the fields and forests and streams of Concord with a classic interest that can never fade."

Hawthorne's first impression of Thoreau was that he was "rather puny-looking" and "one of the not-bad." He once described him too as "the most unmalleable fellow alive—the most tedious, tiresome, and intolerable—the narrowest and most notional," who made one ashamed in his presence of "having any money, or a house to live in, or so much as two coats to wear, or having written a book that the public will read," yet added that "true as all this is, he has great qualities of intellect and character." Hawthorne thought too that Emerson might well have suffered some inconvenience from having Thoreau living in his house. "It may be that such a sturdy and uncompromising person is fitter to meet occasionally in the open air. . . ."

For all that, Hawthorne and Thoreau had much in common. Both were at once realistic and spiritually minded, and both were fascinated by symbols. Both were suspicious of reformers and convinced that the social order could be improved substantially only through improvements in the individuals composing it. Thoreau planted a garden for the Hawthornes when they came to live in Concord and sold Hawthorne a boat in which they went out together, once floating down the river on an ice cake, trailing the boat behind. Once, too, Hawthorne dodged a call from Julia Ward Howe in order to go skating with Thoreau. "I find him a healthy and wholesome man to know, one of the few persons . . . with whom to hold intercourse is like hearing the wind among the boughs of a forest-tree, and with all this freedom, there is high and classic cultivation in him too." All in all, Thoreau and Hawthorne seem to have achieved about as much intimacy as was possible for two such reserved men, and Willard Thorp's judgment—"I am inclined to think that the friend who came closest to appreciating the Thoreau we know was Hawthorne"—is not unreasonable.[18]

The relationship with Emerson was, in the beginning, that of master and disciple, and basically that seems to be what was at last wrong with it. There was never any quarrel or break between them, but as time passed both men realized, though for the most part only confiding the realization to their journals, that the bloom had faded and that the old intimacy was over. Perhaps Emerson was disappointed that Thoreau was not producing enough to justify the early promise he had discerned in him, and perhaps if Thoreau had developed less, he might have been more contented in the old position of discipleship. Emerson was "big medicine"; even Hawthorne was conscious of this "after living for three years under the subtle influence" of such an intellect. Thoreau must have known that Lowell and others considered him a mere imitator of Emerson, and as he grew older he can hardly have relished this. He may also well have felt that Emerson was becoming more conservative and more fastidious as he grew older and more famous. "I doubt if Emerson could trundle a wheelbarrow through the streets," he wrote in 1852, "because it would be out of character. One needs to have a complete character." Thoreau apparently did not address Emerson by his given name until 1848, when he began a letter, "Dear Waldo, For I think I have heard that that is your name," but a few years later he is complaining that Emerson's praise, always discriminating, has "some alloy of patronage and hence of flattery in it." Did Emerson know, one wonders, that Thoreau once recorded that he now rarely looked at one of his friend's books, and that no senior had ever given him any valuable advice? There are indications too that the older man may have felt that Thoreau had in a sense gone beyond him and that this made him vaguely uncomfortable. Emerson called Henry's willingness to go to jail rather than pay his poll tax mean and skulking (both, surely, singularly ill-chosen adjectives, whatever one may think of the action), and though he allowed him to build the Walden cabin on his land, he does not seem really to have approved of the enterprise. "Thoreau gives me . . . my own ethics," he once wrote. "He is far more real, and daily practically obeying them, than I, and fortifies my memory at all times with an affirmative experience which refuses to be set aside."[19]

"Persons with whom he had no sympathy," wrote Ellery Channing of Thoreau, "were to him more removed than stocks and stones." But he also says that "despite his *caveats*, his acceptance was large, he took every bill." The truthfulness of the qualification was never better attested than in the vast toleration Thoreau afforded Channing himself, with all his Harold Skimpole-like irresponsibility.

Thoreau's acceptance of the Reverend William Ellery Channing's nephew and namesake was no less surprising because of his clearsightedness concerning his shortcomings: "He is the moodiest person, perhaps, that I ever saw. As naturally whimsical as a cow is brindled, both in his tenderness and his roughness he belies himself. He can be incredibly selfish and unexpectedly generous. He is conceited, and yet there is in him far more than usual to ground conceit upon." Thoreau complains when Channing tries to tell him a smutty story, but he says nothing about his outrageous irresponsibility toward his wife and family, though we know that Henry once attempted to mediate between him and them.

Channing seems never to have had any qualms about throwing upon others the obligations he ought to have discharged himself.

He disliked Mrs. Thoreau to such an extent that he asked his friend to keep her out of the way when he visited, which Thoreau decidedly refused, though without telling Channing he might stay away himself, as many men would have done. Since Emerson too maintained pleasant relations with him and even Margaret Fuller does not appear to have been wholly estranged by his outrageous treatment of his wife, her sister, Channing obviously had charm when he chose to exercise it. He was intelligent in literary matters, he believed in Thoreau as a writer, and he evidently loved him as a man, as much as he was capable of loving anybody, for, after Henry's death, he told Emma Lazarus that "just half of the world died for me when I lost Mr. Thoreau." Love of nature was another bond between them, though Channing's was conventional, and he had none of Thoreau's mystical sensitiveness nor his feeling of the infinite overtones and signficances of natural phenomena. More importantly perhaps, he shared with Thoreau a tendency to eschew established paths and follow his own way, rejecting economic considerations as of primary importance in the ordering of a life (he had even found his own Walden in a cabin in Illinois). The two men may also have been drawn together by a feeling that Concord's "right-thinking" citizens disapproved of them both, and it has even been plausibly conjectured that since he went so much farther off course than Thoreau himself was willing to go, Channing may have served his friend as a warning or a restraining influence.[20]

Thoreau had other friends and acquaintances with whom there is no need to consider his relations at length. These included people like Daniel Ricketson; Harrison Gray Otis Blake; B. B. Wiley, the Providence and Chicago business man; and the Englishman Thomas Cholmondeley, who sent Henry the Hindu books. In Concord there were Elizabeth Hoar and her brother, Edward Sherman Hoar, with whom Thoreau explored the Sudbury River and set the woods afire; Emerson's eccentric aunt, the aged Mary Moody Emerson, whom Thoreau called "the youngest person in Concord . . . and the most apprehensive of genuine thought, earnest to know of your inner life, most stimulating society, and exceedingly witty withal"; and Mrs. Emerson and her sister Lucy Brown (Margaret Fuller is a more doubtful quantity, as she was certainly not a receptive editor when in charge of *The Dial*, though her brother Richard, who was tutored by Thoreau, warmly admired him);[21] and in New York there were Horace Greeley, who was not only kind to Henry personally but acted as his literary barker, trying to place his work elsewhere in addition to "booming" it in the *Tribune;* and Henry James, Sr., who "naturalized and humanized" the city for Thoreau to say nothing of Whitman, over in Brooklyn.

Thoreau wrote forty-nine letters to Blake, afterwards the editor of four volumes of extracts from his journals. Their relationship, as Blake later looked back on it, seemed "almost an impersonal one," but since he adds that Thoreau's "personal appearance did not interest me particularly, except as the associate of his spirit," this may show more about him than it does about Henry. On the other hand, the latter was pretty high and mighty when Ricketson remonstrated pleadingly but humbly after not having received a letter for some time. He had never promised to correspond with him, said Thoreau, and therefore whatever he did was supererogatory. He rarely made visits, not because he did not enjoy them but because he had other things to do which he enjoyed more. "This life is not for complaint, but for satisfaction. I do not feel addressed by this letter of yours."[22] On the other hand, Henry responded with rather surprising warmth to F. B. Sanborn's first letter, despite the latter's rudeness in telling him that he valued what he had written about nature, but "if any one should ask me what I think of your philosophy, I should be apt to answer that it is not worth a straw."[23] Sometimes too Thoreau could cherish contacts made casually or accidentally. When he went with Channing to Fire Island to look for Margaret Fuller's body, he found instead that of Charles Sumner's brother, who had also been drowned there, which won Sumner's friendship through the rest of Thoreau's life, and in 1837 he wrote Orestes Brownson that the time he had spent with him stayed with him "as a dream that is dreamt, but which returns from time to time in all its original freshness."[24]

V

Thoreau made a strong impression of purity upon all who knew him. Samuel Chase "could not believe he ever did a wrong thing in his life," and Daniel Shattuck said his life was "one of singular purity and kindness." It is as certain as anything of the kind can be that

he never experienced sexual intercourse, but I am sure that he himself would have discerned no necessary connection between the two
sentences I have just written. For idealist though he was, Thoreau
was no prude.

This does not mean that no individual utterance of prudery can be
found in his writings. Probably only anchorites in the desert and
wholly abandoned libertines are completely consistent in their attitudes toward sex; all normal human beings must surely be conscious of a certain ambivalence, a mingled attraction and repulsion.
So I suppose we should not be surprised when we find Thoreau
rather hysterically accusing nature herself of indecency when he
finds the *Phallis impudicus* (fungi in general seem to have been hard-
er for him to accept than almost anything else in nature) taking the
form of the human penis in erection, but neither should we forget
that he made a detailed drawing of it which the 1906 editors of his
journal were too modest to reproduce. (Naturally Jonathan Katz
gives a whole page to it in his *Gay American History!*) And though
twentieth-century readers may find his essay on "Chastity and
Sensuality" naive in some aspects, the fact remains that he did write
it, which is more than many of his peers among nineteenth-century
American writers would have done. Both here and in his other writings he finds it strange that a subject which occupies the thoughts of
all men so much and so importantly affects their lives and characters
as sex should be veiled in such secrecy. "The calmness and gentle-
ness with which the Hindoo philosophers approach and discourse
on forbidden themes is admirable," he says. He observed the copu-
lation of toads, tortoises, and other animals without disgust and discussed it freely. Nor is his use of sexual imagery confined to his
nature writing. The imagination is the "fruit" of the intellect, he
says, and is born of the "marriage of the soul with Nature," and
even in writing "there must be the copulating and generating force
of love behind every effort destined to be successful."

Surely he misrepresented himself when he wrote, "I must confess
there is nothing so strange to me as my own body. I love any other
piece of nature, almost, better." Yet when he recalls his youth, he
remembers that "I was all alive, and inhabited my body with inexpressible satisfaction." On a "delicious evening," he was all "one
sense" which imbibed "delight through every pore." Again he says,

"My body is all sentient. As I go here or there, I am tickled by this or that that I come in contact with, as if I touched the wires of a battery." He scorns the ascetic idea that the soul is benefited by punishing the body, for body and soul are both good, even as wildness and civilization are, and he can even declare without shame that our impressions of nature depend as much upon the state of our bowels as of the stars. "The body is the first proselyte the Soul makes. Our life is but the Soul made known by its fruits, the body. The whole duty of man may be expressed in one line,—Make to yourself a perfect body." I do not think he represents all his thinking fairly when he writes that "we need pray for no higher heaven than the pure senses can furnish, a purely sensuous life. Our present senses are but rudiments of what they are destined to become." He loved Pan, and Richard Drinnon is not absurd when he finds in him "a body mysticism" which placed him "in the tradition of Jacob Boehme and William Blake." Stuart Sherman coined a paradox worthy of Henry himself when he called him "an ascetic of the Epicurean sect," and even Harding calls him "basically sensuous" and finds his ability to express himself "sensuously rather than abstractly" his greatest literary gift. In the light of these considerations, his understanding of Whitman ceases to be surprising. It was not that he never gagged over *Leaves of Grass*, for there are passages in it in which it seemed to him that the beasts spoke and which deepened his conviction of the need for human shame. But even here Whitman had spoken truly, and he wished less that he had not written such things than that men and women were "so pure that they could read them without harm."

For all that, Thoreau was not Whitman. He could anticipate the Freudians by writing that "man begins by quarreling with the animal in him, and the result is immediate disease." He could see too that "this world seems to be thrown away on the saint," and he could respond warmly to a character like Sir Walter Raleigh: "The religion of the hero is the very opposite to that of the ascetic." But he was never in any danger of supposing that Raleigh's way of life, or Whitman's either, was for such as himself. Emerson and Alcott were quite wrong in believing that Henry had no passions or temptations. He was conscious of a "sensual," even "reptile," element in himself, which "perhaps cannot be wholly expelled," and which might perhaps "enjoy a certain health of its own," yet, for all that, it must be overcome. He thought of himself as so impure that if his fellows knew the truth about him, they would shun him, but then again, "when I observe how the mass of men speak of women and of chastity, . . . I feel that so far I am unaccountably better than they." Bradford Torrey quotes "O keep my senses pure!" (which is a very special kind of sensualism, surely) and comments, "For Thoreau the five senses were not organs or means of sensuous gratification, but the five gateways of the soul. He would have them open and undefiled."[25] Nor did he ever delude himself that he could afford to relax discipline because he had God on his side, for he knew that God Himself "is on the side of discipline."[26]

Above all, it should be understood that for Thoreau chastity applied not to sex alone but to all of life. No more than Milton could he have had any truck with the once popular notion that a wanton woman is "bad" and a continent woman "good," regardless of whatever other qualities either might possess. He defines chastity as "perpetual acquaintance with the All," and, as we have seen, he was capable of seeing intemperance in immoderately eating fruit or drinking water. Commenting on the Oriental philosophy referred to at the end of "Higher Laws," Charles R. Anderson declares that chastity is "merely one of the many disciplines by which man aspires toward a higher life," and Charles L. Sanford adds, "Thoreau's major metaphors of merger in nature partook of all the senses reinforcing each other and are easily translated from one to another."[27]

Even when we have made due allowance for the fact that in men of imagination genius can go a long way toward supplying what others must learn through experience, I submit that Thoreau's realization that love subsumes or sublimates lust is remarkable in one who was himself almost certainly virgin. "Love tends to purify and sublime itself," he writes. "It mortifies and triumphs over the flesh, and the bond of its union is holiness." "The intercourse of the sexes," he tells us in "Chastity and Sensuality," "is incredibly beautiful, too fair to be remembered." And yet again: "A true marriage will differ in no wise from illumination. In all perception of the truth there is a divine ecstasy, an inexpressible delirium of joy, as when a youth embraces his betrothed virgin. The ultimate delights of a true marriage are one with this." In itself, then, the sexual act, so far from being degrading, is sacramental. It can be degraded only by the degradation of its participants, as the New Testament says we may eat and drink damnation to ourselves in the Eucharist. *Walden* spells it all out with unmistakable clarity:

> Yet the spirit can for the time pervade and control every member and function of the body, and transmute what in form is the grossest sensuality into purity and devotion. The generative energy, which, when we are loose, dissipates and makes us unclean, when we are continent invigorates and inspires us. Chastity is the flowering of man; and what are called Genius, Heroism, Holiness, and the like, are but various fruits which succeed it. Man flows at once to God when the channel of purity is open.

And surely this is enough abundantly to justify William Wolf's comment: "Thoreau returns again and again to love as the motivating factor in purification. He had much of the spirit of Augustine's dictum that if one loved God he might then do as he wished, the death of all attempts to live in terms of codes or legalism."

In this spirit too he accepted and enjoyed nakedness. To be sure, he grants that bodies need covering in the New England climate and state of society; he even says that "we love to see nature clad, whether in earth or a human body." But he seems to have thought of it as a matter of convention and convenience rather than morality. "In the East, women religiously conceal that they have faces; in the West that they have legs. In both cases they make it evident that they have but little brains." For "nakedness is not so bad a condition after all." It is necessary in hot climates, and if we had it here, it might help us to level ranks and know men by their selves, not merely by their coats and breeches. "Boys are bathing at Hubbard's Bend, playing with a boat (I at the willows). The color of their bodies in the sun at a distance is pleasing, the not often seen flesh color. . . . What a singular fact for an angel visitant to this earth to carry back in his note-book, that men were forbidden to expose their bodies under the severest penalties! . . . I wonder that the dog knows his master when he goes in to bathe and does not stay by his clothes."

That the boys bathed and played naked and that Thoreau did too did not make him, in the modern sense, a "nudist," though the adherents of that cult, always eager to claim converts and cite antecedents, would have it so,[28] for no country man or boy in Thoreau's time or for long after would have dreamed of wearing a "bathing suit." But his passion for bathing ("men stay on shore, keep themselves dry, and drink rum. Pray what were rivers made for?") meant that he spent more time out of his clothes than many. "I love to sit in the wind on this hill and be blown on. We bathe first in air; then, when the air has warmed it, in water." Moreover he shocked Channing by taking "fluvial excursions," treading the river bed wearing only a hat and sometimes a shirt to shield the upper part of his body from the sun. "I wonder if any Roman emperor ever indulged in such luxury as this. . . . What were the Baths of Caracalla to this?"

There is no pornography in Thoreau, but there is a surprising amount of scatology, for even if we do not accept all of Michael West's interpretations,[29] he certainly does show that Thoreau used "foecal and stercoral" imagery. This does not mean that he is ever, in the usual sense of the term, "dirty"; though Chaucer's bawdry apparently did not offend him, he detested Rabelais and was repelled by Channing's coarse jesting. "I lose my respect for the man who can make the mystery of sex the subject of a coarse jest, yet, when you speak earnestly and seriously on the subject, is silent. I feel that this is to be truly irreligious." If the colossal obscenity of the Wellfleet oysterman, "a good Panurge" or "a sober Silenus," offended him less, it seems to have been partly because he expected less of him, and more because the linguist in him for the moment got in the way of the moralist. In much the same spirit he confronted "the poetry of the jakes," which "flows as perennially as the gutter." The rimes he had seen on the walls of privies when he was a boy were still there, word for word. "They are no doubt older than Orpheus, and have come down from an antiquity as remote as mythology or fable. . . . Filth and impurity are as old as cleanliness and purity. To correspond to man completely, Nature is even perhaps unchaste herself."

I do not say that the other great New England writers of Thoreau's time would not have recognized the truth of these observations, but one can hardly imagine Longfellow or Whittier or Lowell making them. They would have preferred to look the other way. Nor would they have written, "What mean these orange-colored toadstools that cumber the ground, and the citron-colored fungus? Is the earth in her monthly courses?" Nor: "When the ice was melting and the trees dripping . . . I noticed that the snow was discolored,—stained yellow by the drip,—as if the trees were urinating." Nor yet: "The sand has begun to flow on the west side of the cut, the east being bare. Nature has some bowels at last."

This last quotation ties up with the great epiphany at the end of *Walden*, the description of the melting railroad bank at which nature is purged. No wonder the great California preacher, Thomas Starr King, called this passage "More weird and winding farther into the awful vitality of nature than any writing that I have yet seen."[30] Thoreau did not look the other way. If he declared bluntly, "What have we to boast of? We are made the very sewers, the cloacae, of nature," he also stands, at the railroad bank, "in the laboratory of the Artist who made the world and me,—had come to where he was still at work, sporting on this bank, and with excess of energy strewing his fresh designs about." For nature cannot be redeemed if you are going to leave what nature rests on out of the reckoning. That is only the way of evasion, which has wrecked half the idealisms of the world and delivered us over to mere sensuality. That the waterlily roots in the mud is not to be lamented. Rather, "it is as if all the pure and sweet and virtuous was extracted from the slime and decay of earth and presented thus in a flower. The resurrection of virtue!"

VI

Emerson said that Thoreau never went through the kitchen where the girls were working without blushing. If so, he must have blushed easily, for he grew up surrounded by women, and his relations with his girl pupils seem to have been quite as easy as those with the boys. He can, to be sure, be very high-and-mighty in his attitude toward the "light and flighty" girls he encountered at a party. The fact that a girl was pretty, he says grandly, was no reason for wanting to talk to her, and anyway he rarely looks at people's faces; but he surely gives himself away when he adds of one of these girls that she "had been accustomed to the society of watering-places, and therefore could get no refreshment out of such a dry fellow as I." Anyway, there is plenty of evidence that he did look at girls, and even at their clothes, and reacted to them strongly; once he was so charmed by the "lively, sparkling eyes" of a girl who combed her long black hair while she talked to him at a house where he had stopped to ask directions that he was sorely tempted to ask if he might not return and remain for a week! The women and girls, "in rude health, with a great deal of color in their cheeks," working in the fields in Canada, also charmed him; he thought them "much more agreeable objects . . . than the men and boys." In 1853 he was "struck by the perfect neatness, as well as the elaborateness and delicacy, of a lady's dress. . . . She wore some worked lace or gauze over her bosom, and I thought it was beautiful, if it indicated an equal purity and delicacy,—if it was the soul she dressed and treated thus delicately." And, per contra, he could react with equal force to unattractive women, like the "pinched up" specimens he saw at the Cape. "They had prominent chins and noses, having lost all their teeth, and a sharp W would represent their profile." Above all, he was horrified by a Nauset woman "of a hardness and coarseness such as no man ever possesses or suggests" and who looked like "one who had committed infanticide; who never had a brother, unless it were some wee thing that died in infancy,—for what need of him? —and whose father must have died before she was born." For that matter, it seemed to him that women, despite the refinement attributed to them, yielded "a more implicit obedience even to their animal instincts than men. The nature is stronger in them, the reason weaker." He knew fewer women than men, for example, who had scruples about eating animal food, and he thought that their "conformity and easy nature" made them less inclined to be reformers.

For all that, no troubadour ever glorified love more than Thoreau. "The music of all creatures has to do with their loves, even of toads and frogs. Is it not the same with man?" And what could he do but "in some shape or other to tell the story of his love,—to sing; and, if he is fortunate and keeps alive, he will be forever in love." Henry found it suitable that "all ideal excellence" should be personified as feminine, and he lamented the lack of a feminine element in the Protestant religion. Even love's failures and tragedies had their dignity, and when he heard that the dead derelict Bill Wheeler had been "what is called love-cracked," he thought there could be no "nobler suffering, and better death, for a human creature."

Yet, though Emerson wrote his brother William that it might sweeten and straighten Thoreau to fall in love, he could never have been an easy lover. With him the imagination was always as important as the heart, nor did the critical faculties ever sleep. "Love is a severe critic. Hate can pardon more than love." He seems to have had the strange idea that love was somehow profaned by confession, not to the world merely but even to the person who had inspired it, and he insisted upon such perfect harmony between lovers that nothing could ever need to be explained. "I require that thou knowest everything without being told anything. I parted from my beloved because there was one thing which I had to tell her. She *questioned* me. She should have known all by sympathy. That I had to tell her was the difference between us—the misunderstanding."

F. P. Stearns has recorded that Thoreau once kicked a skunk cabbage and said, "There, marriage is like that." This can hardly have been more than the expression of a mood, yet it was not quite without meaning. He once called genius hermaphroditic in the sense of being inspired by itself, and he sensed the potentiality of special problems in marriage for men who possessed it or were possessed by it. "They are married to two wives—their genius (a celestial muse) and also to some fair daughter of the earth. Unless these two were fast friends before marriage, and so are afterward, there will be but little peace in the house." Nevertheless Thoreau was far from being cynical about marriage. Instead he thought of it as at its best an exalted state to which many men were quite incapable of aspiring. "To be married . . . should be the one poetical act of a man's life. If you fail in this respect, in what respect will you succeed?" And in 1840 he confided to his journal his desire to live "with some gentle soul such a life as may be conceived, double for variety, single for harmony,—two, only that we might admire at our one-ness,—one, because indivisible."

But whatever theorizing we may indulge in concerning Thoreau's attitude toward marriage must take into account the fact that he did propose to one girl, Ellen Sewall, the daughter of a clergyman in Scituate. In the summer of 1839, when she was seventeen and Thoreau twenty-two, she came to Concord with her brothers, Edmund (eleven) and George (five), for a two-week visit with the Thoreaus and the Wards. She is said to have been beautiful; if this is true, her photographs do not do her justice. Thoreau began writing poems to her at once, and on July 25 he confided to his journal that "there is no remedy for love but to love more." He took her walking, sailing, driving, and to see a giraffe, and at a party where phrenology was the theme, he felt the "bumps" on her head and amused the company by announcing that she had none, which was supposed to indicate either genius or idiocy. In her biography of Thoreau, which was based upon considerable local investigation, Annie Russell Marble recorded that her initials were cut on a bridge between those of Henry and his brother John, Henry's being cut "very neatly and deep."

In March 1840 Edmund Sewall became a pupil in the Thoreau school, and Henry made an entry in his journal about having "no vulgar Cupid for a go-between." In June, Ellen came to Concord again, and he took "a free, even lovely young lady" boating on the Concord River. In July John went to Scituate and proposed marriage to Ellen. She accepted him, then changed her mind, partly on account of her mother, partly, it seems, because she preferred Henry, who, though the matter is somewhat clouded, apparently never knew of John's proposal until after his brother's death. In November Henry himself proposed to Ellen, in a letter addressed to her at Watertown, where she was visiting, and, in obedience to the orders of her father, who may have been antagonized by Thoreau's religious unorthodoxy, she refused him. "I never felt so badly at sending a letter in my life," she wrote her aunt. "I could not bear to think that both those friends whom I have enjoyed so much with would now no longer be able to have the free pleasant intercourse with us as formerly. My letter was very short indeed. . . . I did feel so sorry H. wrote to me. It was such a pity." In later years she told her children that "she had been so distressed and had felt so mortified and worried over her mistaken acceptance of John and the consequent trouble and disturbance that she could only acquiesce in her father's desire with regard to Henry." She was married in 1842 to the Reverend Joseph Osgood, and her relations with the Thoreaus were kept up beyond the end of Henry's life. In 1849 the Osgoods entertained Henry at their home in Cohasset, and later, when Mr. Osgood preached in Concord, he and Henry walked round Walden Pond together.

The wise men have speculated no end about this affair, and we know so little about it that these speculations may easily take almost any turn. Canby doubted that Thoreau really wanted to marry Ellen, and Lebeaux writes, "Even if he avidly thought that he wanted to be accepted, and if he was hurt by the refusal, it is likely that in a way he was relieved by the rejection." One does not need to be a psychoanalyst to grant this possibility. Certainly many men have muffed their chances with women by putting their fate to the test prematurely because, being what they were, they had to relieve the tension and resolve the uncertainty. If Thoreau had married Ellen Sewall or anybody else, he must have radically altered his way of life, for he was no Ellery Channing, to go his own way regardless of his wife's feelings, and "Benedick the married man" could hardly have been the Thoreau we know. On the other hand, he must, like all of us, have had undeveloped possibilities in him, and marriage might well have brought them out. Certainly he was capable of tenderness, and he was always at his best with children. Even at the end of his life, he declared of Ellen that he had "always loved her," and when Ellen's son asked her what she would have done if her father had refused to agree to her marrying Osgood, she replied, "We would probably have got married anyway," which strongly suggests that if she had cared as much for Henry, she would have behaved the same way in 1840.[31]

VII

Were there any other women in Thoreau's life? In his influential 1939 biography, Henry Seidel Canby advanced the view that Thoreau was in love with Mrs. Emerson.

On May 22, 1843, he wrote her that he thought of her as "some elder sister of mine" and "a sort of lunar influence" who had helped to keep his life " 'on loft,' as Chaucer says of Griselda." But the letter which followed on June 20 was much more remarkable. He had received a letter from her in the meantime, and he had taken it "out to the top of the hill at sunset," whence he could see the ocean. "The thought of you will elevate my life." He looked at the letter at midnight, and when morning came he could hardly believe that he still possessed such a treasure. "I feel that I am unworthy to know you."

The mere thought of their acquaintance "will be a new motive for every right action."

Next came a letter, written on July 8 and addressed to both Lidian and her husband, which is very different in tone and probably requires a transcendentalist to interpret. He even writes, "But know, my friends, that I a good deal hate you in all my most private thoughts—as the substratum of the little love I bear you."

This, Canby believed, indicates that the letter of June 20 had frightened Mrs. Emerson to the extent of drawing a rebuke or a chilly reply, whereupon Thoreau, realizing that he had gone too far, drew back and attempted to cover his tracks. On this hypothesis, it was Mrs. Emerson whom Thoreau had in mind when he wrote, "She who was the morning light to me is now neither the morning light nor the evening star. We meet but to find each other further asunder, and the oftener we meet the more rapid our divergence." And Carl Bode even adds: "For Thoreau no woman ever replaced Lidian, and the suffering he felt is reflected periodically in his most private writings."

Canby was certainly correct when he remarked that Thoreau's "obsession with love which is friendship and friendship which is love" makes it difficult to interpret such passages. In general, however, his own interpretation has not been well received. If Perry Miller was the most savage among his critics, accusing Canby of misquoting and misinterpreting, and branding his conclusions "absurdities" and "patent nonsense," even Lebeaux concludes that "it would, I think, be blowing the matter out of proportion to call their relationship a 'romance,' " while Raymond Adams, whose review of Canby's book scrutinized the letters and Thoreau's attitude toward women in general in the context of their time and place, concluded, "I think Mr. Canby shows that there was a slight mother-fixation about the Thoreau-Lidian Emerson relationship, but nothing more."[32]

If Adams was wrong, then both the Emersons were fools, for Thoreau was left in charge of Lidian, her children, and the household while Emerson was in Europe. Obviously, if there ever was any strain or misunderstanding, it was quickly dissipated. "Lidian and I make very good housekeepers," wrote Thoreau to the wandering husband. "She is a very dear sister to me." Moreover, Emerson included the Thoreau letter upon which Canby builds so much in the selection of *Familiar Letters* which he published after Thoreau's death. The most amusing comment on the whole affair and perhaps the final one may well be given to Mrs. Thoreau. When Lidian told her that her son had praised her so highly that she felt humiliated, Cynthia replied, "Yes, Henry is very tolerant."

As has already been noted, Thoreau established a meeting of minds with Emerson's brilliant and eccentric aunt, Mary Moody Emerson, and paid tribute to her wit and vivacity, but naturally there was no question of emotional attachment to a lady of her years. There was probably more emotion in his feeling for another woman older than himself, Lidian Emerson's sister, Lucy Jackson Brown, to whom he wrote a poem and some fairly intimate letters. When Caroline Dall lectured in Concord, he went to hear her, having previously declared his intention not to go, because women never had anything to say, and was so much impressed that he invited her to stay over the next day in Concord with the Thoreau family, which she did.[33] When he went to Staten Island in 1843, Elizabeth Hoar gave him an inkwell, with a friendly note in which she told him that she should miss him and that she wished him well. Bronson Alcott once told William Sloane Kennedy, "with a touch of jocoseness," that Thoreau had "a touch of feeling" for "a wild maiden somewhere in the backwoods."[34] This may have been Kate Brady, but Kennedy unfortunately did not pin down the reference. There is no known foundation for the notions, circulated and revived by sensationalists from time to time, that Thoreau was once engaged to Margaret Fuller or that Louisa May Alcott was in love with him. It is much more reasonable to believe that he had a romantic interest in Mary Russell of Plymouth; at least her husband, Marston Watson, believed that she had been the "Maiden in the East" of Thoreau's poem.[35] As for Kate Brady, he met her at the Ricketsons' in 1857, when she was twenty. Her father was "an Irishman, a worthless fellow, her mother a smart Yankee." The girl had done both sewing and farm work and had taught school; she had also read *Walden* "with great pleasure" and wanted to "live free" in the family homestead, supporting herself by farming, sheepkeeping, etc. She was the only woman Henry ever encountered who could have met him on his own ground, or at least proved an apt pupil, in his fellowship with nature, and it is clear that they liked each other, but neither one seems to have done anything to follow up the contact that had been made. If there is anywhere a tantalizing "might have been" among the women who crossed Thoreau's path, it is Kate Brady.[36]

Yet Thoreau had one experience which many men whose contacts with women have been much more intimate than his have never had; he *received* a proposal of marriage from a woman, to which he "sent back as distinct a *no* as I have learned to pronounce after considerable practice"; he added, "I really had anticipated no such foe as this in my career." This was in November 1847, and the lady was Sophia Foord, sometimes called Ford, who is described as a "dark-skinned, pudgy-featured woman," fifteen years older than the object of her passion. She tutored Emersons, Alcotts, and Channings, and was apparently a highly successful, as we should now say, "progressive" teacher who won and held the affection of her pupils. Louisa May Alcott always kept in touch with her, sent her the news of Thoreau's death and funeral, and wrote a memorial tribute. Once, we hear of her and the young Alcotts wading across a great pond without their shoes, stockings, and "unmentionables," which is an interesting variation of Thoreau's own fluvial excursions. At one time there was a report that she had committed suicide (or was about to do so) for love of Thoreau, and this seems to be what he refers to in one of the chilliest things he ever said: "Hearing that one with whom I was acquainted had committed suicide, I said I did not know when I had planted the seed of that fact that I should hear of it." She waited until the natural end, which came on April 1, 1885, when she was eighty-three, and now rests in Dedham Cemetery, perhaps still believing herself to be Thoreau's "soul's twin," to be united with him in eternity. For his sake, let us hope she was mistaken.[37]

VIII

In an age which has gone stark raving mad on the subject of homosexuality (as Robert Brustein has wittily and caustically observed, the love that once dared not speak its name has now grown hoarse from shouting it), it was no doubt inevitable that Thoreau should be suspected in some quarters not of overt homosexual practices but of a probably latent homoerotic orientation.[38] The only evidence that is worth anything is the poem "Sympathy," written to Ellen Sewall's young brother. It must, I think, be admitted that to Freudianly oriented ears, such verses as "I might have loved him, had I loved him less" and "Each moment, as we nearer drew to each, / A stern respect withheld us farther yet" could be interpreted as Jonathan Katz would have it, and there is also the line "To show you my peculiar love" in another poem. But perverse is surely not the only possible meaning for "peculiar," and if the Sewalls had suspected anything like what Katz suspects, they could no more have sent their boy to school to Thoreau than Emerson could have left him in charge of his household while absent in England, had he agreed with Canby that Thoreau was in love with his wife. As has already been pointed out, Thoreau was transcendentally much given to confusing or equating love with friendship, and it must always be remembered that pre-Freudian writers were much less conscious and wary of such ambiguous references than we are. One need not be a Miss Nancy or a prude to stand on guard against putting oneself into a position where it becomes necessary to regard everybody who has ever felt an impulse of tenderness toward a member of his or her own sex as homosexual, for if everybody is homosexual, then homosexuality ceases to have any particular meaning. If I might engage in a bit of "analysis" myself, I might cite Thoreau's savage account of his encounter in 1853 with the "three ultra-reformers, lecturers on Slavery, Temperance, the Church, etc." who stopped "about our house and Mrs. Brooks's the last three or four days," which strongly suggests his disgust at what may well have been homosexual proclivities in one of them. "It was difficult to keep clear of his slimy benignity, with which he sought to cover you before he swallowed you and took you fairly into his bowels. It would have been far worse than the fate of Jonah. I do not wish to get any nearer a man's bowels than usual." Apparently he was forced to share his bed with one of these men. He seems to have controlled his disgust with an effort, and I have already quoted the reply he made when the one he disliked most declared, "I am going to dive into Henry's inmost depths": "I trust you will not strike your head against the bottom."

One writer, Mary Elkins Moller, has raised the question of

whether Thoreau masturbated, a practice which was considered both harmful and immoral in his time.[39] In a contribution to *The Truth Seeker*, November 20, 1897, an anonymous contributor quoted Thoreau as having said, "I never had any trouble in my life, or only when I was about fourteen; then I felt pretty bad for a little while on account of my sins, but no trouble since that I know of." Since fourteen is the age when puberty is generally achieved, one cannot but remember that many a less idealistic boy than Thoreau has felt himself defiled by his own semen. But this could only be a guess at best, and the statement quoted, whether accurately or not, does not seem true to Thoreau's experience, since, as we have already seen in other connections, he expresses the conviction of his own unworthiness elsewhere again and again. He has more commonly been supposed, as by Perry Miller, to have sublimated his sexual impulses in nature worship.[40] He himself declares that "all nature is my bride," and there is a curious passage in which he writes, "I love and could embrace the shrub oak with its scanty garment of leaves. . . . I felt a positive yearning toward one bush this afternoon. There was a match found for me at last." One understands both Charles Anderson's comment, "This is a curious New England version of the myth of Apollo pursuing the chaste Daphne only to find her transformed into a laurel tree to escape his ravishing embrace," and Wayne Morris' reference to D. H. Lawrence's saying "Absolutely the safest thing to get your emotional reactions over is NATURE." But neither would it be safe to neglect B. R. Harding's reminder that while Thoreau finds the Indian's intimacy with nature "noble and cleanly," he sees "something vulgar and foul" in the gardener's "closeness to his mistress." "The sexual metaphor is not casual; it is evidence enough that Thoreau was aware of, and was rejecting, the sort of intimacy with 'Mother Nature' of which the psychoanalytic critics would accuse him."[41]

CHAPTER THREE

Wider Circles

The universe is wider than our thought of it.
HDT, *Walden*

HENRY JAMES said of Thoreau that "he was worse than provincial
—he was parochial," but this does not seem one of his more per-
spicacious judgments. The perfect comment is that of Charles Ives:
"He was so universal that he did not need to travel round the world
to *prove* it."

It is true of course that of all the Concord writers, Thoreau is the
Concordian par excellence. He signed one letter "Yours Concor-
dially," and there is no better complimentary close on record. And it
is true also that he did not think it worth while "to go round the
world to count the cats in Zanzibar," for, like the other transcendentalists, he held the conviction that all the essential elements of
human experience may be found wherever a person may be. If you
are one of the "jet set" who rush madly about the world to get away
from the place you are tired of in order to reach another that you will
begin to tire of as soon as you get there, then certainly Thoreau was
provincial. But this is hardly a universal criterion.

"I have never got over my surprise," he writes, "that I should
have been born into the most estimable place in all the world, and in
the very nick of time." And he echoes and paraphrases the Psalmist:
"If I forget thee, O Concord, let my right hand forget her cunning.
. . . To whatever quarter of the world I may wander, I shall deem it
good fortune that I hail from Concord North Bridge." Or, to
Mrs. Emerson: "I carry Concord ground in my boots and in my
hat,—and am I not made of Concord dust?" To his way of thinking
it was only folly to try to attempt "to go away from here! When the

constant endeavor should be to get nearer and nearer *here.*" If he could have a draught of wild New England nectar, he did not need the springs of Helicon, and he once declared of a great oak tree that there was enough there "to keep one man happily busy all his life!" Even to walk on the "imported sod" or "English grass" of "culti-vated fields" made his thoughts "heavy and lumpish," as if he were eating turnips. What he wanted was "an American sward in the fine sedge of woodland hollows." There was no point in getting to know Paris better if it made you know Concord less, for "at best, Paris could only be a school in which to learn to live here." For us "God himself culminates in the present moment," and if we do not find Him here, we shall not find Him anywhere.

What saves all this from provincialism is that Thoreau never made the chauvinist's mistake of supposing Concord to be better than other places because he happened to be born in it. It was simply that even as late as "Walking" he was sure he had not exhausted his en-vironment. If a local phenomenon could excite as much interest as the Egyptian pyramids, he could see no point in going to Egypt. Concord was his Rome and her people his Romans and her river as old as either the Nile or the Euphrates. "As the stars looked to me when I was a shepherd in Assyria, they look to me now a New Eng-lander." He found Homer's characters in his neighbors, and reading Virgil's *Eclogues* convinced him that in three thousand years there had been little change. At the end of *Walden*, Walden Pond and the waters of the Ganges are commingled, and elsewhere he writes, "Where is the 'Unexplored land' but in our own untried enterprises? To an adventurous spirit any place,—London, New York, Worces-ter, or his own back yard, is 'Unexplored land,' to seek which Fre-mont and Kane travel so far." But, by the same token, he wanted those who lived elsewhere, like Isaiah Williams in Buffalo, to find their Concord wherever they might be and not come to his in a vain search for it.

For all his attachment to the particular, then, Thoreau never lost the universal. Emerson said that "to him there was no such thing as size. The pond was a small ocean, the Atlantic, a large Walden Pond. He referred every minute fact to cosmical laws," and he him-self said that "to elevate the little into the great is genius" and that "hell itself may be contained within the compass of a spark." When he was a little boy, he asked his mother whether Boston was in Concord. It wasn't, nor did he want it to be, but he came close to putting the world there, and if he preferred the ordinary to the extraordinary, it was simply because he wished to be alive all the time. "I wish so to live as to derive my satisfactions and inspirations from the commonest events, so that what my senses hourly perceive, my daily walks, the conversation of my neighbors, may inspire me, and I may dream of no heaven but that which lies about me." Raymond Adams has acutely analyzed the brilliant description of the battle of the ants in *Walden* as an example of his capacity to create "a macrocosm of time and place," pointing out also that if "embattled insects" are raised to "the importance of men," men are also reduced "to the level of insects," and that if the siege of Troy is burlesqued, so is the fight at Concord, which was considerably more daring in Thoreau's time and place.[1] He never wished to be "rooted to the soil" in Concord or anywhere else. He could fancy himself as "a mail-carrier in Peru, or a South African planter, or a Siberian exile, or a Greenland whaler, or a settler on the Columbia River, or a Canton merchant, or a soldier in Florida, or a mackerel-fisher off Cape Sable, or a Robinson Crusoe in the Pacific, or a silent navigator in any sea," and if the wine or water which would nourish him could be found only on the surface of the moon, he was willing to go there for it, for though he knew he loved his Concord best, he was always glad to discover elsewhere the materials out of which other Concords might be made, but he did not really believe this would be necessary, for often, after having received a rare plant from a distance, he would find the same thing growing in Concord, and he observed in Concord winters many of the phenomena recorded in Kane's account of his Arctic voyage.[2]

It is easy to find passages in Thoreau in which travel as such is downgraded. "I have travelled a good deal in Concord," he says, and he believed that the Farthest Indies might be reached by other means than actual locomotion. He dissents from Burton's "voyaging is a victory," seeing it rather as "a defeat, a rout," leaving the traveler "at home anywhere but where he was born and bred." Travelers are "defended and calloused"; they deal with surfaces and wear a great-coat, and he observes that "the after life of those who have traveled much is likely to be empty and pathetic." Once he even says that a family's going to the beach for six weeks in the summer was a confession that the lives they habitually led spelled "failure and defeat."

But all this of course is relative, and Thoreau, who was so much less an extremist in many things than many persons believe, was certainly none in his attitude toward travel. True, he rejected Isaac Hecker's invitation to join him on a walking tour of Europe, but he was conscious of "a decided schism between my outward and inward tendencies" as he did so. "Channing wonders how I can resist your invitation . . . and so do I. Why—there are Roncesvalles, the cape de Finisterre, and the three kings of Cologne, Rome, Athens, and the rest." He turned down Thomas Cholmondeley's invitation to England also, and both Cholmondeley and Edwin Morton invited him in vain to the West Indies. But he did go three times to the Maine woods, four times to Cape Cod, twice to the White Mountains, to New York City at least three or four times, and to Minnesota, and he would have gone on a government expedition to survey mineral lands in Michigan if he had been able to secure the position. The Canadian jaunt (*mirabile dictu!*) was even made on a twelve-and-a-half-day excursion ticket, and the Minnesota journey, undertaken when he was a dying man, involved stopovers at Niagara Falls, Detroit, Chicago, and St. Paul and consumed almost two full months. All in all, Thoreau probably did about as much traveling as a man in his circumstances and position could have been expected to do. Moreover his traveling was hard work, for he not only observed diligently but read and studied hard both before and after. As he says, "true and sincere traveling is no pastime, but it is as serious as the grave, or any part of the human journey, and it requires a long probation to be broken into it."[3]

Furthermore he traveled in his heart and his imagination. In an excellent book, John A. Christie has demonstrated conclusively that his extensive readings in travel literature significantly widened his vision of the world. Though he had a special interest in the American West, reading at least forty books of Western travel during the 1850s, he did not stop there but embraced Africa, South America, and the Middle and the Far East as well. He claimed that he faced west more readily than east and told Emerson he would rather go to Oregon than to London, but in his time the West was the Maine frontier too, and, as Lawrence Willson has remarked, it was more a spiritual condition than either. "His West was a land of youth and imagination and poetry, with its accent always on aspiration and the morning star," and its geography was that "of the heart and mind and soul of man" and his Westerner "the man who by himself fronts the essential facts."[4] Nor is this all. Thoreau himself calls the traveler "the best symbol of our life. Going ――― toward ―――; it is the history of every one of us." Most of his books and essays resulted from excursions, and even *Walden,* so mistakenly interpreted as the record of an hermitic interlude, is laced with images of travel. As Reginald L. Cook observes, the journey, though predominantly an interior pilgrim's progress, thus becomes "the dominant image" of Thoreau's life.

II

This may well bring us, at last, and for once in the right context, to Walden Pond. Walter Harding has conjured up a Man in the Street who, upon being asked what he knew about Thoreau, might reply, "Oh, that's the fellow who spent half his life in the woods at Walden Pond and the other half in jail." Leaving out the obvious and humorous exaggerations, let it be said here and now that any writer who speaks of Thoreau as "the hermit of Walden" simply proves that he has no qualifications for the subject he proposes to discuss except ignorance. For one thing, Thoreau had more company and entertained more guests during the two years he lived at Walden Pond than does many a lonely city-dweller of today during a comparable period.

By the same token, it is stupid to make fun of him because he settled on Emerson's land and worked with an axe borrowed from Emerson or another, or, as Lowell more pretentiously puts it, that his experiment "actually presupposed all that complicated civilization which it theoretically abjured." Thoreau never abjured it, either theoretically or practically. Whatever else he may have been trying to do at Walden Pond, he was not trying to relive the experience of Robinson Crusoe. When, in Maine, he came across a real hermit, he wondered how the man could endure such separation from humanity.[5]

Obviously he was neither the first nor the last man who chose to live for a spell in a cabin. Ellery Channing had done it in Illinois, and Charles Stearns Wheeler had tried it at Flint's Pond in Lincoln, where Thoreau spent six weeks with him, probably in 1837. Nor, though he said he wished he could live there when he first saw Walden Pond at the age of five, was it the only site considered, for in 1841 he almost bought the Hollowell Place, on the Sudbury River, about two miles southwest of Concord.

Vernon Louis Parrington found the right terms when he called Thoreau the "Transcendental Economist," and the sojourn at the Pond a controlled experiment in economy. Of course Henry was not wholly correct when he declared that "defeat is heaven's success. He cannot be said to succeed to whom the world shows any favor." Though this is a half-truth, it also comes under the heading of selling oneself short, since actually to be able to cope with success affords at least as great a test of character as poverty, and many persons who have experienced both can testify that they have passed one only to fail the other. Though Thoreau's income and outgo always remained small—pitifully small by modern standards —he was always "practical" and scrupulous about discharging his obligations to the halfpenny.

As to the rest, it was not penury by which he was actuated but merely an attempt to order life so that the primary things should not get lost amid the superfluities. Time was life, and he did not propose to exchange it for dross; he once wrote Ellen Emerson that the necessaries of life have no value except to provide undergirding for its dreams. It was not enough to be industrious—the ants were that; the question was what were you industrious about. You must get your living by loving, and many people's work was only a kind of St. Vitus dance. "I love a broad margin in my life," he says. When you earn more than you need, he believed, you simply acquire a more expensive style of living and consequently both limit your freedom and increase your susceptibility to fear lest the means to continue it should be taken from you, at the same time giving hostages to the established order and creating sacred cows for yourself to serve, in the form of the existent vested interests. It hurt him to see his Concord neighbors leading "lives of quiet desperation," at the same time doing penance for owning their possessions, as it were pushing their barns down the road before them, and ultimately themselves being plowed under the soil for compost. Once, at least, in a passage strongly suggestive of a famous tirade in *The House of the Seven Gables*, he suggests that life might be improved by making a periodic holocaust of all the debris of the past.

The purpose of a gainful occupation was, then, to supply the wherewithal to cultivate and support the intellect and the spirit; consequently the less time and energy a human being needed to put into it, the more he would have to devote to the things that make us human. In the larger sense of the term, economy was neither getting nor spending but the intelligent ordering of all life's resources in the interest of the ends sought. The basic difficulty with the factory system as a means of making clothing, for instance, was simply that its principal object is "not that mankind may be well and honestly clad, but, unquestionably, that the corporations may be enriched." Moreover, while hand-craftsmanship tended to preserve the relative importance of men and things, "when labor is reduced to turning a crank it is no longer amusing or profitable." Production becomes more efficient under such a system but the development of the whole person of the worker suffers.

But why, then, Walden in particular, and why did he go there when he did, and why did he leave when he did? There has been no lack of explanations. He had a book to write, and he needed seclusion to do it. He was all wound round with family and boarders, and he had to unwind. Or he had come to a crisis in his relations with Mrs. Emerson. Or he went off in a pique because he was in bad odor with his fellow-Concordians after burning the woods. Or what-have-you.

He himself tells us that he does not know why he went nor why he left. He also suggests that it will be employment enough to watch the progress of the seasons there. But he says other things too; indeed the one thing he does not say is that he was trying to get away from it all. On the contrary, he wanted "to transact some private business with the fewest obstacles."

> I went to the woods because I wished to live deliberately, to front only the essential facts of life, and see if I could not learn what it had to teach, and not, when I came to die, discover that I had not lived. I did not wish to live what was not life, living is so dear, nor did I wish to practise

resignation, unless it was quite necessary. I wanted to live deep and suck out all the marrow of life, to live so sturdily and Spartan-like as to put to rout all that was not life, to cut a broad swath and shave close, to drive life into a corner, and reduce it to its lowest terms, and, if it proved to be mean, why then to get the whole and genuine meanness of it, and publish its meanness to the world; or if it were sublime, to know it by experience, and be able to give a true account of it in my next excursion. For most men, it appears to me, are in a strange uncertainty about it, whether it is of the devil or of God, and have *somewhat hastily* concluded that it is the chief end of man here to "glorify God and enjoy him forever."

It may be objected, of course, that this is rationalizing after the event or that it is literature, and, as we have seen, Thoreau was first and foremost a writer and as such did not hesitate to recharacterize his materials for aesthetic purposes, even when they were derived from his actual experiences. Nevertheless the motives and attitudes here alleged are basically in harmony with what we know about the way he conducted his life.

He was then not trying to break from society, but he did have to get far enough away from it to see it and himself in proper perspective and to sort out what belonged to him from what he had merely taken over from others. In his first letter to Thoreau, written in March 1848, H. G. O. Blake writes: "If I understand rightly the significance of your life, this is it: You would sunder yourself from society, from the spell of institutions, customs, conventionalities, that you may lead a fresh, simple life with God," and though, in his reply, Thoreau disclaims having actually achieved this, he professes his respect for "faith and aspiration" and his conviction that "heroism, magnanimity, truth, sincerity" have proved themselves wherever they have been given a chance. On the other hand, the "respectable daily life" upon which commonsense people stand seems to him "in fact the veriest illusion, and will vanish like the baseless fabric of a vision, but that faint glimmer of reality which sometimes illuminates the darkness of daylight for all men, reveals something more solid and enduring than adamant." He adds that he has "no designs on society—or nature—or God. I am simply what I am, or I begin to be that." As Melvin E. Lyon puts it, "Thoreau's ultimate purpose in going to Walden Pond was to give his 'Genius' (or spiritual intuition) more freedom to pursue its search for greater intimacy with God and a greater spiritualization of himself."[6]

The basic problem then was not economic; neither was the Walden sojourn an experiment in primitivism; nor yet was it intended to set up a pattern for other men to follow. Thoreau eschewed possessions as Saint Francis of Assisi did (though, of course, without going anything like so far) because they were a burden. A man has only so much time, so much energy; he must invest it in that which he needs most. This is not sacrifice but merely intelligent discrimination. As Sherman Paul says, to Thoreau "the way to wealth was not the way to health, but to lives of quiet desperation." His economy was geared to "enrichment, not denial, and he spent lavishly." Or, as Reginald Cook puts it, the Walden experiment is less a one-man revolution than a one-man reformation. What Thoreau is insisting upon is that life must be worth living for its own sake, an end in itself, rather than either a means toward an end or something to be endured.

It has also been pointed out by these critics and others that though the *Week* was the book Thoreau really wrote at the pond, *Walden* was what he lived there, and also that this work itself is full of imagery which was not derived from either solitude or Thoreau's immediate surroundings, thus reinforcing the view that the Walden sojourn was not a retreat from society but rather an attempt to prepare to live in it more effectively.[7] Though the immediate occasion for his leaving when he did may have been that he should take up residence in Emerson's house during the latter's absence in England, this was not fundamental. Since he had never intended a permanent stay, and since he had found himself following "a particular route" and making "a beaten track" from his door to the pond before he had been there a week, there was no reason why he should remain after his experiment had been concluded. "I left the woods for as good a reason as I went there. Perhaps it seemed to me that I had several more lives to live, and could not spare any more time for this one." He did not know why he had left any better than why he had come. "Perhaps it is none of my business, even if it is yours. Perhaps I wanted a change." He says he has often wished himself back, but he also says that "perhaps if I had lived there longer, I might live there forever" and that "one would think twice before he accepted heaven on such terms."[8]

At Walden Pond Thoreau experimented with subsistence agriculture, and, for him, and for the time being, and under the circumstances which existed, it worked well enough, but he was not really
alone there, for he had Concord and his family and Emerson's land
behind him. Leo Stoller has argued at some length that after Walden
he moved in the direction of making terms with the new industrial
economy. It was not that he had ceased to prefer the old ways or lost
his mistrust of the money men. He says that the best thing a rich
man can do for culture is to try to carry out the ideas he conceived
when he was poor, and when the Panic of 1857 struck he told Blake
that he rejoiced in it as showing that "justice is always done. If our
merchants did not most of them fail, and the banks too, my faith in
the old laws of the world would be staggered." So far, so good, but
he is pretty cavalier and high-and-mighty when he continues, "If
thousands are thrown out of employment, it suggests that they
were not well employed." In practice, he was, as usual, much less
the extremist than he was in some of his pronouncements. He
worked as a surveyor; he was an important part of the pencil
business; he had become interested in preventing accidents and
guarding against dangers in factories and on the highways; he
planned for the enrichment of men's lives through leisure time activities. He may have felt "inexpressibly begrimed" as he did some
of these things, as if he had "committed suicide in a sense" or were
on his way to the devil. "My Pegasus has lost its wings; he has
turned a reptile and gone on his belly." Yet he knew that the old
days were gone. Not all men could move to the frontier or take up
bypassed parcels of land in settled areas.

Yet, in a sense, Stoller and those who take their cue from him
exaggerate, for Thoreau had not needed to wait until after returning
from Walden to realize these things. He had never wanted other
men to follow him to the wilds. Even his Harvard discussion of the
commercial spirit saw it as "one more indication of the entire and
universal freedom which characterizes the age in which we live"
and a sign "that the human race is making one more advance in that
infinite series of progressions which awaits it," and he surprises
readers of the Week when he suggests "that the advertisements, or
what is called the business part of a paper were greatly the best, the
most useful, natural, and respectable," though, to be sure, he carefully specifies that those he has in mind "were serious and not of the

modern quack kind." All in all, it was neither industrialism nor commerce in itself that was dangerous but merely allowing them to usurp the place of more important things. Like everything else with Thoreau, it all came back in the last analysis to the decency and capacity of the individual.[9]

Some may feel that there was a histrionic quality in the Walden experiment as, for that matter, in the night spent in jail also. Thoreau, they say, made only a token payment in an area in which other rebels against the state have given all they had, even their lives. This is perfectly true, but Thoreau did not liberate himself from jail, and only a masochist deliberately seeks martyrdom. As Stevenson observes, we do not reject writing which is good simply because it has been done with ease and confine ourselves to praising those writers whom we know to sweat blood over every sentence. Aesthetically gifted persons do have an advantage over the rest of mankind (though they also pay a price for their gifts), and because Thoreau was a man of genius, his symbolic actions cannot but appeal to us more strongly (perhaps even they have done more good in the world) than the more heroic services of less interesting people. Raymond Adams says of Thoreau that he "shared with his mother the ability so to dramatize an act that, however imitative it may have been, it seemed original with him and bore his stamp forever after." It is a serious mistake to regard histrionism as necessarily allied to either insincerity or distortion. The prophets of Israel never stopped with proclaiming their messages; whenever they could, they acted them out. Hosea married a prostitute to symbolize the relationship between Yahweh the faithful husband and Israel the unfaithful wife, and Isaiah walked naked through the streets of Jerusalem to symbolize the desolation which would come upon Judah should she place her trust in Egypt rather than the Lord. In his humble way, Thoreau too existed in a prophetic tradition.

III

In government as such Thoreau had considerably less interest than in economy. To him the ultimate authority of all government rested in the people, that government was best which governed least, and no government at all was the ultimate goal. Not the government but the people themselves had achieved whatever had been accomplished here; "the merely political aspect of the land is never very cheering; men are degraded when considered as members of a political organization." Few people fit to govern were ever willing to take the job, so that the halls of Congress acquired "an ale-house odor" and compelled one to think of human beings as apes and baboons; certainly if the country were to survive, the "wordy wit" heard there must be perpetually corrected by complaints from back home. Patriotism itself, though not necessarily degrading, became only a "maggot" in the heads of those who professed devotion to country without showing any respect for themselves.

Government indeed was an artifical creation, in itself "unreal, incredible, and insignificant"; consequently "most revolutions have not the power to interest, still less to alarm us; but tell me that our rivers are drying up, or the genus pine dying out in the country, and I might attend."

For all that, Thoreau was not an anarchist in the sense that he asked for no government at once; for the time being, at least, he was willing to settle for a better government, especially if he can have one that will leave him alone. He did not vote because he thought voting accomplished nothing. Even what his countrymen called political freedom did not seem very important to him since it did not involve economic and moral freedom. In his eyes a man's attitude toward society was not the great thing either; what he had to do was "to maintain himself in whatever attitude he find himself through obedience to the laws of his being, which will never be one of opposition to a just government, if he should chance to meet with such." Of course when the government interfered with "the laws of his being" by demanding that he perform an action of which his conscience disapproved, the situation changed its aspect. [10]

Thoreau nowhere seems more crotchety or contrary than in his attitude toward philanthropy and reform. "I feel that my connection with and obligation to society are very slight and transient," he says. In *Walden* he confesses that he has "hitherto indulged very little in philanthropic enterprises." "You must have a genius for charity as for anything else," and doing good is an overcrowded profession which does not agree with his constitution. "Probably I should not consciously and deliberately forsake my particular calling to do the good which society demands of me, to save the universe from annihilation; and I believe that a like but infinitely greater steadfastness elsewhere is all that now preserves it." Again he says, "I very rarely indeed, if ever, 'feel any itching to be what is called useful to my fellowmen.' . . . What a foul subject is this, of doing good, instead of minding one's life, which should be his business." Even when his opposition to slavery was at its height, he wrote in his journal, "I do not think it is quite sane for one to spend his whole life in talking or writing about this matter, unless he is continuously inspired, and I have not done so. A man may have other affairs to attend to." And though I, for one, do not think Thoreau was quite sane about John Brown, even here he seems to have kept his balance sufficiently to refuse to put aside his own particular interests and preoccupations to write Brown's life.

Some of the shocking statements I have quoted (one thinks of Emerson's chilly "Are they my poor?") exemplify the familiar Thoreauvian exaggeration and deliberately cultivated individualism. For all that, they have deep roots in his thinking. As has already been said, he based everything on the individual. "Look not to your legislatures and churches for your guidance nor to any soulless, *incorporated* bodies, but to *inspirited* or inspired ones." Moreover he did not believe that a man could improve himself without immensely wanting to do it, and while he had little belief in legislation as a means of inspiring that desire, nor apparently very much in the power of direct exhortation, he did retain considerable faith in the power of example. "It is for want of a man that there are so many men." If it is true that a little leaven leavens the whole lump, then Thoreau's argument—that a man's primary duty is not "to devote himself to the eradication of any, even the most enormous wrong" but to keep his own hands clean—does make sense (he even praises Wendell Phillips for having said that he was born not to abolish slavery but to do right). If we take care "to flourish & smell & taste sweet and refresh all mankind to the extent of our capacity & quality," we shall accomplish all we are capable of and at the same time avoid the superficialities, partialities, and intolerance of reformers who concentrate upon their own pet projects and themselves suffer distortion in consequence. Now, the critic who would present Thoreau, or perhaps any other man, as completely consistent may be trusted to square the circle, but I am persuaded that it is along some such line as this that we must proceed if we would understand how, feeling no genius for doing good, he could still write, "I would fain communicate the wealth of my life to men, would really give them what is most precious in my gift. I would secrete pearls with the shellfish and lay up honey with the bees for them. . . . I know of no riches I would keep back. I have no private good, unless it be my peculiar ability to service the public," nor yet how he could admire as he did only those who labored for the public good, rejecting the pursuit of both money and power.[11] And, perhaps by the same token, it may help us to understand why he favored official encouragement of culture, science, art and education, good roads, crime detection, prevention of fire, and the protection of nature and wildlife.

Thoreau not only recognized the obligation of the state to educate children, both for their welfare and for its own; he wanted education to continue through adult life: "It is time that villages were universities." "Shall the world be confined to one Paris or one Oxford forever? Cannot students be boarded here and get a liberal education under the skies of Concord?" (So, never one to preach without practicing, he served as secretary of the Concord Lyceum.) Libraries and art galleries were equally important, "In this country, the village should in some respects take the place of the nobleman of Europe. It should be the patron of the fine arts." Then too, "every town should have a park, or rather a primitive forest of five hundred or a thousand acres, where a stick should never be cut for fuel, a common possession forever, for instruction and recreation." In these areas at least he came to realize the need for collective action. In the first great age of railroading, he had the wit to see that a few were riding but at the cost of riding over the rest, and he realized that some way must be found to control individual acquisitiveness in the interest of the common welfare.[12]

IV

Thoreau's beliefs about government affected and were affected by his famous doctrine and practice of "civil disobedience" as well as by his attitude toward slavery and the Civil War crisis which developed out of slavery. During most of his life he committed himself only to individual resistance to what he considered unjust laws and immoral pressure upon the individual. "I quietly declare war with the State, after my fashion, though I will still make what use and get what advantage of her I can, as is usual in such cases." Though he thought the law a "humbug," he once seriously considered invoking it against a neighbor whose sow and horse had trespassed upon his property, and he might very well have done this if he had thought it would work. Nevertheless he did not wish "to split hairs, to make fine distinctions, or set [himself] up as better than [his] neighbors," but sought rather "an excuse for conforming to the law of the land." So long as the state left him alone, he would leave her alone, but if she required him to commit injustice, he must resist. "What I have to do is to see, at any rate, that I do not lend myself to the wrong which I condemn." For such resistance, should it be necessary, he recognized that he might have to accept penalty. "Under a government which imprisons any unjustly the true place for a just man is also in prison."

This, of course, is ethical absolutism. Thoreau was not primarily concerned with the social consequences of his action, nor, as Michael J. Hoffman has observed,[13] did he accept "the Kantian ethic whereby the individual determines his actions by whether or not the whole of society ought to act as he does." He knew perfectly well that the whole of society would not, any more than he either expected or desired it to follow him to Walden Pond; he was not proselytizing. His primary responsibility was "to himself and not his need to please others." Among the abolitionists of his time he sympathized most not with Garrison and his stress on political action but with the extreme individualism of Nathaniel Peabody Rogers, editor of *The Herald of Freedom*. Thoreau would wash his hands of guilt by refusing to cooperate with "the *slave's* government." If enough men did that, "a peaceable revolution" would follow. It would be dangerous to assert that he actually expected this to happen, but he did believe that effective revolution was impossible upon any other basis.

Thoreau's method of reform, concentrating upon the individual, goes to the root of the matter, and if it is true that society can never be better than the individuals of which it is composed (while in practice it is always very much worse than the best among them), then this method has one clear advantage over the methods of those who would begin at the other end and reform men from above. As Joseph Wood Krutch remarked, it has the obvious advantage of making it impossible "to indulge in that nerveless self-pity which expresses itself in the tendency to blame everything on 'our times' or 'the present system'; and he puts upon each man the responsibility for himself, at least." Its obvious disadvantage, of course, is that there is much that cannot be accomplished by men working alone but only by men working together. To a limited extent, Thoreau came to realize this as the Civil War approached, though he never worked it out logically nor spelled out all the implications of his at least moderately changing outlook, but Heinz Eulau probably does not greatly exaggerate when he says that his mind was "totally closed to the democratic conception of politics as a never-ending process of compromise and adjustment." Emma Goldman's biographer, Richard Drinnon argues that "his community consciousness was the essential, dialectical *other* of his individuality," but he also thinks that "belief in higher law *plus* practice of individual direct action *equal* anarchism." As the slavery crisis worsened, Thoreau seems to have been willing to accept secession for Massachusetts (New England never really discovered that secession was a wicked doctrine until after the South had taken it up), but in both "Slavery in Massachusetts" and "A Plea for Captain John Brown," he goes beyond this in advocating the secession of the individual also. "Are laws to be enforced simply because they were made? or declared by any number of men to be good, if they are *not* good?" "Let each inhabitant of the State dissolve his union with her, so long as she delays to do her duty." In such utterances, Thoreau does earn Emerson's characterization of him as "protestant *à outrance.*"

About racism itself Thoreau does not seem to have thought very much. He says that "a wise man sees as clearly the heathenism and barbarity of his own countrymen as those of the nations to whom his countrymen send missionaries," but he also writes that "barbarous as we esteem the Chinese they have already built their steamboat," which not only suggests an amazing ignorance of Chinese civilization for one so much interested as Thoreau was in Orientalism but also sets up a criterion for judging civilization itself which might have pleased George F. Babbitt. There is one rather Whitmanesque poem, "Our Country," which suggests both "America the Beautiful" and "An Ode in Time of Hesitation," and which culminates in a vision of "the so long gathering congress of the world" being brought into being in America:

> The Afric race brought here to curse its fate,
> Erin to bless,—the patient German too,
> Th' industrious Swiss, the fickle, sanguine Gaul,
> And manly Saxon, leading all the race.

But even this vision of the melting pot shows racist overtones and would seem more the voice of New England provincialism and snobbery than the utterance of a man who himself bore a French name.

We have no information as to how Thoreau regarded the capacities of the Negro race; his anti-slavery was determined by his basic humanity, but he was even more concerned about what he called "slavery in Massachusetts" than he was about Negro slavery in the South, for slavery existed, he thought, wherever a man "allows himself to be made a mere thing or tool, and surrenders the inalienable rights of reason and conscience." True as this was, a fugitive slave might have found cold comfort in it, but, as we have already seen, here again his practice was warmer than his theory, and though he joined no abolition society, he did not hold himself wholly aloof from Underground Railroad activities. He himself contributed to the legend that the hut at Walden Pond served as a station when he wrote, "I have thought that Walden Pond would be a good place for business, not solely on account of the railroad and the ice-trade; it offers advantages which it may not be good policy to divulge. . . ." One cannot say that there was never a fugitive slave at Walden, but since there were no good places for concealment there, such persons were generally kept at the Thoreau home or elsewhere in Concord. The passage of the Fugitive Slave Act in 1850 made it legally incumbent upon Northerners to act as slave-catchers (even Emerson wrote in his journal, "I will not obey it, by God!"), and the Anthony Burns case and the Sims case roused anti-slavery passions to such an extent as to make subversives out of the New England intellectuals. Thoreau fought the battle for freedom of speech in the Concord Lyceum when it was proposed to bar Wendell Phillips or prevent his discussing slavery there; he arranged for Emerson's address in 1844, celebrating West Indian emancipation, himself ringing the bell to announce the meeting after the sexton had refused to do so; and he delivered "Slavery in Massachusetts" as an address at the same anti-slavery meeting in Framingham, on July 4, 1854, at which Garrison burned the Constitution of the United States as a covenant with death and hell. [14]

Both Alcott and Charles Lane preceded Thoreau in being jailed for their refusal to pay taxes, and though Garrison believed that making it clear the tax was being paid under duress was enough to satisfy conscience, there is considerable reason to believe that resistance in Massachusetts was fairly widespread. No doubt some really were the skulkers that Emerson strangely called Thoreau, but others must have suffered far more than he did, and it is interesting that Longfellow, who, anti-slavery man though he was, would never have dreamed of taking such an action for himself, praised Thoreau for doing it though he never said anything about *Walden*.

In view of the fame it has achieved, it is surprising how little we know about the night Thoreau spent in jail. It is nearly always described as a protest against the Mexican War, yet he seems to have begun defaulting on his taxes at least as early as 1843; it is safer, then, to regard his action as a protest against slavery. "I do not wish, it happens," he wrote in the *Week*, "to be associated with Massachusetts, either in holding slaves or in conquering Mexico. I am a little better than herself in these respects." H. H. Hoeltje has argued that since the tax in question was local, with no relationship "either to the government of the state of Massachusetts or to the Federal Government," Thoreau's money could not possibly have been used to "buy a man or a musket to shoot one with" and that what he did was "as if, in our own day, some villager who disliked federal aid to Tito would therefore refuse to pay a tax for the pavement in front of his own home." Perhaps. On the other hand, Thoreau knew that Massachusetts had her share in supporting slavery in the South and in condoning what, if possible, concerned him even more, the very different but no less wicked forms of what he called "slavery in Massachusetts"; and Concord being a part of Massachusetts, she could not avoid her share of responsibility for this. Thoreau began protesting, as he began everything else, where he found himself.

We do not know the exact date of Thoreau's jailing; it was certainly late in July 1846, but the exact date has been fixed as July 23 or 24 only by conjecture. Why Sam Staples waited until 1846 to arrest him is open to speculation; it may have been because he was soon going out of office and was obliged to clear his books, paying the accumulated fines himself if he could not get them from the defaulters. We do not know who paid Thoreau's tax for him; his Aunt Maria has always been the favorite candidate, but Alcott says it was Squire Hoar, and Edward Emerson nominated either the squire or his daughter Elizabeth. (Emerson says friends continued to pay the tax during succeeding years, "and I believe . . . [Thoreau] ceased to resist.") Questions have even been raised as to whether Henry was as calm and satisfied about his jailing as his own account indicates or as interested in a fellow prisoner and in what he could hear and see of the activities in the nearby hotel, and Staples says he was "as mad as a hornet" about having the force of his protest undercut when his fine was paid for him. He ought to have been "mad as a hornet" against Staples himself for holding him in jail overnight after the fine had been paid, simply because he had taken his boots off and was too lazy to put them on again until morning! And finally, as Walter Harding has now pointed out, Staples' whole action was probably illegal, though apparently neither he nor his prisoner was aware of this. Under Massachusetts law at the time, Staples seems to have had the right to seize Thoreau's goods and sell them for whatever they would bring to discharge his indebtedness but not to lay hands upon his person. [15]

That Thoreau's views and actions with reference to civil disobedience raise fundamental and deep-seated questions concerning the relationship between the individual and society is undeniable, and only a fool could argue that either Thoreau or anybody else has completely solved these problems. Perhaps, indeed, they never can be completely resolved, but unless we are to accept a Hitler-like tyranny, Thoreau's protest still deserves more careful consideration than probably any government on earth would be willing voluntarily to accord it at the present time. Berel Lang says it very well: "Admittedly, it will be difficult to decide when the state has lost its claim to obedience. But this does not differ from the difficulty which figures in the making of any ethical choice; and, difficulties and possibilities of error notwithstanding, we make them." [16]

V

But one cannot go far in considering the problems of government without running into the problem of peace and war. Modern pacifists generally think very well of Thoreau since his championship of civil disobedience makes him their ally whenever they have to take a stand against a warring or threatening state, but if one takes his thought in this area as a whole and interprets it without prejudice, he proves a somewhat weak rod for a pacifist to lean on.

It is not that none of his utterances were ever pacifistic. He must have been playful when, upon visiting Quebec, he thought it well to examine the walls, that "I might be the better prepared should I ever be called that way again in the service of my country." For he goes off from this into a hilarious discussion of the futility and anachronism of fortifications; the only reason they have not been dismantled, he says, is that men's intellects have been. In Quebec the whole exhibition was like "the keeper of a menagerie showing his animal's claws," and the bare-legged Highlanders on guard made it all seem the more ridiculous. "If you wish to study the muscles of the leg about the knee, repair to Quebec." The soldier who would stand guard in winter to have his face frozen lest Wolfe should again attack the Heights of Abraham, or some Malay or Japanese troop be "coming round by the northwest coast . . . to assault the citadel," must surely be "a natural or unnatural fool." It was all about as reasonable as it would be to guard the walls of Nineveh. The only constructive thought he got out of the whole thing was one that brought him close to William James' musings about the possibility of developing a moral equivalent for war. If the "vast centipede of a man" which was the Canadian army could be used "for all sorts of pulling down," might it not also conceivably be employed for some kind of building up? "If men could combine thus earnestly, and patiently, and harmoniously to some really worthy end, what might they not accomplish?"

Nor was it only the soldiers of a foreign power that he viewed with such unanointed eyes. A soldier is a "powder-monkey" and "a fool made conspicuous by a painted coat." Educate him and he will desert, for only the defeated go to the wars in the first place. The heroism of the Light Brigade simply shows that soldiers are machines; even decent men, who behave well when left to themselves, will commit outrages under orders, and he looks forward with horror to the annual state muster which turns Concord into Discord. He doubts that men ever made a trade of heroism even in the Homeric Age, when eating must have been much more important than fighting and Homer himself a greater hero than any of those about whom he wrote. "The weapons with which we have gained our most important victories [and] which should be handed down as heirlooms from father to son, are not the sword and the lance, but the bushwack, the turf-cutter, the spade, and the bog-hoe, rusted with the blood of many a meadow, and begrimed with the dust of many a hard-fought field." As for the moral law, it needed no champion. "Its asserters do not go to war. It is never infringed with impunity." In 1836, when he thought there was danger of war between England and America, he considered both parties candidates for Bedlam. "What asylum is there for nations to go to?" And even when he was losing his head over John Brown, he harked back admiringly to Brown's refusal to train for the army and the price he had paid for this at the age of eighteen. "He said that few persons had any conception of the cost, even the pecuniary cost, of firing a single bullet in war."

Unfortunately for pacifists, however, these utterances are balanced, if not overbalanced, by those on the other side of the argument. It may be well to have the worst of these before us at the outset. "I have a deep sympathy with war," he wrote in 1840, "it so apes the gait and bearing of the soul." And, even worse: "The soldier is the practical idealist; he has no sympathy with matter, he revels in the annihilation of it. So do we all at times. When a freshet destroys the works of man, or a fire consumes them, or a Lisbon earthquake shakes them down, our sympathy with persons is swallowed up in a wider sympathy with the universe. A crash is apt to grate agreeably on our ears." Moreover, when his English friend Cholmondeley went off to fight in the Crimea, Thoreau, though gravely doubting that his cause was that of the people of England, felt bound to add that he had "no sympathy with the idleness that would contrast this fighting with the teachings of the pulpit, for perchance more true virtue is practised at Sebastopol than in many years of peace. It is a pity that we seem to require a war from time to time to assure us that there is still manhood left in man."[17]

The early essay on "The Service," which Margaret Fuller wisely rejected for *The Dial,* and which was not published until 1902, when *The Nation* found in it "the kind of writing which makes the most unintelligible passages of the earlier Emerson seem miracles of clarity" and declared that it would add nothing to the writer's reputation, is important in this connection. Both Matthiessen and Sherman Paul have argued that "The Service" is not so much a glorification of war as of the courage which, until now, has found its most characteristic expression in war (Thoreau himself once wrote in his journal that "war is but a training, compared with the active service of . . . peace"), and logically this view can be defended. Yet the whole essay is vague and highfaluting ("often bordering on the vapid in expression," says Harding), with no trace of Thoreau's later simplicity and concreteness, full of what Carl Sandburg might have called "proud words" because the young writer was not yet quite sure what he was saying. In its attitude toward war, it is, in the most pejorative sense of the term, romantic, and, as I think we shall see soon, Thoreau never wholly threw off this tendency, for it reappears at the very end of his life in what he wrote about John Brown. [18]

It is interesting that Emerson should have found "somewhat military" in Thoreau's nature and regretted that this side of him never found expression in action and command. Certainly he often uses military figures, even in wholly unmilitary connections: "The writer must direct his sentences as carefully and leisurely as the marksman his rifle." I do not recall that he ever quotes the passage from Aeschylus of which Robert Kennedy was so fond, that "man was not made for safe harbors," but he would certainly have found it congenial, for he himself wrote, "It is never enough that our life is an easy one. We must live on the stretch; not be satisfied with a tame and undisturbed round of weeks and days, but retire to our rest like soldiers on the eve of battle, looking forward with ardor to the strenuous sortie of the morrow."

The same temperament shows in his passion for the *Iliad,* which apparently meant much more to him than the more romantic and less warlike *Odyssey,* and even more strikingly in his choice of heroes, a list which includes Bayard, Godfrey de Bouillon, Sir Walter Raleigh, Sir Philip Sidney, George Fox, Socrates, Jesus, Columbus, Martin Luther, Oliver Cromwell, Philip van Artevelde, Sir Harry Vane, Sir Richard Arkwright, and George Washington.

He apparently felt only contempt for Franklin, and his tribute to Washington ends oddly with "But we are not sorry he is dead"! To be sure, these are not all military figures, but soldiers certainly figure importantly in the list. Raleigh is the one he comments upon at greatest length, and nothing he wrote is more fascinating for the student of his complicated temperament. He was well aware that there was much in his hero of which the New England moralist in himself could not approve. An intermixture of Cromwell or George Fox would have improved him, he says, quite disregarding the fact that with such an intermixture he would not have been Raleigh, and he knew that "the stories about him testify to a character rather than a virtue." He is tolerant toward Raleigh's monopolies, less tolerant of his courtier aspects (though "not disappointed to learn that he indulged in a splendid dress"), and though he blames him for his relations with Cecil and Essex, he enters a generous interpretation of his motives as an explorer and admires him greatly for the way his nobler nature emerged under misfortune. All in all, he was clearly fascinated by the "bloom and halo" which clings to this dazzling figure and makes no real attempt to resist it; instead he says frankly that it "defies a close and literal scrutiny, and robs us of our critical acumen." For Thoreau in certain moods, it is clear, the hero was what Nietzsche might have seen as "beyond good and evil." "His action had a right to be done however wrong to the moralist it might be." And however odd such a conclusion may seem, it was not wholly out of harmony with Henry's acceptance of even those aspects of nature which seem most wholly indifferent to or even hostile toward human standards of right and wrong.

V I

Thoreau faced a war situation with both the Mexican War and the Civil War. His opposition to the first does nothing for his pacifism, for the Mexican War was a war for slavery and not even a militarist believes in war for the wrong cause. The Civil War was quite another matter. As early as 1837 Thoreau recognized that sectional feeling was tearing the country apart, and in 1856 he thought he heard "distant mutterings" of war. There had been no real unity of feeling in America for many years, he wrote Cholmondeley, nor would be so long as slavery was among us; apparently he would have been willing to accept disunion even in 1861.[19] "I only wish that Northern—that any men—were better material, or that I for one had more skill to deal with them; that the north had more spirit and would settle the question at once, and here instead of struggling feebly and protractedly away off on the plains of Kansas." Yet he adds that what he now admires "is not the regular governments but the irregular primitive ones, like the Vigilance committee in California and even the free state men in Kansas. They are most divine. . . ." However unstatesman-like, this view was quite in harmony with Thoreau's general tendency to trust the heroic individual rather than government action, an attitude which also helps to explain why he was so much more impressed by what John Brown did than by any of the actions of the army.

Yet however impractical all this may have been, it was much less solipsistic and detached from reality than what he wrote Parker Pillsbury on April 10, 1861. He is ignoring Fort Sumter, he says, "for that is the most fatal weapon you can direct against evil ever; for as long as you *know* of it, you are *particeps criminis*. What business have you, if you are 'an angel of light,' to be pondering over the deeds of darkness, reading the New York Herald, & the like? I do not so much regret the present condition of things in this country . . . as I do that I ever heard of it." It is clear that he had little or no confidence in the Lincoln administration, for Bronson Alcott records that during his final illness he spoke impatiently of "what he called the temporizing policy of our rulers" and even thought Seward's letter to Earl Grey over the Mason and Slidell case humiliating to America. Moncure D. Conway adds that though all the rest of Concord, including the Emersons, was steeped in gloom after Bull Run, Thoreau was "in a state of exaltation about the moral regeneration of the nation," which is surely quite as romantic as anything in the Pillsbury letter, and, according to his best early biographer, Henry S. Salt, he said he would never recover while the war lasted, which indeed he did not, though, the circumstances being what they were, he would not have recovered if it had ended either.

In considering Thoreau's attitude toward the Civil War, it must not be forgotten that he died in 1862, which was a year before the Emancipation Proclamation was issued. Nevertheless it is hardly an exaggeration to say that for him the war was John Brown's War. When the news of the raid on Harper's Ferry reached Concord, and even the abolitionists were condemning Brown, Thoreau, on his own initiative and in defiance of all advices ("I did not send to you for advice, but to announce that I am to speak"), delivered an address in his defense at the town hall, ringing the bell himself to announce the gathering; and on the day Brown was hanged, he was foremost among those involved in arranging for a memorial meeting.

It has often been pointed out that though Emerson, Thoreau, and Alcott had all associated with Brown during his visit to Concord, only Sanborn was privy to Brown's plan to foment a slave insurrection when he set out for Harper's Ferry. What if anything Thoreau knew about the Pottawatomie massacres, in the course of which the old fanatic had hacked even the children of slaveholders to pieces, on the ground that "nits grow to be lice," is perhaps still unsettled; he certainly was not familiar with the findings of modern historians who see Brown as "an embezzler, a murderer, a cattle thief, and an inveterate liar."[20] Sanborn, to be sure, says that when he left Brown with Thoreau at his house, "the Thoreaus received him gladly, knowing his brave deeds in Kansas," and that when he himself left, Brown was "describing to Henry his fights on the prairie," and Channing adds that Thoreau found pleasure in a remark of Brown's about "a border ruffian he had despatched," who "had a perfect right to be hung." But surely it must have been a somewhat edited account of his exploits with which Brown regaled Thoreau, and we cannot be sure what Henry would have said if he had known what we know now. Nevertheless it would be idle to pretend that he ever imagined Brown was making omelettes without breaking eggs. "The question," he says, "is not about the weapon, but the spirit in which you use it," and he derides those who imagine themselves able to free the slave by "the quiet diffusion of the sentiments of humanity." "It was his peculiar doctrine," he writes of Brown, "that a man has a perfect right to interfere by force with the slaveholder, in order to rescue the slave. I agree with him," and he goes further still when he declares that he will not "complain of any tactics that are effective of good, whether one wields the quill or the sword, but I shall not think him mistaken who quickest succeeds to liberate the slave. I will judge of the tactics by the fruits." He even attempts to defend Brown by pointing out that we condone violence all through our society. "We preserve the so-called peace of our community by deeds of petty violence every day. Look at the policeman's billy and handcuffs! Look at the gallows! Look at the chaplain of the regiment! We are hoping only to live safely on the outskirts of the provisional army." But however true all this may be, it is surely factitious to attempt to justify one deed of violence by pointing out that others exist.

Thoreau exposed the fundamental romanticism of his nature over John Brown as he never did over anything or anybody else. Consider the following from the journal of 1859: "The preachers, the Bible men, they who talk about principle and doing to others as you would that they should do unto you,—how could they fail to recognize him, by far the greatest preacher of them all, with the Bible on his lips, and in his acts, the embodiment of principle, who actually carried out the golden rule?" Was ever any more completely wrong-headed eulogy ever pronounced over a man of blood? But though all this has been discussed at length from the point of view of its inconsistency with that whole side of Thoreau's thought and nature which expressed itself in his advocacy of civil disobedience and non-violent resistance, this is by no means its most interesting aspect for the student of his character. He had never been completely consistent in his attitude toward government. When the state of Massachusetts placed its forces at the disposal of the slavecatchers, as in the Sims and Anthony Burns cases, it was guilty of iniquity, but he would have had no objection to its interfering in *defense* of the fugitives. Why, he asks, should the state train soldiers if they cannot prevent such outrages as these? And if the state will not act, then others must. Still characteristically holding himself aloof from group action (the closest he ever came to this was when, like much of Concord, he was involved in protecting Sanborn from arrest after Harper's Ferry), he did not, like Higginson, and even, up to a point, Alcott, take an active part in trying to rescue Burns; nevertheless he not only approved of what they were trying to do but found in it the only authority he could respect. "They are lovers of law and order, who observe the law when the government breaks it." "Pray, is virtue constitutional, or vice? Is equity constitutional, or iniquity?"

"While they are hurrying off Christ to the cross, the ruler decides that he cannot *constitutionally* interfere to save him." Well, Brown acted alone, even more than these men, in obedience to his own conscience, or what he regarded as such; violent and bloody though he was, he was still motivated by the self-reliance which the transcendentalists valued so highly and was never a cog in a killing machine set in motion by the impersonal power of the state.

This, essentially, is the "line" that Thoreau takes up in his defense; John Brown becomes a transcendentalist or Cromwellian hero, a kind of divine avenger of the wrongs of the slave, and the man himself tends to disappear in the myth which is largely the creation of his defender's own imagination. Howells gives us the key when he tells us that when Thoreau spoke of Brown, "it was not the warm, palpable, loving, fearful old man of my conception, but a sort of John Brown type, a John Brown ideal, a John Brown principle, which we were somehow . . . to cherish and nourish ourselves upon." Or, as Virginia Woolf would say, he was attached not to John Brown but to John Brownness. It would be quite fair, I believe, to say that the man who, of all the Concord men of his time, had the firmest hold on actualities, lost it at this point, but if we are to say this, we must also remember that, as Ethel Seybold wrote long ago, he always "inclined to believe that the events themselves were unimportant and that only the courage and wisdom—or the lack of them—with which men met events had value as history, that history became truth only as it approached the mythical or apocryphal."

If Emerson was right in seeing Thoreau as temperamentally a man of action, there was certainly nothing of the statesman about him; his whole attitude toward the Civil War in general and John Brown in particular shows him as not only indifferent but impervious to all the considerations of policy and expediency. At no point does he even raise the question of what Brown's raid accomplished, or might have accomplished. So far as he was concerned, it was heroism for heroism's sake; whether it failed or succeeded was hardly worth considering; at one point he even says he was afraid Brown might *not* be martyred! This is the artist, the idealist, the moralist, the ethical absolutist, the man of generous passions on an emotional jag, but it is certainly not the statesman.

Stanley Edgar Hyman underlines the importance of the aesthetic element in all this when he remarks that about all Brown and Thoreau had in common were principle and literary style. There is no denying the eloquence and, if you can forget their background, the nobility of Brown's utterances after his arrest, and Thoreau makes it abundantly clear that he was deeply moved by them. Surely this must have been as large an element in his Brown-intoxication as the eloquence of Bartolomeo Vanzetti was to be in rallying the intellectuals to his defense and that of Nicola Sacco in the 1920s. Sacco and Vanzetti may, for all I know, have been as innocent as Brown was guilty, but we shall never know how much less passionate the protest in their behalf would have been had Vanzetti had no more eloquence than Sacco. And it often seems that those who are themselves most unmistakably the masters of words are the ones who are most easily taken in by them.[21]

CHAPTER FOUR

The Seen

I want a whole continent to breathe in,
and a good deal of solitude and silence, such as Wall Street cannot buy,
—nor Broadway with its wooden pavement.
HDT, 1843

FOR MANY YEARS, Thoreau was known mainly, almost exclusively, as a "nature writer" and the founder of a whole school of "nature writers," and, though this was never in itself an adequate definition of his work, there is no denying the importance of nature in either his life or his appeal.[1] He came by his interest in it honestly, by association with both his parents and his brother John. His early reading of Audubon and of Emerson's *Nature* must surely have contributed. He felt that he needed at least four hours a day in the open air to preserve his health and spirits, walking sometimes up to twenty miles, staying out after sunset and occasionally even all night, "sauntering through the woods and over the hills and fields, absolutely free from all worldly engagements." He would have hesitated to be born, he said, if he had thought he would be cut off from roaming over the fields.

The corollary of his love of the country was of course dislike of the city. He exalts Concord even above Harvard College in the autobiography he wrote for his class book, and he thought even villages could be called beautiful only in comparison with other villages. Arnold Bennett once said that the only good thing about Boston was the five o'clock train to New York, and the only room in Boston Thoreau cared much for was the one in the Fitchburg depot, where he waited for the train to take him out of town. Unlike Bennett, however, he thought New York even worse than Boston; to him indeed the pigs in the street were the most respectable part of the population there. Boston was quite bad enough however; once when he encountered South End children on an outing, with boys of twelve sucking on cigars, he decided that it must be impossible to keep children either morally or physically clean in the city, and he wondered how shopkeepers and mechanics who were cooped up indoors all day could possibly avoid suicide.

Since he was a writer, steeped in literary associations, Thoreau necessarily sometimes thought of nature and literature together. Thus a ferry across the Merrimack suggests Charon and Styx, "Ledyard or the Wandering Jew," and Dante and Virgil, and the western landscape of an early morning reminds him "of the shadowy realms of Pluto," with the trees trailing Virgilian associations. Nature delivered him from the bondage of time and space also, since, for all his emphasis upon the importance of living in the present, he did not wish to be imprisoned there. It was pleasant to sit on a stump "whose rings number centuries of growth" and "to remember, as I sit by my door, that I too am at least a remote descendant of the heroic race of men of whom there is tradition." The sound of the harvest-fly reminded him that "there were ears for these sounds in Greece long ago, as Anacreon's ode" will show, thus helping to establish "the identity of human nature in all ages." When the snow covered the ground in Massachusetts, it was pleasant to read in Audubon of the magnolia and the Florida Keys, and when he listened to the "*troomp, troomp, troomp*" of the bullfrogs at night, he thought of it as not merely a Concord phenomenon but part of "an incessant and uninterrupted chain of sound . . . from the Atlantic to the Pacific." Yet nature did not need either literary or metaphysical associations to charm him, nor even, in the conventional sense, beauty—any more, say, than it does for his great modern heir and admirer, Andrew Wyeth. Indeed the highest praise he can give literature is to say that it seemed as if nature spoke through her, and the values attached to gold and jewels seemed to him artificial and factitious when compared to the beauties of nature.

> My books I'd fain cast off, I cannot read,
> 'Twixt every page my thoughts go stray at large
> Down in the meadow, where is richer feed,
> And will not mind to hit their proper targe.

So Homer himself must "wait till I the issue learn" of the battle of the ants, and Shakespeare

> attend some leisure hour,
> For now I've business with a drop of dew.

All this is in harmony with what is perhaps his best epigram:

> My life has been the poem I would have writ,
> But I could not both live and utter it.

It is also of course Wordsworthian and in tune with Chaucer's praise of spring:

> whan that the month of May
> Is comen, and that I here the foules sprynge,
> Farwel my book, and my devocioun!

He passionately enjoyed the "crackling fire" of blazing color in the New England autumn, but "the beauty of those terrestrial browns" he had seen recently in the rain also haunted him. He simply could not spare being "abroad in the morning red" when "the forms of the leafless eastern trees" were outlined against the sky, with the cocks crowing and "a thin low mist" hanging over the meadows, and he was even willing to sacrifice income from his own lectures if it gave him more time for nature. The dicksonia fern had a "wild and primitive fragrance," like "the early morning fragrance of the world, antediluvian, strength and hope imparting." In Maine the sight of wild fir and spruce was "like the sight and color of cake to a schoolboy." The "mere remembrance" of pine woods was like a crust of bread to a hungry man, and he was not sure that a pine wood was not "as substantial and as memorable a fact as a friend." During his final illness he was deeply distressed when one of his white pines was bent over by snow and he was not well enough to go out and straighten it and he felt greatly encouraged when, a few days later, it straightened itself. To cast a stone against a chestnut tree to shake down the nuts seemed to him an act of sacrilege, and he was sure that a grove of elms was better worthy of representation at the General Court "than the barroom and victualling cellar and groceries they overshadowed."

These were all trees of repute. But Thoreau's affections were not limited to such. He even sympathized with weeds, "perhaps more than with the crop they choke," because of their vigor, and some-times too for their beauty—the hogweed, for example, being "a fairy's wand." When he lay on his deathbed, it was a grief of mind to him that he could not scrape the frost from his windowpane so that he might at least see the out-of-doors from which he was now ex-cluded. He was well aware of the religious element in all this ("I suppose that this value, in my case, is equivalent to what others get by churchgoing and prayer"), and he would not have been ashamed to take a shrub oak for his coat-of-arms or regard one as his "parish minister, regularly settled."

I believe that his becoming, in Robert Frost's phrase, "acquainted with the night" was a comparatively late development in Thoreau, which testifies strikingly to the way he continued to explore nature and penetrate more deeply into her secrets as long as he lived. "I love the night, for its novelty," he says; "it is less prophaned than the day," and he came to think of moonlight as "like a cup of water to a thirsty man" and "more favorable to meditation than sunlight," in which last aspect, though gentler, it might be said to stand for him to daylight much as winter did to summer. Certainly some of the most beautiful things he ever wrote about nature are in the little book called *The Moon*, originally published in part as the essay "Night and Moonlight": "How insupportable would be the days, if the night with its dews and darkness did not come to restore the drooping world! As the shades begin to gather around us, our prim-eval instincts are aroused, and we steal forth from our lairs like the inhabitants of the jungle, in search of those silent and brooding thoughts which are the natural prey of the intellect." "The moon is a mediator. She is a light-giver that does not dazzle me." "By moon-light we are not of the earth earthy, but we are of the earth spiritual."[2]

Another subject that has received increasing attention during re-cent years is Thoreau's relationship to water.[3] Thus Canby remarks that "as he grew older, his travels in Concord became more and more fluvial"; indeed the Concord River was so much alive to him that he wondered how it could run heedless to the sea without his being there to see it. There is an interesting little paradox here: though Thoreau knew he was basically a land animal, he also thought of water as "much more fine and sensitive an element than earth." Islands fascinated him also, even if they only stood at the junction of two rivers. As for sailing, he found it pleasant and exhilarating to feel the boat in which he was riding tossed up and down by the waves. "It is flattering to a sense of power to make the wayward wind our horse and sit with our hand on the tiller. Sailing is much like flying, and from the birth of our race men have been charmed by it." Thoreau would certainly have taken a dim view of both the motorcar and the plane, but such a passage shows that he might well have relished the physical sensation of guiding either one.

I do not know whether Thoreau ever pondered or debated in his mind the question whether the true, the good, and the beautiful were one, but his natural tendency was to associate nature with both goodness and health. "The constant inquiry which nature puts is: 'Are you virtuous? Then you can behold me.' Beauty, fragrance, music, sweetness, and joy of all kinds are for the virtuous." He called the buds of the poplars "our little vegetable redeemers" and believed that if we would be well, we must go out every day and really ourselves with nature. His own beanfield at Walden attached him to the earth and renewed his strength, even though he did not himself like beans, and once he climbed a hill to recover his sanity by watching the sun go down. "Show me two villages," he writes, "one embowered in trees and blazing with all the glories of October, the other a merely trivial and treeless waste, with only a single tree or two for suicides, and I shall be sure that in the latter will be found the most starved and bigoted religionists and the most desperate drinkers."

For if nature was health and strength and goodness, he knew only too well that our harmony with her can be destroyed by grief or disappointment or sin. When John Brown was sentenced to be hanged, a cloud passed over Thoreau's landscape. He was well aware that there is no objective seeing. We see only what we look for. "There is no beauty in the sky, but in the eye that sees it." "There is just as much beauty visible to us in the landscape as we are prepared to appreciate," and if nature is "a fountain of health to the healthy," she is "sickly to the sick." When, after having been sick himself, he heard the cattle lowing in the streets again with "a healthy ear," he was sure he was on the mend. For if disease was "the *rule* of our terrestrial life," it was also "the prophecy of a celestial life," and though no man was completely healthy, every invalid still thought of health as the norm and of himself as the exception from it, and it was here that our hope lay and the final testimonial to man's basic soundness. "Man begins by quarreling with the animal in him, and the result is immediate disease. In proportion as the spirit is the more ambitious and persevering, the more obstructions it will meet with. It is as a seer that man asserts his disease to be exceptional." Such an utterance brings to mind such different persons as Sigmund Freud and Mrs. Eddy, though Thoreau here ignores the fact that much of our disease is the result not of quarreling with but of indulging the animal in us.

I I

Joseph Hosmer says that as a boy Thoreau hated sports and games, also "street parades and shadows, with their band accompaniment." Artificial methods of exercise, as carrying dumb-bells on journeys to exercise with, also seemed ridiculous to him. "I see dumb-bells in the minister's study, and some of their dumbness gets into his sermons." (I wonder how he knew, since he never heard them.) On the other hand, as Emerson sums it up, "he was a good swimmer, runner, skater, boatman, and would probably outwalk most countrymen in a day's journey." He proved himself a good mountain climber in Maine, and at the age of forty he records having skinned up a 15- to 18-foot tree to look into a nest. When he was at Walden, the pond in winter gave him a skating rink of more than sixty acres. In 1851 he skated to Sudbury over meadows just frozen enough to bear his weight, and in 1855 he skated up the river through the snow, sometimes taking a spill from drifts or concealed unevenness in the ice, but he "would not have missed the experience for a good deal." Mrs. Hawthorne thought the "dithyrambic dances and Bacchic leaps" he performed on the ice "very remarkable, but very ugly," but she was contrasting both them and Emerson's way of "pitching head-foremost, half lying on the air," as if he were "too weary to hold himself erect," with the grace of her handsome husband, who, "wrapped in his cloak, moved like a self-impelled Grecian statue, stately and grave," and she was not an unprejudiced witness. Bathing, however, was Thoreau's great passion. To be sure, there were limitations to his appetite for it. At Cohasset the water was so cold he could swim only a stroke or two, and on September 11, 1860, he wondered whether bathing might not be over for the season. But since we also have record of his getting up to bathe at 1:30 in the morning, his toleration for cold must have been reasonably hearty.

One form of outdoor sport he generally eschewed: it was only in his first thoughtless youth, if he ever had any, that Thoreau could take any real pleasure in hunting. Falconry, to be sure, was associated for him with "nobleness and poetry," but this was literary, not experiential. Everything in him that attracted him to wildness and convinced him that in wildness lay the preservation of the world attracted him to the hunter over the agriculturalist. "I am convinced," he writes, "that my genius dates from an older era than the agricultural. I would at least strike my spade into the earth with such careless freedom and accuracy as the woodpecker his bill into a tree. There is in my nature, methinks, a singular yearning toward all wildness," and he adds that though gardening is civil and social, it still "wants the vigor and freedom of the forest and the outlaw." Yet while he was drawn toward hunters and trappers by their nearness to nature, he could not help thinking that the evolutionary process had somehow been arrested in them and that their life was not for him. If violence and killing represented a necessary stage in the development of life, this was nevertheless for men a stage that must be passed *through*. It was quite in character that when he heard of Emerson on his Adirondack jaunt shooting a peetweet for Agassiz or cracking an ale-bottle with his rifle, he should have been appalled, and that when he read a book in which the writer wrung his hands over the ferocity of the wildcat and then turned about to praise hunting, he should cry, "Physician, heal thyself!"[4]

Of course he was not completely consistent about it; when was he ever that about anything? When he met little Johnny Riordan wearing his woodchuck cap (which encounter N. C. Wyeth painted so charmingly in *Men of Concord*), he commented merely that it was worn "as fresh and handsome as if the woodchuck wore it himself." But he opposed squirrel hunts on the ground that while squirrels devoured a little corn, they also planted acorns and that, for this reason alone, it would be more sensible to have "some significant symbolical ceremony" once a year in honor of this great service than to slaughter them. In Maine Thoreau attended a moose hunt for what he could learn from it, but found it too much "like going out by night to some woodside pasture and shooting your neighbor's horses," while as for destroying a muskrat's house, this was an act which boded no good end for any who performed it.

Very occasionally Thoreau could bring himself to kill a specimen for scientific study but never without protest. He believed there was much more to be learned from live creatures than from dead ones and preferred holding one in his affections rather than his hand, and once, when he was asked why he did not shoot an animal if he wished to study it, he replied, "Do you think I should shoot you if I wanted to study you?" To him killing was inconsistent with the "poetic perception" which he always preferred to the scientific, and he prayed "that I may walk more innocently and serenely through nature. No reasoning whatever reconciles me to this act. It affects my day injuriously. I have lost some self-respect. I have a murderer's experience in a degree."

Thoreau was one of the pioneer American conservationists, functioning long before most of his countrymen had begun to grasp the fact that our resources are not inexhaustible. He had more respect for the scavengers who clear the Paris sewers than for the employees of the Hudson's Bay and Northwest Fur companies, nor could he entertain any great regard for "the most tender-hearted and delicately bred lady, perhaps the President of the Antislavery Society," who was attired in skins and furs. Not only did he issue a call for public parks, creating such preserves in the name of the people as kings used to do for their private playgrounds; he wanted falls and river banks kept free from the intrusion of mills and factories, so that beauty could be preserved everywhere in a rational manner, and it would not be necessary for New Englanders to rush off to the White Mountains and elsewhere to see it. The destruction of a great tree, especially for trivial purposes, seemed to him comparable to the killing of a great man ("why does not the village bell sound a knell?"), but he was not obscurantist about it, for his 1860 lecture on "The Succession of Forest Trees" showed his grasp of the beginnings of the principles which govern modern forestry and his real-

ization that it is possible for a developing economy to use the land
without destroying it. It has taken us a century and more to catch up
with him in this perception.

The best and most penetrating thing ever said about Thoreau's attitude toward animals was written by William J. Wolf, in his authoritative study of Thoreau's religion:

> What the ecological crisis of our day is plainly demonstrating to us, and
> what Thoreau so well anticipated, is that neighbor love needs to be ex-
> tended to include all creation, inanimate as well as animate. The parable
> of the good Samaritan with its decisive question, "Who is my neigh-
> bor?" leads to the wider answer of Francis of Assisi in his "Canticle of
> the Sun" and on to Thoreau's recognition of the kinship of all created
> reality. Even Albert Schweitzer's magnificent "reverence for life" needs
> to be expanded to include matter, the foundation of all life, as Teilhard
> de Chardin does in his "Hymn to Matter."

The journal contains remarkable and loving descriptions of an en-
gaging heifer named Sumach and of his sympathy with two toil-
worn oxen ("it is painful to think how they may sometimes be over-
worked"), and James T. Fields was impressed by his loving memory
of a cow he had known as a child. The muskrat who chewed its leg
off to escape from a trap exemplified "heroic virtue" in Thoreau's
eyes, worthy of prayer and praise, and in 1852 he was shocked when
neighbors' boys made a football of a slaughtered pig's bladder before the animal was cold.

Thoreau necessarily missed the "nobler animals" in the Concord
environs, but he went out at night in Maine hoping to meet a moose
or a wolf. He did not believe that moderns were in any position to
reproach the ancient Egyptians for their idolatry toward animals,
and he would have liked to bridge the gulf between man and beast
and mend the estrangement between them. "I am attracted toward
them undoubtedly," he writes, "because I never heard any nonsense from them. I have not convicted them of folly, or vanity, or
pomposity, or stupidity, in dealing with me." At one point he even
suggests that they "may have something divine in them akin to revelation,—some inspiration allying them to man as to God." Certainly there can be no question of his ability to get on with them.
Frederick L. H. Willis reports (and his account is corroborated in almost every detail by Mary Hosmer Brown): "Stepping quickly to the

cabin door, he gave a low and curious whistle; immediately a wood-chuck came running towards him from a nearby burrow. With vary-ing note, yet still low and strange, a pair of gray squirrels were summoned and approached him fearlessly. With still another note several birds, including two crows, flew towards him, one of the crows resting on his shoulder." It is no wonder that he loved "The Nun's Priest's Tale," and Canby's tribute to him as himself an ac-complished beast fabulist was honestly earned.

Charles Anderson counts more than seven hundred references to animals in *Walden* alone, of which he reports that less than one-fifth are figurative but that these are the most significant of the lot. I should not say that Thoreau never anthropomorphizes his refer-ences to animals, any more than I could honestly claim that there is no sentimentalism in his interpretations of natural phenomena in general, but when he is compared to other writers in his place and time, this tendency does not predominate in either area. Sometimes he indulges himself by half playfully attributing his own emotions and reactions to animals. Thus the eyes of the young partridge "suggest not merely the purity of infancy, but a wisdom clarified by experience." A newly hatched turtle "meditates how it may reach the water in safety." A shoat whom he has been pursuing through a harrowing afternoon and has finally cornered sits "resting quietly on his belly . . . thinking unutterable things." "*See there, see there,*" says a red squirrel to himself, "who's that? O dear, what shall I do?" And as for the parent fishes, in view of all the perils that exist in pond and river, if they care anything for their offspring, how can they bear to leave them out of their sight? Once at least he even an-thropomorphizes a machine; to him, as to Emily Dickinson, the locomotive is an iron horse who makes the hills "echo with his snort like thunder, shaking the earth with his feet, and breathing fire and smoke from his nostrils." Thoreau can even "hear him in his stable blowing off his superfluous energy of the day, that he may calm his nerves and cool his liver and brain for a few hours of iron slumber." But such passages are the exceptions. Much more typical is the real-istic, deeply sympathetic but unsentimental feeling expressed in his description of the rabbit, now mere skin, bones, and mould, found starved to death in a box trap. "What a tragedy to have occurred within a box in one of our quiet swamps! The trapper lost his box,

the rabbit his life. . . . After days and nights of moaning and struggle, heard for a few rods through the swamp, increasing weakness
and emaciation and delirium, the rabbit breathes its last."

Obviously it is easier to sympathize with some animals than with
others, but Mary P. Sherwood must stand alone in noting a "curious
lack of enthusiasm throughout Thoreau's writings for the bird inhabitants of his beloved fields and woods." Surely Robert Henry
Walker comes much closer to the truth in his more comprehensive
and authoritative study, where he finds Thoreau's bird notes
"remarkably free of errors" and based on sound ornithological
knowledge. "He does not condescend, he does not go too far in per-
sonalizing his creatures, he does not moralize; instead he finds his
way into their lives as far as his knowledge and understanding
will permit."[5] Their ethereality charmed him, and he resented the
human tendency to consider only their practical use, disregarding
their dispositions, their beauty, or the loveliness of their song, while
as for basing their right to live on their usefulness to man, "it is as if
the question were whether . . . Jenny Lind . . . did more harm or
good, should be destroyed or not, and therefore a committee should
be appointed not to listen to her singing at all, but to examine the
contents of her stomach and see if she devoured anything which
was injurious to the farmers and gardeners, or which they cannot
spare." No wonder birds seemed more afraid of man than of any
other creature, being well aware that to them he is "a beast of prey"
and "not humane, as he pretends to be." As for Henry himself, to
him the song of the chickadee celebrated the praise of heroes and the
loveliness of virtue, and surveying became a noble employment
when it brought him within hearing distance of the first brown
thrasher of the season. In Maine he thought the voice of the loon so
thrilling that he could have lain awake for hours listening to it, and
he could not have forgiven himself if he had let the fox-colored spar-
row migrate to Rupert's Land before he had appreciated it. He always taught boys who collected birds' eggs to leave some for the
mother bird to hatch, and when he found a hawk's nest in a pine
tree, he climbed the tree every day to watch the young develop. "I
would rather," he says, "never taste chickens' meat nor hens' eggs
than never to see a hawk sailing through the upper air again," and if
this seems kinder to hawks than to hens, we must remember that

Thoreau also found in the crowing of cocks "an illimitable holiness, which makes me bless God and myself," and that though the hooting of owls might be "idiotic and maniacal," they still represented his own "stark, twilight, unsatisfied thoughts," and he would rather hear them hoot than the most eloquent man of the age speak.

He would have liked to meet a man capable of living on nuts and berries alone, but he did not wish to rob the squirrels, "who, before any man, are the true owners" of such things. At one time he made a close friend of a mouse, and there are some wonderful passages on woodchucks, with one of whom he once spent a half-hour in mutual contemplation. "I think I might learn some wisdom of him. His ancestors have lived here longer than mine." At Walden he once killed a woodchuck, but he caught another one in a box trap and released it several miles away. On his trip to Minnesota, sick as he was, he noted three different varieties of prairie gophers.

Though he seems to have been less squeamish about fishing than hunting, he still observed fish very closely, became sufficiently familiar with them to be able to handle them, and even felt himself amphibious and a "fellow in a degree." He was particularly impressed by the beauty of pickerel, though he admits their voraciousness, and he calls the horned pout "a bloodthirsty and bullying race of rangers."

The most famous insect passage is of course the famous battle scene in *Walden*, which is more remarkable for observation than affection. He loved the song of the cricket ("a glorifying of God and enjoying him forever")—as who does not?—and he seems to have lived in peace with wasps at Walden Pond, though not with hornets. Here too the mosquito made an "invisible and unimaginable tour through my apartment at earliest dawn. . . . It was Homer's requiem, itself an Iliad and Odyssey of the air, singing its own wrath and wandering." Certainly such a description must have flattered the mosquitoes if a mosquito were capable of being flattered by anything, but there is another passage in the journal in which he speaks of mosquitoes tormenting him.[6]

Probably the animal man hates most is the snake. Though Thoreau was fascinated by the movement of serpents, I find no reason to suppose that he liked them, but the only expression of horror comes in connection with his description of one found swimming in the water, with his head a foot above it, "darting his tongue at it." "A snake thus met with on the water appears far more monstrous, not to say awful and venomous, than on the land." Yet he allowed it to curl round the paddle and took it into the boat and goes on record that it was killed about 2:00 P.M.; he does not say why or by whom, but he continues, "I have the same objection to killing a snake that I have to the killing of any other animal, yet the most humane man that I know never omits to kill one." There is also one description of a "repulsive and gluttonous-looking eel." "It is more repulsive to me than a snake, and I think must be less edible," and there is a horrible journal entry, probably not meant to be taken literally, about swallowing a small snake while drinking at stagnant waters, which may possibly have a connection with Hawthorne's story, "Egotism; or, The Bosom Serpent."

One thing is certain: the dislike of snakes which some persons extend to lizards, frogs, toads, etc., Thoreau did not share. There is one passage in which he compares such creatures to fungus, but I have found no parallel to this. There is a long, loving, and winning description of a wood frog whose confidence he won to the extent of being allowed to pat it, and then, "having passed, it occurred to me to return and cultivate its acquaintance," which he did, and there is another touching description of how he thawed out a frozen frog. "In the evening, the moon being full," he writes in 1858, "I paddle up the river to see the moonlight and hear the bullfrogs." There is also a description of his remaining in a constrained position for three-quarters of an hour or more to watch a painted tortoise lay her eggs, with his face only eighteen inches away from her.

Dogs I think he sympathized with less than with most animals. Once, at some risk to himself, he rescued a little dog from half a dozen big ones who were pursuing it and the next day the beneficiary of his bounty barked at him, causing him to quote Shakespeare's "Blow, blow, thou winter wind," and once, having saved some cows from dogs who were deviling them, he wondered whether devilish boys might perhaps be reincarnated as dogs. On the whole, he thought he preferred foxes to dogs because of their greater independence, and when he came across dogs glutting themselves on carrion, he exclaimed, "surely they are foul creatures that we make cossets of." There is a very sensitive, sympathetic tribute to the fox in "The Natural History of Massachusetts," and once he trailed a fox, not maleficently, for sport, somewhat factitiously justifying the action by "hoping this experience would prove a useful lesson to him." One winter morning he even saw the tracks of the fox as an expression of the Divine Mind. "If these things are not to be called up and accounted for in the Lamb's Book of Life, I shall set them down as careless accountants."

Thoreau's name does not occur in Christabel Aberconway's supposedly definitive *Dictionary of Cat Lovers,* nor are there any selections from his writings in any of the multitudinous cat anthologies with which I am familiar, but I am afraid this proves only that their compilers have been too lazy to read his journal. There can be no question that the cat was his favorite animal. His account of the antics of his cat Min in the very last pages of his journal contains some of the very best descriptions of feline behavior extant, and his story of the tiny, unweaned kitten which, having been dumped into the river, swam out to hail his passing boat is as good a cat story as we have in all literature. He thought the movement of cats the most graceful of any quadruped, their rhythm being identical with that of nature itself, and in Quebec he saw one parading the walls "as serene as Wisdom herself, and with a gracefully waving motion of her tail, as if her ways were ways of pleasantness and all her paths were peace." In fact, the only expression of impatience with cats I have ever found in Thoreau relates to the night he tried to sleep in an attic bedroom at an inn, and they kept him awake with their performance on the neighboring roofs and threatened to come in at his windows—

> "Soon as the evening shades prevail,
> The cats take up the wondrous tale"—

and even then he was less annoyed by the cats than by the bedbugs. "It would be worth while to send a professor there," he says, "one who was skilled in entomology."

As to the famous Min, she distinguished herself as a kitten by jumping out the attic window and coming back unharmed—early one morning, five days later, over snow-covered ground, after she had been given up for dead—and waking up the whole house with her mewing. "She is a mere wrack of skin and bones, with a sharp nose and a wiry tail. . . . There is as much rejoicing as at the return of the prodigal son, and if we had a fatted calf, we should kill it." As it was, she was "fed with the best that the house affords, minced meats and saucers of warmed milk," and recuperated with unstinted sleep in every lap in the house in succession. Thereafter she became an excellent mouser, sharpened her claws "on all the smooth hair-bottomed chairs and sofas, greatly to mother's vexation," and once chose to go to sleep on the bread dough, allowing it to rise about her form.[7]

Indians seemed to Thoreau to live closer to nature without trying to dominate it than any other humans. He murmured "moose" and "Indian" on his death bed, and this has sometimes been interpreted as an expression of regret that he could not live to write the book about Indians for which he had accumulated such immense materials. Edwin S. Fussell expressed the opinion that this work would have made Thoreau "the greatest historian of the age," but Robert B. Sayre, the author of the most recent and detailed study of Thoreau's interest in the Indians, does not believe that he would ever have written it except to the extent that he did write it in *The Maine Woods.*

Thoreau's interest in Indians was part of his interest in early Americana; if we were to study "the indigenous animals" of our country, it seemed stupid to overlook "the indigenous men." As a teacher, he interested his pupils in Indian arrowheads, which, at that time, he might pick up wherever he chose to stoop in Concord, and his collections of Indian materials were ultimately very large. "I have not decided whether I had better publish my experience in searching for arrowheads in three volumes, with plates and an index, or try to compress it into one."

Sayre's basic thesis is that in the beginning Thoreau's conception of the Indian was a literary construct, derived from the Romantic conceptions of savagism and primitivism prevalent in his time. This was modified through diligent reading and study, carried out in quite as scholarly a fashion as was possible with the resources available to him, and through contact with actual Indians, notably Joseph Aitteon and Joe Polis on his second and third trips to Maine, through whom he began to see Indians as individuals, even though his more conventional early notions were never altogether thrown off. Harding even believes that a certain measure of disillusionment followed. Thoreau had idealized the native American as "a 'noble savage' who lived in perfect communion with Nature. In real life the Indian proved to have no cultural nor aesthetic interests. He was interested only in where his next day's food was coming from." Thoreau speaks of the mendacity of the Indians, of "their dishonesty, their lasciviousness, the 'unspeakable filth' of their bodies, their houses, their habits, their cookery," and saw their "fixed habits of stagnation" as robbing them of the ability he thought the Negroes did possess of adjusting themselves to the changed conditions under which they must live if they were to survive. The wastefulness of their indiscriminate slaughter in moose hunting disgusted him, and though he expressed indignation over the white man's obvious patronage of the Indian and assumption of his own superiority, he seems to reveal a touch of condescension himself when he refers to Joe Polis as "the Indian" rather than by his name.[8]

Nevertheless the value of the Indian remained as clear as his right to exist. He "stands free and unconstrained in Nature, is her inhabitant and not her guest and wears her easily and gracefully." Indians had their legitimate place "as a distinct and equally respectable people" who stood in no need "to be inoculated with the twilight civilization of the white man." In an early piece about this, Thoreau invokes Homer, Pindar, and Isaiah. Even if history has passed a sentence of doom upon them, she has certainly not called upon the white man to execute it, for the savage and the civilized alike trace back to a common father, and "inside the civilized man stands the savage still in the place of honor." He praises Sir Walter Raleigh for his consideration for the Indians, and one of the few things he finds to approve of in the conduct of the early French explorers is that "to a certain extent [they] respected the Indians as a separate and independent people." The last time George William Curtis saw him, Thoreau talked about the Indians "and of our obligations to them and our ingratitude."[9] But even then comparisons between the races did not leave whites with all the advantages. With all their shortcomings, the Indians in Maine were still more agreeable and refined company than the white lumberers. "The thought of a so-called savage tribe is generally far more just than that of a single civilized man." And in spite of the Indian capacity for cruelty, he was impressed by the dignity and decorum with which Indians could negotiate treaties. "These savages are equal to us civilized men in their treaties, and, I fear, not essentially worse in their wars."[10]

III

Was Thoreau's interest in nature, then, a scientific interest? He once expressed the view that the day might come when the same formula could express the rules of moral philosophy and of arithmetic, yet when, in 1853, the secretary of the American Association for the Advancement of Science proposed him for membership and asked him to describe his scientific interests, he replied:

> I feel that it would be to make myself the laughing-stock of the scientific community to describe or attempt to describe to them that branch of science which specifically interests me, inasmuch as they do not believe in a science which deals with the higher law. . . . The fact is that I am a mystic, a transcendentalist, and a natural philosopher to boot. Now that I think of it, I should have told them at once that I was a transcendentalist. That would have been the shortest way of telling them that they would not understand my explanations.

In 1860 he probably destroyed his chances for a lecture tour of the middle west by telling two correspondents that if he came his lectures would be transcendental rather than scientific and that most of his hearers would probably find them moonshine.

He praised the establishment of a scientific school at Harvard, but he also called science inhuman. "Things seen with a microscope begin to be insignificant. . . . Suppose I should see and describe men and houses and trees and birds as if they were a thousand times larger than they are!" He was repelled by what seemed to him the coldness and arrogance of science, the attempt to treat phenomena "as something independent of you and not as it is related to you." "A fact stated barely," he says, "is dry. It must be the vehicle of some humanity in order to interest us. . . . A man has not seen a thing who has not felt it." Science "does not embody all that men know, only what is for men of science," and he was convinced that "we shall see but little way if we require to understand what we see. How few things can man measure with the tape of his understanding!" If you had to choose, it was better to know nothing about a subject and realize it than to know something and imagine you know it all. There is little point in studying nature as if it were a dead language, for we cannot "probe with our fingers the sanctuary of any life, whether animal or vegetable." Even "the chief value and significance of flowers to man" escapes the Linnaean classification: "I suspect that the child plucks its first flower with an insight into its beauty and significance which the subsequent botanist never retains." Even scientific nomenclature may be a barrier to understanding, for it does not belong to the object but is simply something men have imposed upon it, and having done so, they run grave danger of never getting beyond it to the thing itself. In confrontation with nature as with other things, the soul does not inspect but beholds, and "knowledge does not come to us by details, but in flashes of light from heaven." If it is insight you are after, you had better, then, avoid anatomy and give yourself up to nature as the first men did, "letting her make what impression she will on you." She will not yield her secrets to one "who goes forth consciously as an observer"; it is the "free sauntering of the eye" that is congenial to her. Like the Gorgon Medusa, she is not to be looked at directly. How could it be otherwise with one whose desire is not merely to understand the object before him but to see it in its relationship to everything else and "communicate with the spirit of the Universe"?

Poetry, wonder, imagination, religion, love, and the capacity to surrender to delight—all these are necessary equipment, then, in the laboratory of anyone who would see beyond the end of his nose. That was why Thoreau preferred the descriptions of animals in Edward Topsell's *The History of Four-Footed Beasts* (1607) and the descriptions of plants in Gerard's *Herbal* to those of modern scientists. "Modern botanical descriptions approach ever nearer to the dryness of an algebraic formula, as if $x + y$ were $=$ to a love letter," and though it was true that some of Topsell's animals existed only in the imagination, they had vitality there, while most modern authors failed either to imagine or to realize the actual animals that they described. For you have not described anything until you have told what it means to man. "Surely the most important part of the animal is its *anima*, its vital spirit, on which is based its character and all the peculiarities by which it most concerns us." Unwelcome though it might be, such considerations drove Thoreau to the conclusion that "men are probably nearer to the essential truth in their superstitions than in their science." A natural phenomenon must satisfy the imagination as well as the understanding. "It is what it suggests and is the symbol of that I care for, and if, by any trick of science, you rob it of its symbolicalness, you do me no service and explain nothing." But the last word always must go not even to understanding but to love. "I have a friend among the fishes." Their chief use was their poetry; their flesh was only their "lowest use. The beauty of the fish, that is what it is best worth while to measure." Unfortunately, as boys grow older, they generally lose some of their "perception and . . . interest" in these things and degenerate into mere fishermen or ichthyologists."[11]

About technology he felt very much as he did about science, only, as the saying is, more so. Though he was always interested in the discovery of new uses for materials, he remained wary of machines; once he even expressed doubt of the wisdom and legitimacy of man's using the labor of animals. His reading of J. A. Etzler's *The Paradise Within the Reach of All Men* (1842) left him with the feeling that "there is a Transcendentalism in mechanics as well as in ethics," yet he could not believe that work might be shirked or that anything else could take the place of industry, and he dissented sharply from Etzler's mistrust of the individual as the source of progress and achievement. Etzler failed in idealism, he thought, his book painting "a Mahometan's heaven," aiming only at "the greatest degree of gross comfort and pleasure" and overlooking the "moral reform" which must underlie any real progress.

The technological advances which came closest to him were the telegraph and the railroad. Both stimulated his imagination, but, as we have already seen, the principal appeal of the telegraph was aesthetic; he loved the humming sound of the wires. As to the function for which it was designed, "we are in great haste to construct a magnetic telegraph from Maine to Texas; but Maine and Texas, it may be, have nothing important to communicate." The Fitchburg Railroad he could see from Walden Pond, and it seemed to link him to society. Though he knew that much of its business was trivial, the enterprise, confidence, and serenity of commerce appealed to him; here as elsewhere he avoided the extremism for which he has so often been reproached. During his second winter at Walden he used a stove instead of the open fireplace and admitted that it was more economical, and if we may judge by the accounts he gives of his later visits to a gingham mill and a steel mill, I think we must admit that he saw the necessity of making some terms with industrialism. Since he thought it "so much pleasanter and wholesomer to be warmed by the sun while you can than by an artificial fire," he must surely have approved of solar heating. Surely he would not object to those who invoke his name while demonstrating at the sites of nuclear power plants, and though, generally speaking, he did not care much for sermons, he certainly would have approved of the one Donald Harrington preached in New York in connection with the 1962 exercises, when he cited Thoreau's thankfulness that men had not yet learned to fly and asked, "What would he think of the world today where we supinely allow essentially insane governments . . . to make a radioactive sewer of the sky itself?" Essentially, however, J. Lyndon Shanley's comment sums up the matter best: "His criticism was not of the improvements themselves, but of men's too great concern for them."[12]

As himself a scientist and even as an observer of nature, Thoreau has been disparaged by Fannie Eckstrom, John Burroughs, Bradford Torrey, Havelock Ellis ("his science is that of a fairly intelligent schoolboy—a counting of birds' eggs and a running after squirrels"), Sherman Paul, Leo Stoller, and others, and defended by Kathryn and Philip Whitford, James S. Bishop and Edward S. Deevey, Jr., Aldo Leopold and Sara E. Jones, Mary P. Sherwood, Raymond Adams, Alec Lucas, Donald G. Quick, and Lawrence Willson.[13] He could display Sherlock Holmes-like powers of observation,[14] and he could also overlook even very obvious things (ornithologists now seem inclined to believe that it was the common oven-bird that he called the night warbler). In fidelity to the old New England principle of never buying anything you did not need, he handicapped himself for years by studying birds without a glass, and though he did read *The Origin of Species* in 1860 and concluded that "the development theory" implied "a greater vital force in nature, because it is more flexible and accommodating, and equivalent to a sort of constant *new* creation," this was too late in his life to exercise much influence upon his work; through most of his career he was more under the influence of Agassiz than of Darwin. Yet he has been credited with pioneering work in limnology, dendrochronology, ecology, and phenology. He anticipated the future in studying the age of trees by the rings shown in the stump, and nobody questions the originality of his address to the Middlesex Agricultural Society in 1860, in which he attempted to discover why when a pine wood was cut down, an oak wood commonly succeeded it, and vice versa; Deevey says no other important studies on ecological succession were made for a generation after him, and Kathryn Whitford declares that the similarities between his study and those which have followed "are too great to be obscured even by the changes which more than eighty years have made in the vocabulary of science." During his later years he spent much time measuring the depths of water and snow, and later surveys have confirmed the remarkable accuracy of his soundings at Walden Pond.[15]

Thoreau's apparently increasing interest in observing and recording phenomena in his later journals has distressed many of his admirers. Canby thought it had a depressing influence upon his style, and even the editors of the *Correspondence* believed that though his eye for nature had sharpened, his eye for transcendentalism had "definitely clouded." Thoreau himself lends support to this view when he writes in 1851, "I fear that the character of my knowledge is from year to year becoming more distinct and scientific; that, in exchange for views as wide as heaven's scope, I am being narrowed down to the field of the microscope. I see details, not wholes nor the shadow of the whole. I count some parts, and say 'I know.' "

The rock on which this view begins to founder is the fact that Thoreau seems even more convinced of the limited value of scientific investigation in his final phase than he had been before.[16] Harding, consequently, no longer adheres to the view advanced in the *Correspondence;* neither is it supported by either Shanley or Sherman Paul. Though Emerson probably did not understand all the implications of his own statement when he said that the scale upon which Thoreau's last studies were being prosecuted "was so large as to require longevity," he was on the right track nevertheless, and Thoreau himself gives us the essential clue when he writes, "Let us not underrate the value of a fact; it will one day flower into a truth." But until that happened he had no more use for it in his final phase than he had ever had. Facts were always the "frame" to his pictures, the "material" of the "mythology" he was writing.

After 1850, as Paul has remarked, he "began the staggering task of charting every phenomenon in the hope of finding in the cycle of the year correspondences to the seasons of man." Accumulations were vast—journals, Indian notebooks, and various data, charts, and indexes—but he did not live to produce the "Kalender" he planned as a study of the whole economy of Nature. "I wish to know an entire heaven and an entire earth," he said. And again, "I pray for such explanation as will make nature significant." Let us not make the mistake of supposing that he had settled at last for counting the cats in Zanzibar, nor in Concord either; he was reaching out toward a total, all-comprehending grasp of the "flower in the crannied wall" and everything connected with it, that is, everything that is. But the complete understanding of natural phenomena, vast as it was in itself, was for him only a means, a way station on the road to the knowledge of "what God and man is," and if there had ever been any solipsism in his vision of nature, he was freeing himself of it, still cherishing those "flashes from heaven" which to him meant true knowledge, but now realizing that they came only out of rich accumulations of data. It is true that what he was reaching for is something that mortal man cannot fully grasp, but surely this does not make his endeavor either less audacious or less admirable, and, as Browning says, you must mix some doubt with faith if you would have faith be. Moreover his endeavor was all the more remarkable as coming from a writer who had been brought up on old-fashioned classificationism and taxonomy, for no modern scientist/philosopher/religionist has attempted more.[17]

IV

In the last analysis, then, the only thing of supreme importance was nature's relevance to man. To be sure, Thoreau sometimes thought of nature as "holy and heroic" while people were "mean and trivial," and turned to her therefore as a refuge against them. Few humans, he felt, were fit to be likened to Walden Pond, though even those who passed it by night on the train might be refreshed by the sight of it. Man indeed was much better at contaminating nature than redeeming her (if she needed redemption); if you wanted steadiness and solidity, you might find them in the rocks, and if you sought honesty and sincerity you had better look to the animals. In 1853 especially there is a series of journal entries which show Henry turning to nature as a refuge from a humanity which has obviously in some connection bitterly disappointed him. Human relations were "full of death and decay, and offended the nostrils," and he loved nature because she was "not man, but a retreat from him." Occasionally indeed he advanced the idea that intimacy with nature kills the need for association with humans (if it stimulates a desire for society, it also unfits you for it), and once at least he tried to lift himself above a merely human outlook by arguing that the notion that the proper study of mankind is man is a mere expression of human egotism. The universe is too vast to have been designed merely for man's abode, and man's concerns cannot fill it. "It appears to me that, to one standing on the heights of philosophy, mankind and the works of man will have sunk out of sight altogether."

But Thoreau does not often reach the heights of ideality or inhumanity (whichever you choose to call it) which have been indicated here. "We soon get through with Nature," he writes. "She excites an expectation which she cannot satisfy." Ideally he wanted a "perfect correspondence" between man and nature, but he knew that the ideal is not often achieved, and he shifted his emphasis to correspond to his changing moods. Thus he can declare both that he would not wish to live in a city built on the site of a more ancient city, where "the dwellings of the living are the cemeteries of the dead, and the soil is blanched and accursed," and that he loves the sight of Indian blood on the rocks because it shows that men have lived, enjoyed, and suffered there, and "that the mould I tread on has been animated, aye humanized." "It was the Greeks made the Greek isle and sky," he cries, and he would like to meet men in the woods, not merely moose and caribou, for

> Though all the firmament
> Is o'er me bent,
> Yet still I miss the grace
> Of an intelligent and kindred face.

"Nature must be viewed humanly to be loved at all," he says; "that is, her scenes must be associated with humane affections. . . . She is most significant to a lover. . . . If I have no friend, what is Nature to me?" Nor does Genesis itself go further than he goes when he declares that "it is for man the seasons and all their fruits exist. The winter was made to concentrate and harden and endure the kernel of his brain, to give tone and firmness and consistency to his thought." Indeed he goes further still: "Man is all in all, Nature nothing, but as she draws him out and reflects him." And again: "The universe is a sphere whose center is wherever there is intelligence. The sun is not so central as man." And, most striking of all: "If it is possible to conceive of an event outside to humanity, it is not of the slightest significance, though it were the explosion of a planet." It is interesting that H. G. O. Blake should have observed that Thoreau showed little interest in astronomy "as compared with studies relating more directly to this world." "The milky way," he says, "yields no milk." Though it is almost as difficult to get a thing exactly wrong as exactly right (even a stopped clock is right twice every day), Canby would seem to have achieved it when he objected to the limitations of Thoreau's science on the ground that it "was intended to make not so much better science as better men." Unless what you want is that humanity should destroy itself, that is exactly what science and every other branch of learning should do; otherwise we steer straight toward the imbecility of the president of a great technological school who once declared that research must continue no matter where it might lead (which, if it means anything, means that man was made for research, not research for man) and that of the mad surgeon who gravely reported that the operation was a success except that the patient died.

Thoreau's attitude toward nature was certainly conditioned by the fact that he lived in Concord, where, in spite of hot summers and cold winters, nature seems built upon a comparatively moderate, *gemütlich*, reasonably modest scale, with which human beings can make terms which would be more difficult to accomplish in either arctic or subtropical regions. To be sure, the agonies of birth and death were the same in Concord as they were everywhere else, and so too were the horrors of disease. "There is not a lily pad floating on the river but had been riddled by insects. . . . Now, at midsummer, find me a perfect leaf or fruit." Moreover, besides disease there was hideous cruelty. Thoreau kept on his mind for days and wondered about the voracity of the pickerel who had three fresh perch in his belly and part of another in his maw, and tried to figure out how many he would devour in the course of a year. Once too he found a turtle with its entrails torn out, probably by a long-beaked bird. "Such is Nature, who gave one creature a taste or yearning for another's entrails as its favorite tidbit." He was equally shocked when he saw a shrike pecking a small bird to pieces and flying off with it in his beak. "I find that I had not associated such actions with my idea of birds. It was not birdlike." Or was it, after all?

It was not that nature gave death the last word. If the earth was a necropolis, was it not also a granary, filled with the seeds of life? And, for that matter, did not decay itself produce fertility, and was not the matchless purity of the waterlily nourished by the rich, black, slimy mud of a dead stream? In some moods, Thoreau could even be cheered by the sight of "the vulture feeding on the carrion which disgusts and disheartens us, and deriving health and strength from the repast. . . . I love to see that Nature is so rife with life that myriads can be afforded to be sacrificed and suffered to prey on one another," and this is the kind of utterance which impelled William J. Wolf to observe that "he had a feeling for the wholeness of nature, partly the result of mystical intuition and partly the result of the kind of observation that was leading Darwin and others to the panorama of organic evolution." But to maintain such a viewpoint consistently would be either to sink below the human level or rise above it, and Thoreau did neither.

In his explorations he was capable of voluntarily embracing what most of us would regard as great hardships. He speaks of the satisfaction of being wetted clear through in a storm and of the "pleasing challenge" of a tempest which "puts to rout the trivialness of our fair-weather life and gives it at least a tragic interest." Darkness had no terrors for him either, and he speaks of having traveled hundreds of miles "without taking any meal in a house, sleeping on the ground when convenient," and finding it "in many respects more profitable" than staying at home.

Nothing is more interesting in this connection than his attitude toward winter. He admitted that November is the month in which "a man will eat his heart out" if he ever does, yet he would often tramp as far as ten miles "through the deepest snow to keep an appointment with a beech-tree, or a yellow-birch, or an old acquaintance among the pines." Long walks of this kind, confronting brute nature, kept his spirits up, and he thought winter ought to appear in the almanacs not "as an old man, facing the wind and sleet, and drawing his cloak about him" but rather "as a merry woodchopper, and warm-blooded youth, as blithe as summer." For all that, one cannot avoid the conclusion that a large part of the pleasure Thoreau derived from winter came from his conviction that he could conquer it. He says that his hands began to "die" with the first cold blasts from the north and that "if we had not gone through several winters," he might very well be dismayed at the approach of yet another one. "How pleasant a sense of preparedness for the winter— plenty of wood in the shed and potatoes and apples, etc., in the cellar, and the house banked up! Now it will be a cheerful sight to see the snows descend and hear the blast howl." That and the feeling that the greater "inwardness" winter brought with it, encouraging thought, were precious to him. Without these things, his approach to it might have been very different, for indeed he says that "perhaps what most moves us in winter is some remembrance of far-off summer. . . . The cold is merely superficial; it is summer still at the core, far, far within."

"I love the wild not less than the good," says Thoreau, but as Garber has pointed out, he obviously didn't, for the true antithesis of wild is not good but tame, as the true antithesis of good is not wild but evil. "I find an instinct in me conducting to a mystic spiritual life," he says, "and also another to a primitive savage life," but he adds significantly that "a risen man never returns to where he began." Or, as Mary Johnston was to express it, many years later, in her novel, *Michael Forth:* " 'I won't say a word against the ancient sea. When we were in it, if we were sincere, it was all that we could do. It has its own powers, beauties, and truths. But the winged thing mustn't return to the finned thing.' " To lose hold on the primitive altogether was to lose hold on all that was vital and fertile in life. The whole side of Thoreau that loved mythology beyond anything else that followed in literature fought on this side. "Mythology is the crop which the Old World bore before its soil was exhausted, before the fancy and the imagination were affected with blight; and which it still bears, wherever its primitive vigor is unabated." Yet there were times when even nature as he was most familiar with it seemed too big so that Henry's thoughts turned to being absorbed in it like leaves and acorns. Actually the range within which he felt completely at home in nature was comparatively narrow. He loved the "smooth but still varied landscape" around Concord, but he did not want even that smoothed out to anything resembling a formal or cultivated park or garden.

The two experiences which made it most difficult for Thoreau to come to terms with nature and see it as something friendly to man and in harmony with his spirit were in his encounter with the shipwreck, as recorded at the beginning of *Cape Cod*, and his account of his ascent of Mount Ktaadn, which is the first episode in *The Maine Woods*. The shipwreck was not the only shock he encountered at the Cape: it must not be forgotten that he himself was nearly drowned there when, not understanding the tides, he attempted during his 1857 visit to cross from Captain's Hill in Duxbury to Clark's Island on the flats. But he escaped from the incoming tides, while, for all the meanings that various writers have read into it and out of it,[18] the shipwreck spelled death and destruction and though, as McIntosh has clearly demonstrated, Thoreau first attempted to view the catastrophe in the chilly light of cosmic perception rather than in terms of naked, individual, human isolation, and then sheered off from a desolating naturalism by about as clear an affirmation of the Christian hope of spiritual triumph beyond the wreck of everything human as he ever achieved, the fact remains that he had here come face to face with what must be in itself either a blind or a malevolent natural force, unmoved by individual misery and destiny.

But bad as the Cape was, Ktaadn was worse, when Thoreau climbed it in September 1846, pulling himself up above the tree line and into the clouds, away from his companions, "probably," says Harding, "the fifth or sixth man in history" to perform this feat. At the Cape nature may have been hostile to man, but at least and at worst she recognized his existence and accepted him as an adversary. At Ktaadn all attempt to establish a contact between nature and the human spirit failed. Here there were only gray, silent rocks, as old as the Flood, not Mother Nature but mere nature, vast, titanic, inhuman, terrific matter, drear, savage, awful, the unhandseled globe. Here were "Chaos and ancient Night"; such a phenomenon might belong to the gods perhaps, but man had no place in it, nor could there be anything to ask him here save why he had come; if this was what God had used to make the world, it had nothing to do with either religion or humanity as Christians and Americans understood it.

Yet, traumatic as the experience was, it is a mistake to suppose, as writers ignorant or careless of chronology have sometimes assumed, that it permanently altered Thoreau's attitude toward nature or plunged him into a permanent depression. It came early, not late, in his career, before he had written either *Walden* or the *Week*, and it may even be that the inconsistency between the three works under consideration is more apparent than real, for *Walden* too shows Thoreau's knowledge of how frail is the tenure by which human beings cling to their life on this earth. "It would be easy to cut their threads with a little sharper blast from the north. We go on dating from Cold Fridays and Great Snows; but a little colder Friday, or a greater snow would put a period to man's existence on the globe."

Garber says that Ktaadn showed Thoreau that "nature refused to be anything but its own strange self, overwhelmingly literal, and [that] his habitual bent toward the figurative was shown to be an irrelevance," but I think Harding puts it better when he says that after the experience on the mountaintop, Thoreau "returned to Concord a soberer man and with a fuller realization that what he wanted at heart was not an escape from civilization but an accord between man and nature, a blend of civilization and of wildness." And indeed Garber himself is fundamentally in accord with this when he writes of Thoreau that "his suppositions were so firm that even Ktaadn could not obliterate them entirely, however much the events in Maine established a series of contervailing patterns to his habitual attitudes." And Wolf adds that his climb "cured him of any sentimental or romantic feelings about nature he might have had, probably strengthened his perception that God was to be found in human communities wrestling with historic responsibilities as well as in nature. . . . The experience of terrifying aloneness on Ktaadn drove him down to rejoin his comrades, abandoning the earlier-mentioned possibility that he might leave them for further solitary exploration of the range."[19]

V

But what now, finally, *was* nature to Thoreau? Trees and rivers and flowers and stars? Or was it something beyond itself of which these and all other physical manifestations were but symbols, capable of inducing an epiphany or theophany? Joel Porte[20] is the scholar who has most strenuously insisted upon detaching Thoreau from the usual transcendental tendency to make nature the symbol of spirit and the search for what Swedenborg and others called correspondences, making him in effect a Lockean or anti-Hegelian and, as he sees it, allying him with such later writers as Poe, Pater, and Santayana. Thoreau, says Porte, "detested moralizing and spiritualizing in literature. His dislike of Ruskin also stemmed from exactly this difficulty." He either sought or achieved "total vision . . . through the five senses, a purely sensuous life," or attained philosophical insight by purely sensuous means. I realize that this is a somewhat crude and oversimplified statement of Porte's position, but he is not entirely alone in maintaining it. Thus McIntosh says that "in Thoreau, the natural details are more than mere symbols. Thoreau is so interested in them as things that their symbolic meaning is half forgotten in the process of perception. They call attention to themselves as real and independent facts." Charles Anderson too thinks Henry "came to believe that the poet must create the symbols that go into his work," observing and describing realities so as to raise them to the status of symbols, though he also admits that the shift of interest from philosophy to art was never really completed.

Though Porte seems to have convinced few scholars that Thoreau ever totally abandoned either the symbolic interpretation of natural phenomena or the search for correspondences between matter and spirit, he has performed a valuable service in demonstrating Thoreau's ability to stick to the "thing-in-itself" (as he himself says, "Let me not be in haste to detect the universal law; let me see more clearly the particular instance of it") and to refuse to allow this world to sink into the transcendental bog which engulfed so many of his contemporaries. And I call this a valuable service, for if there is nothing in this present life which cannot be acquired elsewhere, then it was obviously a great mistake not to form us so that we might, whatever Macbeth may have meant by that expression, "jump the life to come." "Oh, if I could be intoxicated on air and water," is Thoreau's cry, and Porte compares this with Keats' "O for a Life of Sensations rather than of Thoughts" and with Emily Dickinson's "inebriate of Air—am I— / And Debauchee of Dew." In one mood at least, Thoreau believed that "to see the sun rise or go down every day would preserve us sane forever" (though I think we must admit that many a lunatic still at large has achieved this without visible effect), and there is above all the challenging passage in the *Week* in which he declares that nature is herself that of which she is commonly taken as merely the sign, something real and solid and sincere that you cannot put your foot through, and that if you train the senses away from their present "trivial" and "groveling" uses, you may even see God by this means.

Only, as usual, Thoreau cannot be summed up so simply and uncontradictorily. Dismiss if you like the comparatively few passages in which he takes his place with the nineteenth-century nature sentimentalizers; you do not thereby wipe them out of existence. So the lily is the traditional symbol of purity. A green fern is an argument for immortality, and "the brave spears of the skunk cabbage buds," of all things, cure melancholy. The stars in heaven, like the fireflies on earth, show their light for love, and God cultivates flowers in heaven as men do here, with the rainbow as the faint vision of His face. The willow, far from being "the emblem of despairing love" which some would make it, is "rather the emblem of love and sympathy with all nature," while as for the mountains on the horizon, what are they but steppingstones to heaven? Dismiss these things if you will; we can afford to let them go. But they do not leave us with a naturalistic or materialistic attitude toward nature on Thoreau's part.

"I do believe," he says, "that the outward and the inward life correspond." He read *The Human Body and its Connection with Man* (1851), by the English Swedenborgian James John Garth Wilkinson, and commented upon it admiringly, and though he admitted he had not read much Swedenborg at first hand, he praised him for his "wonderful knowledge of our interior and spiritual life" and seemed to accept his views on a correspondence between the "interior and spiritual" and the world of sense.[21] We human beings are not wholly involved in nature, nor does she cast her pearls before swine, but only reveals herself to those who are fit to look upon her, perceiving the correspondences. "The actual alone is a sort of vomit in which the unclean love to wallow." "It is more proper for a spiritual fact to have suggested an analogous natural one, than for a natural fact to have preceded the spiritual in our mind," and the poet who uses nature "as raw material for tropes and symbols with which to describe his life" sees into her far more deeply than the scientist. Thoreau admits that the most significant incidents in his own life had "allegorical significance and fitness; they have been like myths or passages in a myth, rather than mere incidents in history which have to wait to become significant." Therefore he believed that the poet must "be something more than natural—even supernatural." Nature spoke not through him merely but along with him, and he did not become a poet until he had taken the fact out of nature and poeticized it. So Thoreau himself prayed "for such inward experience as will make nature significant."

The reader will already have observed that in some of these utterances the creative element is at least as much human as divine and as much imaginative as actual, but this should not greatly trouble those who have learned, or ought to have learned, from Walter de la Mare that it is not safe to rely upon the testimony of the senses alone for the simple reason that the senses "can tell us only what they are capable of being sensitive of," that "what we see and hear is only the smallest fraction of what is," and that even when the phenomena the senses register are frightfully "real," "it doesn't follow . . . that they didn't mean something else too." This we can find illustrated in Thoreau in such essays as "Autumnal Tints" and "Wild Apples," which are developed matter-of-factly, with material classified in scientific fashion, but without permitting this method to inhibit either the play of his fancy or his search for meaning. Red here is "the color of colors which speak to our blood." Falling leaves "teach us how to die. One wonders if the time will ever come when men . . . will lie down as gracefully and as ripe,—with such an Indian-summer serenity will shed their bodies, as they do their hair and nails." Trees should be set in our streets "with a view to their October splendor." The red maple swamp all ablaze suggests "a thousand gypsies . . . or even the fabled fauns, satyrs, and wood-nymphs come back to earth." If it is true then that Thoreau tried to find a spiritual significance in things themselves, it is equally true that they do not remain mere things. He says, "I find the actual to be far less real to me than the imagined." So Richard Tuerk, insisting that Thoreau "is clearly interested in things-in-themselves as well as their relation to man and God," also admits that it is "through a close vision of the concrete, physical object that he "communicates intimations of the divine," and Porte himself compares him with Plotinus in his realization that epiphany was rare and needed to be carefully prepared for by keeping the senses pure. "For it is exactly in the present moment that Thoreau discovers his religious experience."[22]

CHAPTER FIVE

The Unseen

*My profession is to be always on the alert
to find God in nature, to know his lurking-places,
to attend all the oratorios, the operas, in nature.*
HDT, 1851

THEY TELL OF A Concord lady who used to decorate the graves of Thoreau's peers in Sleepy Hollow Cemetery and who, having done so, would leave his with a curse: "No flowers for you, you dirty little atheist!" This warm-hearted Christian was no doubt misled by the many harsh things Thoreau says about the church. He signed off from First Parish in Concord, refusing to pay his church tax, on January 6, 1841,[1] and he refused to attend services there even with Ellen Sewall. There are, I fear, many men in America who refuse to go to church with their wives, but when a young man refuses to attend the girl he is in love with to divine service, he must feel rather strongly about the matter.

Part of this was probably due to Thoreau's indignation over the failure of the church to take an unequivocal stand on slavery, as may be seen in his splendid blast against the American Board of Commissioners for Foreign Missions after it had refused even to adopt a resolution condemning the slave trade. Part of it too was his well-known anti-institutionalism. He is just about as critical of schools, governments, medicine, and newspapers, and if his opposition to the church proves that he was anti-religious, then he must have hated learning too because of what he says about the schools. He believed "that a human institution is almost by definition conservative and that no matter what its theoretical idealism, it tended to have a stultifying effect on those who circumscribe their lives to its tenets and practices." Once a temple was " 'an open place without a roof,' whose walls served merely to shut out the world, and direct the mind toward heaven; but a modern *meeting house* shuts out the heavens, while it crowds the world into still closer quarters," and it would hardly have been reasonable to expect a man like Thoreau to believe that one who did not revive with nature in the spring could do so when "a white-collared priest" prayed for him. Real goodness was "original and as free from cant and tradition as the air" and "heathen in its liberality and independence of tradition," while as for truth, as soon as it became "known and accepted," it began to be "bad taste to repeat it." Those who swear by ancient revelations may think they love God; actually they love only his old clothes, "of which they make scarecrows for the children," and the clergyman, a man of straw who speaks of God as if he owned Him, is committed to defending the system in which he has a vested interest and is obliged to adjust his standards to those of his congregation. It would be better, he thought, to consult a chickadee that a D.D.—"the fungus of the graveyard, the mildew of the tomb"—and he loved the story of the boy who was making a meetinghouse out of mud and hoped to have enough left over so that he could make a minister too. "What great interval is there between him who is caught in Africa and made a plantation slave of in the South, and him who is caught in New England and made a Unitarian minister of?"[2]

Much of what Thoreau says about the church is thus violent enough so that one can understand why the Concord lady mistook him for an atheist. The church is "a baby-house made of blocks" which subsidizes "lifelong hypocrisy." Its piety is like stale gingerbread, its voice less brave and cheering than what may be heard from the frog ponds. It is suitable that it should be the ugliest building in the village, "because it is the one in which human nature stoops the lowest and is the most disgraced": "every kernel of truth" has been swept out of it; even the barrooms in country towns sometimes reach higher. Its only really useful function nowadays is to conduct funerals. "Our manners have been corrupted by communication with the saints. Our hymn-books resound with a melodious cursing of God and enduring him forever." He thought we might learn more from an Indian than from a missionary, and he wanted boys to go paddling along the river and read *Robinson Crusoe* rather than polish their shoes, brush their clothes, go to church, and read Baxter's *Saints' Rest*. When he gave "Walking" as a lecture at an orthodox church, he hoped he had undermined it. Once he even rudely compared churches to outhouses.

To be sure, this savage antagonism sometimes relaxed a little. Once at least he admitted that the church had improved, and once he granted that some Christians feel the same exaltation in church that he experiences in the mountains. Once he even went so far as to say that the life of the priest "approaches most nearly to that of the ideal man." When he shocked one of his Indian guides by telling him that he did not go to church, he at least tried to meet the man halfway by describing himself as a Protestant, and in *Cape Cod* he lingers over the records of hellfire clergymen who had preached in the camp meetings at Millennium Grove and then ends the account on an amazingly conciliatory note: "Let no one think I do not love the old ministers. They were, probably, the best men of their generation, and they deserve that their biographies should fill the pages of the town histories." He did go to hear sermons by Samuel Ripley, Henry Ware, Jr., Henry Whitney Bellows, Daniel Foster, Henry Ward Beecher, and "Father" Edward Taylor, and when he was in Chicago, he called on Robert Collyer. Beecher, for some reason, he thought "pagan," though Alcott was pleased by him, but he respected Taylor and Foster.

Toward the Roman Catholic Church, with which he had little or no direct contact until he went to Montreal, he shows both more and less sympathy than toward the Protestant churches. Lawrence Willson speaks of and documents in part his "prodigious reading in the literature of Catholic America," inspired by his desire to learn more about the Indians; there are 312 pages of notes from the Jesuit reports among his Indian notebooks. He respected the character and devotion of these missionaries, thought they showed more sympathy toward Indian culture than the English did, and in general believed the French historians the more reliable. But he also thought the Catholics had a strategic advantage over the Protestants because their own religion was more superstitious and barbaric, and he could see no point in trying "to convert the Algonquins from their own superstitions to new ones."

Arriving in Montreal, he went at once to the church of Notre Dame. "The Catholic are the only churches which I have seen worth remembering, which are not almost wholly profane." He was impressed by "the quiet, religious atmosphere" of the place. But the priests and the worshipers had "fallen far behind the significance of their symbols." It was "as if an ox had strayed into a church and were trying to bethink himself." If the priests looked effeminate, the nuns had "cadaverous faces" and "looked as if they had almost cried their eyes out, their complexions parboiled with scalding tears; insulting the daylight by their presence, having taken an oath not to smile," so that all in all the Catholic religion would be an admirable one only if you could take the clergy out of it. For that matter, the whole atmosphere of French Canada, from the church to the military, was a holdover from the Middle Ages.[3]

The Quakers fared better. When he visited his Quaker friend Ricketson at New Bedford in 1854, Thoreau thought the Quaker meetinghouse "an ugly shed, without a tree or bush about it" and "altogether repulsive to me, like a powder-house or grave. And even the quietness and perhaps unworldliness of an aged Quaker has something ghostly and saddening about it, as it were a mere preparation for the grave." Both in New York and at Eagleswood, New Jersey, however, his contacts with Quakers were much happier. For all his sensitiveness to sound, he had always appreciated the values of silence, "the ambrosial night in the intercourse of men in which their sincerity is recruited and takes deeper root." In 1843 he heard Lucretia Mott speak in meeting and was pleased not only by what she said about slavery but by Quaker ways in general— "their plainly greater harmony and sincerity than elsewhere." But his closest contact with Quakers came in New Jersey, when he went there as a surveyor and encountered Theodore Weld, the Grimké sisters, James G. Birney, and Edward Palmer, and almost permitted himself to be lionized. He took the regular Saturday night dance, at which attendance was regarded as almost a matter of course, in his stride, though there is no reason to suppose he joined in, and was, for him, amazingly cooperative about speaking in meeting on Sunday morning, "where it was expected that the spirit would move me (I having been previously spoken to about it) & it, or something else did, an inch or so. I said just enough to set them a little by the ears &

make it lively." Afterwards he told the children his "moose story" from the Maine woods with great success, and subsequently gave two lectures—"Walking" and "What Shall It Profit?"[4]

I find little evidence to show that Thoreau accepted any of the distinctively Christian doctrines or the traditional Christian scheme of salvation, though there is more in the early writings than in the later ones. "The wisdom of the Creator has ever been the theme of the Christian's admiration and praise," he writes in 1836; Christ is "our Savior," and fear is the ruling principle of superstition but not of "our religion." The essay on Carlyle too finds his "brotherliness" Christian and would like to know more about his inner life, his "hymn and prayer." There are references also to Henry's talking to young people about both Christ and Moses and using the argument from design for the existence of God.

The attitude toward fear was permanent. "Nothing is so much to be feared as fear," he said, in the words paraphrased by F.D.R. in his First Inaugural. "Atheism may be comparatively popular with God himself." And if atheism, then certainly doubt, for doubt too may have "some divinity" about it. "If one hesitates in his path, let him not proceed." Once at least, citing Byron of all people, he even argues that rebellion against conventional or "vulgar" religion is a necessary prerequisite to moral excellence.

When Mrs. Webster wanted to make him a Methodist, he told her he was "too hard a nut to crack," and he told Samuel Chase that in fifty years most people would believe as he did. In 1843 he wrote Emerson that Lidian "almost persuades me to be a Christian, but I fear I as often lapse into heathenism." He did not believe that every man was qualified to be a Christian; it was "a matter of constitution and temperament. I have known many a man who pretended to be a Christian, in whom it was ridiculous, for he had no genius for it." There were other standards of excellence in the world. "The hero obeys his own law, the Christian his, the lover and friend theirs; they are to some extent different codes. . . . My neighbor asks me in vain to be good as he is good. I must be good as I am made to be good, whether I am heathen or Christian."

Sometimes his rejection of dogmatic Christianity seems a part of his repudiation of all systems. "Yes and No are lies. . . . All answers are in the future, and day answereth to day." "The old Jewish scheme," if held as dogma, became an obstacle to understanding. "Even Christ, we fear, had his scheme, his conformity to tradition, which slightly vitiates his teaching." Sometimes, however, he enters more specific objections. He speaks of "the Christian fable." "Christianity only hopes. It has hung its harp on the willows, and cannot sing a song in a strange land." Having "dreamed a sad dream," it "does not yet welcome the morning with joy." Yet he once declined to lecture at Plymouth on the ground that he had no lecture suitable for delivery on the Sabbath day, and I am amazed that he should have thought *The Pilgrim's Progess* the best sermon ever preached on the New Testament, for where is there a more rigid "scheme"?

The Trinity he rejected, though recognizing that to some Father, Son, and Holy Ghost are "like the everlasting hills," for in all his wanderings, he "never came across the least vestige of authority for them." I recall no reference to the Incarnation or Atonement. He once said that what was religion in others was love of nature with him, and this was true in more than the obvious sense, for he had his own kind of equivalent of the Puritan saving grace, though it is more antinomian than Calvinistic. No more than Jonathan Edwards did he conceive of himself, or of any man, as living in a state of perpetual illumination (instead he thanks God for "a moment of special awareness"), but he did not believe that such awareness was bestowed by arbitrary divine fiat or that it was the monopoly of any "elect" or exclusive group, though, as a practical man, he knew too that there were many natures too coarse or too material to be capable of receiving it at any time.[5]

Like many who dissent from orthodox religion, Thoreau was inconsistent in being quick to reproach Christians whenever their conduct disappointed him. "The nation is not Christian," he says, "where the principles of humanity do not prevail, but the prejudices of race. I expect the Christian not to be superstitious, but to be distinguished by the clearness of his knowledge, the strength of his faith, the breadth of his humanity." And he cites specifically the discrimination from which Africans suffer in America, "exactly similar to, or worse than, that which the American meets with among the Turks, and Arabs, and Tartars." But if Christianity is not superior to the religions of these other peoples, then obviously it must be unfair to hold those who profess it to a higher standard.

Thoreau's reference to the Bible as "an old book" in *Walden* gave offense to some readers, but this form of reference is not necessarily disrespectful. John Robert Burns, who studied Henry's use of the Bible in a Ph.D. dissertation for Notre Dame University in 1966, found that he used Scripture to add authority and weight to his style but also saw him using it for both comic and dramatic effect. Obviously, however, such things are a matter of judgment, which is inevitably influenced by the commentator's own religious beliefs. When Horace Greeley questioned the propriety of Henry's New Testament references, the Concordian's "one thought" was that it would give him "real pleasure" to know that Greeley loved the book "as sincerely and enlightenedly" as he did. Channing says that at the end of his life Thoreau wished he had studied the Bible more, but Wolf counted about five hundred references to it, with far more in *Walden* than in the *Week*, which is especially interesting since many profess to see a certain decline in Thoreau's interest in religion as he grew older.[6] In "Resistance to Civil Government" he recommends the precepts of the New Testament to legislators and declares that "they who know of no purer source of truth, who have traced the stream no higher, stand, and wisely stand, by the Bible and the Constitution, and drink at it there with reverence and humility." That something higher, of course, was direct revelation, what Quakers call the "Inner Light," and so we find him writing elsewhere that "the love of Nature and fullest perception of the revelation which she is to man is not compatible with the belief in the peculiar revelation of the Bible which Ruskin entertains."

Thoreau was not completely consistent in his references to Jesus Christ. He complained that Christ's concerns were too exclusively ethical (he "taught mankind but imperfectly how to live; his thoughts were all directed to another world. There is another kind of success than his"), and when, in 1846, Alcott said that Christ "stood in a more tender and intimate nearness to the heart of mankind than any [other] character in life or literature," Thoreau thought he "asserted this claim for the fair Hebrew in exaggeration." He is reported (though not perhaps on completely established testimony) to have remarked on his deathbed that a snowstorm meant more to him than Christ. But in the *Week* he says that it is not necessary to be Christian to appreciate the beauty and significance of Christ's life. He quotes Thomas Dekker's reference to Christ as "the first true gentleman that ever breathed," and though Wolf complains that he removes "the joyous references" to him as "Incarnate Redeemer" when he quotes from the metaphysical poets, he still declares that Christ yet "awaits a just appreciation from literature"; he felt this specifically in connection with both *Heroes and Hero-Worship* and *Representative Men.* He also calls Christ "the Prince of Reformers and Radicals," not only "a child of God" but "a brother of mankind" ("the day began with Christ"), and, significantly, places him above Brahma for courageously assaulting evil rather than tolerating it, ignoring it, or seeking merely to starve it out. He invests John Brown with Christ-like characteristics, and when he sees slaves being returned to captivity, he asks, "Do you think he [Christ] would have stayed here in liberty and let the black man go into slavery in his stead?"

Both Raymond Adams and Mary Elkins Moller have assembled and studied the quotations bearing upon Thoreau's attitude toward the immortality of the soul. Adams believes that faith is indicated; Ms. Moller finds belief and disbelief about equally balanced.[7] My own feeling agrees with that of Adams. To be sure, Thoreau can be as crotchety and contrary on this subject as he is on others. When his Calvinistic Aunt Louisa asked him on his deathbed whether he had made his peace with God, he replied that he was not aware they had ever quarreled, and when Parker Pillsbury inquired whether he could see the farther shore, he replied, "One world at a time." But I must say that these are just the answers I should have expected him to return to such questions, nor can I attach much weight to his impatience with those who seem more interested in the next world than in this and live only on "hope deferred." It is certainly not the Christian view that we become immortal through dying, but rather through the putting on of Christ, and the deathbed testimony is far more positive than negative. Thoreau had thought it was only his body they locked up when they put him in jail; now he felt it was only his "envelope" that was sick. When Edmund Hosmer described a beautiful walk he had had in the country, Thoreau replied, "Yes! This is a beautiful world; but I shall see a fairer," and when Blake came in from skating, he said, "You have been skating on this river; perhaps I am going to skate on some other." And again: "Perhaps I am going up country." On the very day he died, his sister

Sophia having read to him from the *Week*, he whispered, just before breathing his last, *"Now comes good Sailing."*[8]

Moreover the deathbed utterances do not stand alone. "There is no continuance in death. It is a transient phenomenon." Thoreau hated cemeteries and thought it would be better for a farmer "to leave his body to Nature to be plowed in" and restore the fertility of the land rather than be carted to the graveyard, but if there were to be monuments, he wanted them not flat but "star y-pointing," with inscriptions proclaiming "There rises," not "Here lies." The reawakening of the earth in spring at the end of *Walden* and the hatching of the beautiful bug out of the old table are symbols, not dogma, of course, but it is Thoreau himself who asks, "Who does not feel his faith in a resurrection and immortality strengthened by hearing of this?" and the faith involved in his description of the shipwreck on Cape Cod seems unquestioning. The Irish immigrants who perished there had "emigrated to a newer world than ever Columbus dreamed of," he says, "yet one of whose existence we believe that there is far more universal and convincing evidence—though it has not yet been discovered by science—than Columbus had of this." And he even adds that "we have reason to thank God that they have not been 'shipwrecked into life again' " and that "the strongest wind cannot stagger a Spirit; it is a Spirit's breath."

Thoreau shocked the religious sensibilities of many of his contemporaries by seeming to put the sacred scriptures of other religions on a level with or even higher than the Bible, and it is true that he called the religion of the Hebrews wild and rude compared to the subtleties and refinements of that of the Hindus. "Beside the vast and cosmogonal philosophy of the Bhagavat-Geeta," he writes, "even our Shakespeare seems youthfully green and practical merely." He can tolerate all philosophies, he says, and all philosophers. "It is the attitude of these men, more than any communication which they make, that attracts us." "Any sincere thought is irresistible." He can admire the "superstitious rites" of the heathen, including the Indians, and he finds no very important difference between the religion of a New Englander and that of a Greek or Roman. Once he suggests that demons are merely dethroned gods. He feels the need of a feminine element in religion and "discovers" Ceres, but surely he might have found this need supplied in the Church of Rome. He would like a world Bible too, but he ignores the question of how contraries might be reconciled in it, and at times he seems to assume that any religion is better than no religion, ignoring the fact that there are bad religions as well as good ones and that many men have been worse, not better, for what they believed.

In the *Week* Thoreau thought Jehovah less a gentleman, "not so gracious and catholic . . . as many a god of the Greeks." And there is the famous (or, as some thought it, infamous) passage: "In my Pantheon, Pan still reigns in his pristine glory, with his ruddy face, his flowing beard, and his shaggy body, his pipe and crook, his nymph Echo, and his chosen daughter Iambe; for the great god Pan is not dead, as was rumored. No god ever dies. Perhaps of all the gods of New England and of ancient Greece, I am most constant at his shrine." Yet though at one point he admitted a prejudice against the New Testament by early unpleasant associations with church and Sunday school, Henry later came to love it. "Having come to it so recently and freshly, it has the greater charm." Some New Englanders have junked Christianity for Buddhism; Thoreau was not one of them. He liked to remember both his French inheritance and his Viking ancestry, but basically he remained Anglo-Saxon and Puritan, for he was too much a free spirit to be capable of rejecting the tradition in which he had been born and bred only to bind himself over to another. The Christian heaven is superior to the Muslim, he says, and though there are numerous passages which indicate that the idea of the transmigration of souls appealed to him in certain moods, he never actually committed himself to it. The pessimism, the extreme asceticism, the indifference or hostility to progress, and the caste structure of Orientalism were all antipathetic to him. He stands for moderation, not denial for denial's sake, and he has no desire to be absorbed into the Godhead or anything else. As Kenneth Lynn remarks, "the Hindu mystic wishes release from the unending cycle of rebirth, whereas *Walden* glorifies it." From Oriental sources as from all others, he took what was congenial to him, what, as Willa Cather would say, "seemed destined" for him, and let the rest go.[9]

II

Some of Thoreau's critics, like Holbrook Jackson and Daniel Gregory Mason,[10] not content with delivering him from Christian orthodoxy, insist upon seeing him as basically committed to aesthetic rather than moral principles, and it is true that he has much to say about morality which might have come from Nietzsche or Blake in their most cryptic moods. "I don't like people who are too good for this world," he says. And again, "We cannot do well without our sins; they are the highway of our virtue." Our lives are "not all moral," nor need we always insist that men incline to the moral side of their being. He himself would like to read "a sonnet, genial and affectionate, to prophane swearing, breaking on the still night air, perhaps like the hoarse croak of some bird," and what offends him most in his own writings is their moralism. "Strictly speaking," he says, "morality is not healthy," and he advises H. G. O. Blake not to be too moral. "You may cheat yourself out of much life so. Aim above morality. Be not simply good—be good for something. —All fables have their morals, but the innocent enjoy the story." "Almost all that my neighbors call good I believe in my soul to be bad. If I repent of anything, it is of my good behavior. What demon possessed me that I behaved so well?" Once he even says that we need to stop striving upwards from time to time to "wallow in meanness," though this is evidently only so that, when we recover, we may know that we are no longer mean. Even more metaphysical, in a perverse kind of way, are such statements as "the greatest impression of character is made by that person who consents to have no character," and the declaration in the *Week* that "at rare intervals we rise above the necessity of virtue into an unchangeable morning light, in which we have only to live right on and breathe the ambrosial air."

The attentive reader will already have noted that several of these utterances oppose morality from a highly moral point of view, but let us disregard that for the moment and give our attention to other statements of Thoreau's which seem completely opposed to them. Habitually he connects the beauty of both nature and music with purity and moral aspiration; if he so much as encounters a scamp in his afternoon walk, it spoils his day. He guards the purity of his mind, to keep it a thoroughfare for mountain springs, not town sewers, crying "No Trespassing" not only to the details of cases before the criminal court but also to "idle rumors, tales, incidents, even of an insignificant kind." In "Higher Laws," "our whole life is startlingly moral. There is never an instant's truce between virtue and vice." We should allow "the religious sentiment to exercise a natural and proper influence over our lives and conduct—in acting from a sense of duty, or, as we say, from principle." He praises a young farmer for having fired a hired man who had "one day let drop a prophane word" and wishes others would follow his example. The State of Maryland is a "fungus" for maintaining a lottery. "Her offense is rank; it smells to heaven"; she is doing the devil's work. Ellery Channing declares of Thoreau that "the high moral impulse never deserted him, and he resolved early to read no book, take no walk, undertake no enterprise, but such as he could endure to give an account of to himself," and then, lest the reader should judge his hero a prig, he adds that "on our estimate of his character, the moral qualities form the basis; for himself rigidly enjoined; if in another, he could overlook delinquency."

Though Thoreau rejected foreordination and total depravity, it is clear that he had far more of the Calvinistic conviction of human sinfulness than Emerson. It is true that Channing says that when he was sick and was told he would need a father confessor, he replied, "I have nothing to confess," and he does seem to have felt that to cultivate conviction of sin was merely to set up another barrier between God and the soul. God, he thought, would rather be approached thoughtfully than shockingly and with passion. "Sin, I am sure," he says, "is not in overt act, or indeed in acts of any kind, but in proportion to the time which has come behind us and displaced eternity, to the degree in which our elements are mixed with the elements of the world."

But no matter what sin was, there can be no question that he was aware of its existence and that it depressed him. Sometimes he even felt that he had grown worse as he grew older. "In our holiest moments our devil with a leer stands close at hand. He is a very busy devil." Like Hawthorne, he even wondered whether we might not incur guilt from what we do in dreams, "for in dreams we but act a part which must have been learned and rehearsed in our waking hours, and no doubt could discover some waking consent thereto." Certainly "an unwavering and commanding virtue would compel even its most fantastic and faintest dreams to respect its ever-wakeful authority; as we are accustomed to say carelessly, we should never have *dreamed* of such a thing."

He also believed, as we have already seen in other connections, that he lived in a moral universe, a world which expressed the decency of God and into which it had been wrought. "In all ages and nations we observe a leaning toward a right state of things." In this life "there is never an instant's truce between virtue and vice. Goodness is the only investment that never fails." The laws of the universe "are forever on the side of the most sensitive," and every zephyr brings a reproof for wrongdoing. "Neither an individual nor a nation can ever deliberately commit the least act of injustice without having to pay the penalty for it." We are all related to truth "in the most direct and intimate way" when we do not "believe" but know. Generally he seems to think of these things in spiritual terms; evil is punished inevitably because whatever a man does, he does to himself, and if he destroys himself as a spiritual being without realizing it, his state is all the more pitiable. At least once, however, he seems to materialize it. This is when he assumes the "avenging power of nature" against wrong in his musings over the men who had been blown up in a munitions explosion. Their lives were not innocent, he says, as they had been engaged in making means of destruction.

III

Whatever else may be said of Thoreau's religion or religious consciousness, I do not believe that any writer since Chaucer, who, like Gerard Manley Hopkins, would have understood his blessing the Lord for crows and hens, has spoken of God more freely, naturally, and without cant or embarrassment. "My desire for knowledge is intermittent," he says, "but my desire to commune with the spirit of the universe . . . is perennial and constant." "the unconsciousness of man is the consciousness of God," and "man flows at once to God when his channel of purity is open." Without religion and devotion nothing great has ever been accomplished. The physical is important only as it ministers to the spiritual, and education is good "if it tend to cherish and develop the religious sentiment—continually to remind man of his mysterious relation to God and Nature." Even his famous "Let God alone if need be" is not out of tune with this if it be quoted, for once, in context:

> When we would rest our bodies we cease to support them; we recline on the lap of earth. So, when we rest our spirits, we must recline on the Great Spirit. . . . What an infinite wealth we have discovered! God reigns, *i.e.*, when we take a liberal view, —when a liberal view is presented to us.
>
> Let God alone if need be. Methinks, if I loved him more, I should keep him,—I should keep myself rather,—at a more respectful distance. It is not when I am going to meet him, but when I am just turning away and leaving him alone, that I discover that God is. I say, God. I am not sure that is the name. You will know whom I mean.

Emily Dickinson could not have said it better. And Thoreau says much the same about nature. We need to "saunter" at times, not confront her too directly, and it is precisely when we do this that she gives us some of her best revelations of herself. Everybody realizes that when we try too hard to love or to be kind both love and kindness turn sour; why should not the limitations of effort be equally clear in other areas, including that of religion?

To Thoreau God was "the Artist who made the world and me," "the Maker of this earth," "the greater Benefactor and Intelligence that stands over me the human insect." He wished modern farmers had the religious awe of the old Romans when they cut woods. Walden Pond was "God's Drop"; He "rounded this water with his hand, deepened and clarified it in his thought, and in his will bequeathed it to Concord." God makes all times and places indifferent. "I feel as if [I] could at any time resign my life and the responsibility of living into God's hands, and become as innocent, free from care, as a plant or stone." Thoreau could not think of even snowflakes or dewdrops as mechanically cohering or simply flowing together, but rather as products of "*enthusiasm*, the children of an ecstasy, finished with the artist's utmost skill." "I may say that the maker of the world exhausts his skill with each snowflake and dewdrop that he sends down."

Was Thoreau, then, a mystic? This depends upon what one understands by mysticism. He lived during the first great wave of

American interest in spiritualism. He took no stock in it, but, like Hawthorne, he rejected it not because he was a materialist but because he found it materialistic. He was appalled by the puerility of the "messages" which came through the knockers and the mediums (the howling of owls and the croaking of frogs seemed to him "celestial wisdom in comparison"), and if he could believe in their validity, he was sure he would be tempted to "make haste to get rid of my certificate of stock in this and the next world's enterprises, and buy a share in the first Immediate Annihilation company that offered." His most amusing reference to spiritualism is in his essay on love: "What if the lover should learn that his beloved dealt in incantations and philters! What if he should hear she consulted a clairvoyant!" Certainly the spell must then be broken. Yet he would have liked to believe in wood spirits or fairy visitors too ethereal to leave their footprints in the snow. He was much interested in dreams too; once at least he dreamed a dream so strange that it seemed to have come out of "a previous state of existence," and once he wrote that in sleep the soul deserted the body to sleep in God. In 1858 he was inclined to credit his discovery of the location, some two hundred years ago, of the Winthrop family's front door to his "occult sympathy" with them, but there is nothing in his account of how he did it that reasonable intelligence could not account for.

He speculated enough about time and space to cause one to believe that he might have been much interested in J. W. Dunne's theories about time-traveling which had such a great influence upon creative writers more than a generation ago.[11] "Time," he says, "is but the stream I go a-fishing in." He saw the present as "the meeting of two eternities, the past and the future," and, as we have already seen, he saw God culminating in the present moment, which, as has been pointed out by others, is close to Christ's "The Kingdom of God is within you." Likewise, his refusal to be imprisoned in the moment is quite in line with Matthew Arnold's emphasis on the importance of living *sub specie aeternitatis*. "What news!" he cries, "how much more important to know what that is which was never old!" When he saw the northern lights over his shoulder it was pleasant to remember that the Eskimos could see them too, for he felt "related to the most distant inhabitants of the globe as to the nearest." Even to see the sun rise and set every day was of value because it related us to a universal fact.

Since there are as many definitions of mysticism as definers, it is not surprising that not all Thoreau's critics should see eye to eye upon this point. There can be no question that he desired the mystical experience, for he says he would "give all the wealth of the world, and all the deeds of all the heroes, for one true vision." But it also seems evident enough that he sometimes attained clear vision, even if not so completely or permanently as he could have wished (what mystic ever did?). As a child he lay awake looking at the stars and trying to see God behind them; as a man he was convinced of the superiority of imagination to "reality" and was sure that his charter to travel his own course had been given him by the Grace of God. "We know the world superficially—and the soul centrally," he says, "and the soul does not inspect but behold." Music reminded him "that we live on the verge of another and purer realm, from which these odors and sounds are wafted over to us," and there was an ethereal music too which brought "indescribable, infinite, all-absorbing, divine, heavenly pleasure, a sense of elevation and expansion." In the *Week* he writes "I see, smell, taste, hear, feel, that everlasting Something to which we are allied, at once our maker, our abode, our destiny, our very Selves," and he told Isaac Hecker that he returned "from every external enterprise" to "a kind of Brahminical Artesian, Inner Temple life."[12]

Pantheism is another fighting word in connection with the discussion of Thoreau's religion. There is one very pantheistic passage in the 1856 journal, where primitive, uncultivated land gives him almost a sense of "the personality of such planetary matter" that he can feel "something akin to reverence for it, can even worship it as terrene, titanic matter" or "love it as a maiden." It would be restorative, not degrading, if mankind were to become elevated enough to, in this sense, "truly worship stocks and stones."

This is misleading, but it is sufficiently seductive so that one need not wonder that many have been misled. As a matter of fact, however, Thoreau did not identify even man with nature. "He must be something more than natural," he wrote, "even supernatural. Nature will not speak through him but along with him. . . . His thought is one world, hers another. He is another Nature,—Nature's brother." And if man must be supernatural, surely less cannot be said of God.

Robert Dickens writes justly that "the traditional theological analysis cannot handle Thoreau's ideas about God. If it gives him the pantheist label (as has often been the case), it fails to do justice to his idea of God as Transcendent Creator." But "if, on the other hand, his thought is labeled 'orthodox theism,' one fails to do justice to his idea of the immanence and temporality of God." But it remained for an accomplished theologian, William J. Wolf, to describe his position as that of panentheism which *The Oxford Dictionary of the Christian Church* defines as the belief that while every part of the universe exists in God, God is still "more than, and is not exhausted by, the universe." As Wolf sees it, transcendence is far more important in Thoreau's thought of God than it is in Emerson's, and he is, in this sense, closer to the Jewish-Christian tradition. God "remains . . . over and beyond his intimate association and presence in all the orders of his own making." And Thoreau himself asks, "If Nature is our Mother, is not God much more?" Though God is *like* the world and the creatures He has made, "likeness . . . is not identity." Thoreau calls man "the crowning fact" in creation, "the god we know," and finds that the existence of "one just man" attests to the existence of God. But he remains fundamentally Christian in refusing to allow the Maker to be swallowed up in what He has made.[13]

Thoreau's God was, then, a Personal God, not in the sense of being a big man sitting up in the center of the universe running things, but because he possessed consciousness and benevolence.[14] He "did not make this world in jest; no, nor in indifference." Moreover, He not only created it but informs it, and it is a mistake to speak of Him as "the Almighty Designer" because this makes Him "a total stranger."[15] "I know that another is who knows more than I, who takes an interest in me, whose creature, and yet whose kindred, in one sense, I am." When he asserts the freedom of his own will, man does not seek to be free of God, for "if God shapes my ends—he shapes me also—and his means are always equal to his ends." Thus Henry wrote after John's death, thanking God even for sorrow: "Is he not kind still, who lets this south wind blow, this warm sun shine on me?" Even when we cannot understand we can trust, and he quotes Coleridge: "He that loves, may be sure he was loved first." "The love wherewith we are loved is already declared, and afloat in the atmosphere, and our love is only the inlet to it"; Thoreau found it as unbelievable as did Browning in "Saul" that the creature could have surpassed the Creator in the one way of loving. "God for Thoreau," says Wolf, "even at the time of maximum Emersonian influence, is still one who is believed capable of answering petitions for concrete requests" (it was no merit, he thought, to have stopped asking a blessing at table), and He is also quite as able to achieve the appointment of a man to do His work in the world today as ever He was in Bible times.

NOTES

The following abbreviations are used in the bibliography and notes:

AL	*American Literature*
AM	*Atlantic Monthly*
AQ	*American Quarterly*
ATQ	*American Transcendental Quarterly*
BNYPL	*Bulletin of the New York Public Library*
BPLQ	*Boston Public Library Quarterly*
CLQ	*Colby Library Quarterly*
CS	*Concord Saunterer*
CW	*Classical Weekly*
ELH	*English Literary History*
ELN	*English Language Notes*
ESQ	*Emerson Society Quarterly*
HDT	Henry David Thoreau
HT	Henry Thoreau
JEGP	*Journal of English and Germanic Philology*
MinnH	*Minnesota History*
MLN	*Modern Language Notes*
NEQ	*New England Quarterly*
PMLA	*Publications of the Modern Language Association*
SAQ	*South Atlantic Quarterly*
SP	*Studies in Philology*
SR	*Sewanee Review*
T	Thoreau
TJQ	*Thoreau Journal Quarterly*
TSB	*Thoreau Society Bulletin*
TSLL	*Texas Studies in Language and Literature*
TWASAL	*Transactions of the Wisconsin Academy of Sciences, Arts, and Letters*
UTQ	*University of Toronto Quarterly*
UTSE	*University of Texas Studies in English*
WHR	*Western Humanities Review*
YR	*Yale Review*

END AND BEGINNING

1   Lowell's essay, written in 1865, may be read in *My Study Windows* (1871); his *North American Review* piece on the *Week,* reprinted in his *The Round Table* (Richard G. Badger, 1913), is considerably more sympathetic. See Austin Warren, "Lowell on T," *SP,* 27 (1930), 442–62, and Wesley Mott, "T and Lowell on 'Vacation': *The Maine Woods* and 'A Moosehead Journal,' " *TJQ,* 10, July 1978, pp. 14–24. Stevenson's paper appeared in the *Cornhill Magazine* in 1880 and was reprinted in *Familiar Studies of Men and Books* (1882), whose preface, written after the author had been enlightened by H. A. Page (A. H. Japp), takes much of it back, unfortunately on somewhat sentimental and not wholly accurate grounds. Stevenson admitted that Thoreau had had considerable influence upon his own writing and declared that he would be willing to "give up most other things to be so good a man as Thoreau."

2   See *TSB,* No. 50 (1955), p. 1. The most important studies of the Thoreau-Gandhi matter are George Hendrick, "The Influence of T's 'Civil Disobedience' on Gandhi's *Satyagraha,*" *NEQ,* 29 (1956), 462–71; Elizabeth T. McLaughlin, "T and Gandhi: The Date," *ESQ,* No. 43 (1966), pp. 65–66; Nissim Ezekiel, "The T-Gandhi Syndrome," *Quest,* 59 (1961), 21–26, reprinted in the Harding-Brenner-Doyle collection. See also Henry S. Salt, "Gandhi and T," *Nation and Athenaeum,* 46 (1930), 728, reprinted in Harding's anthology, *Thoreau: A Century of Criticism* (Southern Methodist University, 1954). C. D. Narasimhaiah has an important statement of "Where T and Gandhi Differed," *TJQ,* 7, July 1975, pp. 11–19. Elizabeth McLaughlin writes, "Satyagraha originated in a spontaneous impulse to action and only later gained a name, a rationale, and literary antecedents."

3   V. F. Calverton, *The Liberation of American Literature* (Scribners, 1932); Granville Hicks, *The Great Tradition* (Macmillan, 1935); Bernard Smith, *Forces in American Criticism* (Harcourt, 1939).

4   George Hendrick, "T, F.D.R., and 'Fear,' " *TSB*, No. 62 (1958), p. 2. When Edith Bunker quoted F.D.R.'s statement to Archie, unwillingly facing a strike, in the TV series, *All in the Family*, Archie replied, "Yes, but he was workin' when he said it."

5   The best place to begin the study of Thoreau's reputation and influence is Chapter 5 of Harding's *A T Handbook* (New York University Press, 1959), but see also the Princeton edition of *Walden*, pp. 368–77. The early vicissitudes are well described by Raymond Adams, "The Day T Didn't Die," in Harding's *The T Centennial: Papers Marking the Observance in New York City of the One Hundredth Anniversay of the Death of HDT* (State University of New York, 1964). K. W. Cameron, "Damning National Publicity for T in 1849," *ATQ*, No. 2 (1969), pp. 18–27, reprints and analyzes the newspaper comment which followed Greeley's blowing the horn for him in the *New York Tribune*, May 25, 1848. John C. Broderick shows that early neglect has sometimes been exaggerated in "American Reviews of T's Posthumous Books, 1863–1866," *UTSE*, 34 (1955), 125–39. George Hendrick, "Henry S. Salt, the Late Victorian Socialists, and T," *NEQ*, 30 (1977), 409–22, is important for Thoreau's early reputation in England. Clarence A. Manning, "T and Tolstoy," *NEQ*, 16 (1943), 234–43, sums up the resemblances and the differences between the two. Cameron, "T's Disciple at Walden: Edmond S. Hotham," *ESQ*, No. 26 (1962), pp. 34–45, is about a Yankee who lived at Walden in imitation of Thoreau in 1888. Donald M. Murray has a discussion of "T and Hemingway," *TJQ*, 11, July–Oct. 1979, pp. 13–33, and Charles Child Walcutt, "T in the Twentieth Century," *SAQ*, 39 (1940), 168–84, maintains his relevance, finding a special affinity to Aldous Huxley's *Ends and Means*. Willard Uphaus tells his own story in "Conscience and Disobedience," *Massachusetts Review*, 4 (1962), 104–08. Eugene Timpe, ed., *T Abroad: Twelve Bibliographical Essays* (Archon Books, 1971) is by far the most detailed account of its subject, but see also James F. Lacey, "T in German Criticism: An Annotated Bibliography," *TSB*, No. 104 (1968), pp. 4–6; Richard Fleck, "A Report on Irish Interest in T," *TJQ*, 6, Oct. 15, 1974, pp. 21–27; and, on Russian translations of Thoreau, *TSB*, No. 150 (1980), pp. 1–3. Finally, anybody who doubts that Thoreau still has enemies might take a look at the two Leon Edel items listed in the selected bibliography; Vincent Buranelli's "The Case Against T," *Ethics*, 67 (1957), 257–68, with Ralph T. Ketcham's reply, 69 (1959), 206–08, and Buranelli's rejoinder, 70 (1960), 64–65; Richard C. Crowley's review of the *Correspondence*, in *Commonweal*, 70 (1959), 186; and Ray Gagnon, "T: Some Negative Considerations," *TSB*, No. 121 (1972), pp. 5–7; as well as the hysterical articles in *Paunch*, No. 24 (1965).

6   For the Wyeths, see N. C. Wyeth, "T, his Critics, and the Public," *TSB*, No. 37 (1951), pp. 1–3, and Betsy James Wyeth, ed., *The Wyeths: The Letters of N. C. Wyeth, 1901–1945* (Gambit, 1971). For Sinclair Lewis see *The Man f.om Main Street*, ed. Harry S. Maule and Melville H. Caine (Random House, 1953), p. 241.

BIOGRAPHY

1   Odell Shepard, ed., *The Journals of Bronson Alcott* (Little, Brown, 1938), p. 127n.

2   Kenneth W. Cameron has published much material which throws important light

on Thoreau's years of study. See "T Discovers Emerson" *BNYPL*, 57 (1953), 319–34; "Chronology of T's Harvard Years," *ESQ*, No. 15 (1959); "T's Harvard Textbooks: A College Reading Record," *ESQ*, No. 23 (1961), pp. 19–111; *T and his Harvard Classmates: Henry Williams' Memorials of the Class of 1837, with a Commentary and an Index* (Transcendental Books, 1965); "T and Orestes Brownson," *ESQ*, No. 51 (1968), pp. 53–65; "Young T and the Classics: A Review: The Curriculum of the Concord Academy, Probabilities and Evidence," *ATQ*, No. 35 (1977); "T's Schoolmate, Alfred Munroe, Remembers Concord," *ATQ*, No. 36, Part I (1977), pp. 10–38. See also Raymond Adams, "T at Harvard: Some Unpublished Records,"*NEQ*, 13 (1940), 24–33; Frederick T. McGill, "T and College Discipline," *NEQ*, 15 (1942), 349–53; H. H. Hoeltje, "T and the Concord Academy," *NEQ*, 21 (1948), 103–09.

3   See Louis B. Salomon, "The Straight-Cut Ditch: T on Education," *AQ*, 14 (1962), 19–36.

4   On Thoreau's lecturing see Hubert H. Hoeltje, "T as a Lecturer," *NEQ*, 19 (1946), 485–94; Walter Harding, "T on the Lecture Platform," *NEQ*, 24 (1951), 365–74; Robert C. Albrecht, "T and his Audience: 'A Plea for Captain John Brown,' " *AL*, 32 (1960–61), 393–402; K. W. Cameron, "T in the Pulpit: Report of a Lost Address," *ATQ*, No. 20, Suppl. (1973), p. 1; John J. McAleer, "The Therapeutic Vituperation of T," *ATQ*, No. 11 (1971), pp. 81–87.

5   See John D. Gordan, "A T Handbill," *BNYPL*, 59 (1955), 253–58. There is also a map inscribed "Henry D. Thoreau, Civil Engineer."

6   For further interesting data on the family business, see Harding, *A T Profile* (Hill and Wang, 1971), Chapter 12, and F. B. Sanborn, *The Life of HDT, including Many Essays Hitherto Unpublished and Some Account of his Family and Friends* (Houghton Mifflin, 1917), p. 212. Harding, *The Variorum Walden* (Twayne, 1962), p. 301, says part of the business was making sandpaper, and Annie Russell Marble says they also made marbled paper.

7   See Gay Wilson Allen's amusing article, "T's Boots for Mrs. Emerson's Hens," *TJQ*, 5, July 1973, pp. 4–5.

8   Raymond Adams, "T's Burials," *AL*, 4 (1940–41), 105–07.

CHAPTER ONE. HIMSELF

1   Ricketson's amusing sketch of Thoreau has been reproduced in many books, but see also Thomas Blanding, "Daniel Ricketson's Sketch Book," in Joel Myerson, ed., *Studies in the American Renaissance, 1977* (Twayne, 1978).

2   See Lawrence Willson, "T's Medical Vagaries," *Journal of the History of Medicine*, 15 (1960), 64–74. Though Willson finds Thoreau inconsistent and impractical, he concludes that he was "ahead of his time in some ways." Certainly he realized that a healer must minister to mind as well as body.

3   Kenneth Allen Robinson, *T and the Wild Appetite*, Thoreau Society Booklet, No. 12

(1957) calls Thoreau "an epicure, a gourmet, a connoisseur—of the Wild Appetite."
See also Joseph Jones, "Transcendental Grocery Bills: T's *Walden* and Some Aspects
of American Vegetarianism," *UTSE*, 36 (1957), 141–54, which relies especially on
comparisons with *The Young House-Keeper* (1838), by William A. Alcott, Bronson's
brother.

4   The most famous crux in *Walden*—"I long ago lost a hound, a bay horse, and a
turtle-dove, and am still on their trail"—has tempted many interpreters, who do not
seem to have satisfied anybody except themselves. The views which had been advanced up to 1962 are summarized by Harding in *The Variorum Walden* (Twayne,
1962), pp. 270–72. Kenneth G. Johnston, "The Star-Spangled Losses: The Hound,
Bay Horse, and Turtle Dove," *TJQ*, 3, Oct. 15, 1971, pp. 10–19, works out a detailed
astronomical interpretation, and Michael A. Burr, "T's Love and Doubt," *ATQ*,
No. 24, Suppl. (1974), pp. 22–25, sees the passage as an anagram. George Whicher
(*Walden Revisited* [Packard and Company, 1945], p. 21) says Thoreau told Ellen
Sewell's aunt that he was thinking of Edmund Sewall, his own brother John, and Ellen herself. See also Robert Marquis, in *CS*, 14, Fall 1979, pp. 11–13; Arthur Volkman,
in *TSB*, No. 103 (1968), pp. 6–7; Leon Edel, *HDT* (University of Minnesota, 1970),
pp. 34–35. On the famous passage about the bug and the old table at the end of
Walden, cf. Harding's "The Apple-Tree Table Tale," *BPLQ*, 8 (1956), 213–15, which
sees the incident as based on fact and a scientific possibility.

5   In his "T, Rice and Vose on the Commercial Spirit," *TSB*, No. 141 (1977), pp. 1–5.

6   See Francis B. Dedmond, "T and the Ethical Concept of Government," *Personalist*, 36 (1935), 36–46.

7   "HT in Our Time," in *The Personal End* (World, 1963).

8   Different as her two subjects were in their particular interests, the appetence they
shared gives point to Elsa Nettels' penetrating article, " 'A Frugal Splendor': T and
[Henry] James and the Principles of Economy," *CLQ*, 12 (1976), 5–13. The essential
points of resemblance between the two writers are "their abiding interest in the nature of consciousness, their affirmation of the uniqueness of each person's view of the
world, their conception of art as the expression of the character and temperament of
the creator, their distrust of preconceived theories and systems as a basis of judgment, their celebration of seeing and feeling as the primary way of knowledge." To
live with such intensity may well impose as great a strain in its way as what Thoreau's
Puritan ancestors experienced in their religious anxieties. In his introduction to the
journals in 1906, Bradford Torrey wrote: "Possibly it is not quite wholesome, possibly, if one dares to say it, it begets something like priggishness, for the soul to be
keyed up continually to so strenuous a pitch."

9   Richard Colyer's discussion of what the color red meant to Thoreau in "T's Color
Symbolism," *PMLA*, 36 (1971), 999–1007, is interesting in connection with his intensity. But Melvin E. Lyon, "Walden Pond as Symbol," *PMLA*, 82 (1967), 289–300, finds
his dynamism decidedly limited and exemplifying "a more limited romanticism than
that of Emerson or Whitman."

10   John Burroughs, *Indoor Studies* (Houghton Mifflin, 1889).

11   "The Significance of *Walden*," *The Humanist*, 5 (1945), 115–21. The most detailed examination of Thoreau's humor is that of J. Golden Taylor, *Neighbor T's Critical Humor* (Utah State University, 1968). See, further, Richard F. Fleck, "T's Mythological Humor," *CS*, 10, June 1975, pp. 1–7, and the references there cited; also M. Thomas Inge, "T's Enduring Laugh," *TJQ*, 2, Oct. 15, 1970, pp. 1–9; Harold F. Mosher, Jr., "The Absurd in T's *Walden*," *TJQ*, 3, Oct. 15, 1971, pp. 1–9; Sidney Poger, "T as Yankee in Canada," *ATQ*, No. 14 (1972), pp. 174–77, which stresses the humor in the work under consideration and insists that the satire is directed against the Americans and Thoreau himself as well as the Canadians; Paul Brawner, "T as Wit and Humorist," *SAQ*, 44 (1945), 170–76. Edward L. Galligan, "The Comedian at Walden Pond," *SAQ*, 69 (1970), 20–37, has much of interest even if one is not prepared to read the entire work under consideration in comic terms. Galligan is good also in his comments on Miller's and Paul's interpretations of Thoreau's "decline" during his later years.

12   In J. Lyndon Shanley, *The Making of Walden, with the Text of the First Edition* (University of Chicago, 1957) and in his contribution to Harding, *The T Centennial* (State University of New York, 1964). See also the essays collected by Joseph R. McElrath, Jr., in *T: A Symposium*, published as *ESQ*, Vol. 19, 3d Quarter 1973; Paul O. Williams, "T's Growth as a Transcendental Poet," *ESQ*, 17 (1973), 189–98; Gary Simon, "1845 and Walden: Triumph and Despair," *TJQ*, 9, July 1977, pp. 1–10. For Thorp, see *TSB*, No. 40 (1959).

13   Janet Adam Smith, *John Buchan, A Biography* (Little, Brown, 1965), p. 300.

14   "T in the Context of International Romanticism," *TSB*, No. 73 (1960), pp. 1–4.

15   See W. D. Templeman, "T, Moralist of the Picturesque," *PMLA* 47 (1932), 864–89, and James G. Southworth's reply, 49 (1934), 971–74; Gordon V. Boudreau, "HDT, William Gilpin, and the Metaphysical Ground of the Picturesque," *AL*, 45 (1973), 357–69; John Stephen Martin, "The 'Mirage' of the Sublime in Walden," *TJQ*, 8, Jan. 1976, pp. 3–15.

16   "T as Artist," *SW*, 29 (1921), 2–13, reprinted in Harding: *T: A Century of Criticism*, (Southern Methodist University, 1954).

17   Besides Charles R. Metzger, *T and Whitman* (University of Washington, 1968), see William J. Griffin, "T's Reactions to Horatio Greenough," *NEQ*, 30 (1957), 508–12; Theodore M. Brown, "T's Prophetic Architectural Program," *NEQ*, 38 (1965), 3–20; William J. Scheick, "The House of Nature in T's *A Week*," *ESQ*, 26 (1974), 111–15; Ronald Marken, " 'From Within Outward,': T, Whitman, and Wright on Domestic Architecture," *Wascana Review*, 11, Fall 1976, pp. 21–34.

18   See also Michael West, *PMLA*, 89 (1974), 1057.

19   See Caroline Moseley, "Some Observations on the T Family's Sheet Music," *TSB*, No. 142 (1977), pp. 3–4, which deals with the collection given to the Concord Public Library by Sophia Thoreau. Mendelssohn seems to be the only standard com-

poser represented. Two abolitionist songbooks which belonged to Thoreau have survived.

20   Both the words and the music are in *TSB*, No. 51 (1955), p. 2. See also Eugene H. Walker, "T, Tom Bowling, and Charles Dibdin," *CS*, Sept. 1973, pp. 3–6; Caroline Moseley, "HDT and his Favorite Popular Song," *Journal of Popular Culture*, 12 (1979), 624–29.

21   Elliott S. Allison, "HT and Horace Greeley Attend *I Puritani*," *CS*, 10, Dec. 1975, pp. 10–12.

22   Caroline Moseley, "T, Emerson, and the Rainers," *CS*, 12, Winter 1977, pp. 9–11.

23   Charles Ives, *Essays Before a Sonata*, ed. Horace Boatright (Norton, 1961), p. 51.

24   The fullest study of Thoreau's attitude toward and adventures with music is in Kenneth W. Rhoads, "T: The Ear and the Music," *AL*, 46 (1974), 313–28. It should be noted that he also praises silence but in a rather special way: "I wish to hear the silence of the night, for the silence is something positive and to be heard." The silence which was "merely negative, in arid and barren waste," caused him to shudder. Sound, he says, is when we hear outwardly, silence when we hear inwardly. See also Sherman Paul, "The Wise Silence: Sound as the Agency of Correspondence in T," *NEQ*, 22 (1949), 511–27, and William Lambdin, "Sounds in Silence," *Colorado Quarterly*, 18 (1969–70), 59–64.

25   H. W. L. Dana, *Longfellow and T*, Thoreau Society Booklet, No. 1 (1942), pp. 14–16.

26   The ideas involved in the preceding two paragraphs have been widely considered from many points of view. Norman Foerster's "The Intellectual Heritage of T," *Texas Review*, 2 (1916–17), 192–212, reprinted in Richard Ruland, *Twentieth Century Interpretations of Walden* (Prentice-Hall, 1968), was the earliest important study; see also E. Earle Stibitz, "T's Humanism and Ideas on Literature," *ESQ*, No. 55 (1969), pp. 110–16; Douglas Myers, "The Bean-Field and the Method of Nature," *TJQ*, 4, Apr. 15, 1972, pp. 1–19; K. W. Cameron, "Transcendentalists and Minerva," *ATQ*, No. 18 (1973), Parts 3–5. The most interesting and penetrating discussion of Thoreau's interest in myth and his own mythologizing is in Robert D. Richardson, Jr., *Myth and Literature in the American Renaissance* (Indiana University Press, 1978), but see also C. Grant Loomis, "HDT as Folklorist," *Western Folklore*, 16 (1957), 90–106; James T. Jenkins, "T, Mythology, Simplicity and Self-Culture," *TJQ*, 4, July 15, 1972, pp. 1–15; Katherine D. Brogan, "T's first Experience with Myth in *A Week*," *TJQ*, 7, Jan. 1975, pp. 3–9; and three articles by Richard F. Fleck: "T as Mythologist," *Research Studies Washington State University*, 40 (1972), 195–205; "T's New England Mythology," *TJQ*, 4, Jan. 15, 1972, pp. 1–9; "T as Mythmaker and Fabulist," *Rendezvous*, 9 (1974–75), 23–32.

27   Thoreau's 1836 paper on the Greek classic poets (*Early Essays*, pp. 50 ff. in the Princeton edition) is largely a summary of Henry N. Coleridge's statement of the Homeric problem. Clarence Gohdes, "HT, Bachelor of Arts," *Classical Journal*, 23

(1927–28), 323–36, was an early general account of his classical reading. Joseph N. Millichap, "Plato's Allegory of the Cave and the Vision of *Walden*," *ELH*, 7 (1969–70), 274–82, questions his alleged indifference to Plato. On his interest in the Hymns of Orpheus, especially in connection with "Smoke," see Barbara Harrell Carson, "An Orphic Hymn in *Walden*," *ESQ*, 20 (1974), 125–30. On the agricultural writers, see J. P. Pritchard, "Cato in Concord," *CW*, 36 (1942), 3–4, and Francis L. Utley's amusing "T and Columella: A Study in Reading Habits," *NEQ*, 11 (1938), 171–80, with which cf. Odell Shepard's comment on pp. 605–06. Leo M. Kaiser establishes Thoreau's knowledge of Greek in his "Remarks on T's Translation of the *Prometheus*," *CW*, 46 (1953), 69–70, but finds the work "no more than a faithful and literal transcript un-imaginatively rendered, evidencing frequent and painful adherence to the Greek word order."

28   The references to Arthur Christy are to his book, *The Orient in American Transcen-dentalism* (Columbia University, 1932). S. D. Stracner's "T's Orientalism: A Prelimin-ary Consideration" is in *TJQ*, 6, July 1974, pp. 14–17. Frank McShaine, "*Walden* and Yoga, *NEQ*, 37 (1964), 322–42, makes interesting distinctions and sees Thoreau's as a highly selective yogism. William Bysshe Stein, "The Yoga of Reading in *Walden*," *TSLL*, 13 (1972), 481–90, develops the suggestion that for Thoreau reading was itself a kind of yoga; see also his "A Bibliography of Hindu and Buddhist Literature Avail-able to T through 1854," *ESQ*, No. 47 (1967), pp. 152–56, and "The Hindu Matrix of *Walden*: The King's Son," *Comparative Literature*, 22 (1970), 303–18. See further three articles on Chinese themes: Lyman V. Cady, "T's Quotations from the Confucian Books in *Walden*," *AL*, 33 (1961–62), 20–32; Jeffrey M. Jeske, "*Walden* and the Con-fucian Four Books," *ATQ*, No. 24, Suppl. (1974), pp. 29–33; Roger C. Mueller, "T's Selections from *Chinese Four Books* for *The Dial*," *TJQ*, 4, Oct. 15, 1972, pp. 1–8.

29   McIntosh, *T as Romantic Naturalist* (Cornell University, 1974), pp. 69 ff., has the best discussion of what Thoreau had in common with Goethe and how he differed from him. On Dante, see Mathews, "T's Reading in Dante," *Italica*, 27 (1950), 77–81; on Pellico, John C. Broderick, "T and *My Prisons*," *BPLQ*, 7 (1955), 48–50. See also Adolph B. Benson, "Scandinavian Influences in the Writings of T," *Scandinavian Studies*, 16 (1941), 201–11, 241–56.

30   James Stronks, "*The Rivals* as a Possible Source for *Walden*," *TSB*, No. 95 (1966), p. 5.

31   On the last point, see Caroline Moseley, "HDT and Felicia Dorothea Hemans," *CS*, 13, Summer 1978, pp. 5–8. Since he admitted that "novelists sometimes speak the truth," Thoreau was not completely consistent in his disdain for fiction, but he la-ments what he considers its tendency to neglect the near and familiar and seems to think that history takes its place with mature people. When his attention was arrested by the print of a man's naked foot beside a Maine stream, he was reminded of *Robin-son Crusoe*. He oddly couples Dickens with De Quincey on the ground that both lack moderation and "flow too freely," and in 1843 he wrote Emerson that he was reading *The Advancement of Learning* with great delight and finding it "more like what Scott's novels were than anything." I cannot imagine what he thought they had in common.

His reading apparently grew less belletristic in later years. He liked to supplement his own experience with reading; upon returning from Canada, he hurried to the Harvard Library to read about the country, and after he had had his teeth drawn, he read up on dentistry! Even his classical reading was much more concerned with the agricultural writers than that of most classicists, and he was an indefatigable reader of books dealing with the discovery, settlement, and early history of New England, the local records of states and towns, and the white man's predecessors here. Lawrence Willson, "Another View of the Pilgrims," *NEQ*, 34 (1961), 160–77, describes Thoreau's attitude toward his New England ancestors, whom he criticized for their lack of interest in nature, failure adequately to explore their environment, sharp dealing with Indians and desecration of Indian sacred places, and their failure to achieve religious freedom and encourage freedom of thought. See also Eugene Green, "Reading Local History: Shattuck's *History*, Emerson's *Discourse*, and T's *Walden*," *NEQ*, 50 (1977), 303–14, and Philip F. Gura, "T and John Josselyn," *NEQ*, 48 (1975), 505–18.

32   It is difficult to read Thoreau on this subject without being reminded of Theodore Roosevelt's brilliant 1912 address before the American Historical Association on "History as Literature," which afterwards lent its name to the book of that title. Roosevelt maintained that it would be better to lose every Greek inscription than to give up "the chapter in which Thucydides tells of the Athenian failure before Syracuse," but he also knew that without accuracy in historical writing, you get "merely a splendid bit of romance-writing, like Carlyle's 'French Revolution.' " Nevertheless, the historian must write vividly in order to write truthfully, "for no amount of dull, painstaking detail will sum up the whole truth unless the genius is there to paint the truth."

33   Cf. Thoreau's *Early Essays and Miscellanies*, p. 81, and *Reform Papers*, p. 59, both in the Princeton edition. "Autumnal Tints" misquotes Emerson's "The Problem." See Wendell Glick, "T's Use of his Sources," *NEQ*, 44 (1971), 101–09, and Douglas A. Noverr's note on it, pp. 475–77; also Raymond Himelick, 'T and Samuel Daniel," *AL*, 24 (1952–53), 177–85, and Edward Stephanson, "Longfellow Revised," *TSB*, No. 118 (1972), pp. 4–5. Ethel Seybold says Thoreau deliberately mistranslated Horace and Persius and found Anacreon "always elevated above the sensual" to make them more congenial to himself. His taking what he needed from wherever he found it and treating it without reference to context is documented in one area by Carl V. Hovde, "Literary Materials in T's *A Week*," *PMLA*, 80 (1965), 76–83. "Thoreau uses his literary sources imperiously."

34   See, in this connection, Joel Porte, "Emerson, T, and the Double Consciousness," *NEQ*, 41 (1968), 40–50.

35   Philip Van Doren Stern traces the development of the drummer passage through Thoreau's writing in *The Annotated Walden* (Clarkson N. Potter, 1970), pp. 442–44. But I have nowhere seen in Thoreauvian commentary any mention of the use Arthur Meeker, Jr., made of it in his fine novel about early Chicago, *The Far-away Music* (Houghton Mifflin, 1945).

36   Virginia Woolf's paper, originally in the London *Times Literary Supplement*,

July 12, 1917, has been reprinted in Mary Lyon, ed., *Books and Portraits: Some Further Selections from the Literary and Biographical Writings of Virginia Woolf* (Harcourt Brace, 1977). In "An Analysis of T's Handwriting," *TSB*, No. 113 (1970), pp. 4–5, Lynn and Bill Lee find Thoreau's writing very much like Beethoven's, showing great individualism and force, "fantastic tempo," and "an inordinate amount of drive and follow-through." He guards against "becoming a prey to the demands of society." His was "an affirmative philosophy of life struggling with depression. He refused to be chained to rigid and traditional rules and precepts."

37   See H. H. Waggoner, " 'Grace' in the Thought of Emerson, T, and Hawthorne," *ESQ*, No. 54, Part I (1969), pp. 68–72: "The heart had to be carefully prepared to hear the voice; or, as the Puritan forefathers on one side of the family might have put it, to receive the free gift of grace in the form of assurance of salvation."

38   See E. Earle Stibitz, "T's Humanism and Ideas on Literature," *ESQ*, No. 55 (1969), pp. 110–16.

39   See William Drake, "Spiritual Ideals and Scientific Fact: T's Search for Reality," in *The Western T Centenary Papers*. "Few men have written so much about their personal experience, and have yet concealed so much of themselves as HDT. . . . Even his letters are literary productions."

40   The pioneering study of Thoreau's poetics was Fred W. Lorch, "T and the Organic Principle in Poetry," *PMLA*, 53 (1938), 286–302. As Thoreau saw it, men possessed genius to the extent that the divine came to expression through them, with inspiration coming "from a transcendent rather than from an immanent deity." But intuitions must be carefully tested for source and validity, and inspiration or genius could avail little without talent to impose form upon it. To Thoreau style as mere embellishment was "varnish and filigree," but he respected it when it was "ingrained polish" like that of a diamond, and he did not reject traditional forms unless they were mechanically applied or produced sterility. In his *A T Handbook* (New York University, 1959), Harding says bluntly that most of Thoreau's poetry is bad. "Much of it deserves no better name than doggerel. When it is regular, it is singsong; when it is free verse, there seems little point to the freedom." Harding calls "Smoke" (which Emerson thought better than Simonides), "Fog," and "Haze" the best poems and also praises "My Prayer," "A Gentle Boy," and "Sic Vita." The first considered evaluation of Thoreau's poems after the publication of the collected edition was that of Henry W. Wells, "An Evaluation of T's Poetry," *AL*, 16 (1944), 99–109, reprinted in Harding's *Century* anthology. Wells sees many influences, some from as far back as the Middle Ages, and much anticipation of later developments. He finds that Thoreau imitated Skelton more often than the seventeenth-century metaphysicals he is supposed to have loved. Subsequent commentary has been voluminous. See Arthur L. Ford, *The Poetry of HDT* (Transcendental Books, 1970), also in *ESQ*, No. 61, Part 1 (1970), and, among articles, Carl Dennis, "Correspondence in T's Nature Poetry," *ESQ*, No. 58 (1970), pp. 101–09; Robert G. Evans, "T's Poetry and the Prose Works," in W. B. Stein, ed., *New Approaches to T: A Symposium* (Transcendental Books, 1969), pp. 4–52; Laraine Ferguson, "Wild Nectar: The Language of T's Poetry," *CS*, 12,

Spring 1977, pp. 1–7; Richard C. Gurney, "The Worst of T," *Connecticut Review*, 3, Apr. 1970, pp. 68–71; William Hasselberger, "T's Poetics," *CS*,7, Dec. 1972, pp. 1–4; Lauriat Lane, Jr., "Finding a Voice: T's Pentameters," *ESQ*, No. 60 (1970), pp. 67–72; Frederick P. Lenz III, "HDT: The Forgotten Poems," *CS*, 11, Mar. 1976, pp. 1–10; and two articles by Paul O. Williams, "The Concept of Inspiration in T's Poetry," *PMLA*, 79 (1964), 466–72, and "T's Growth as a Transcendental Poet," *ESQ*, No. 72 (1973), pp. 189–98.

41   See Raymond Adams, "T's Literary Apprenticeship," *SP*, 29 (1932), 671–29; Wendell Glick, "Go Tell It on the Mountain: T's Vocation as a Writer," *ESQ*, No. 72 (1973), pp. 161–69.

42   An interesting article by Annette M. Woodlief, "The Influence of Theories of Rhetoric on T," *TJQ*, 7, Jan. 1975, pp. 13–32, deals with Richard Whately's *The Elements of Rhetoric* (1828), which was an important text during Thoreau's sophomore year. Without insisting that Thoreau consciously followed Whately's principles, Ms. Woodlief finds them compatible with his "artistic aims without clashing with his demand for an organic style."

43   Michael West, "Charles Kraitsir's Influence upon T's Theory of Language," *ESQ*, 19 (1973), 262–74, argues that T's "punning etymologies and grotesque comparisons . . . derive directly from some of the wilder doctrines that marked early nineteenth-century philosophers of language in England and America, and especially from John Horne Tooke." See also Ted Billy, "A Check List of Wordplays in T's *Week*," *CS*, 14, Fall 1979, pp. 14–19.

44   Perry Miller's *Consciousness in Concord* (Houghton Mifflin, 1958), contains much the best detailed demonstration of how Thoreau used his journals in the writing designed for publication. See also Carl V. Hovde, "Nature into Art: T's Use of his Journals in *A Week*," *AL*, 30(1958–59), 165–84. Harding's "The Influence of T's Lecturing upon his Writing," *BNYPL*, 60 (1956), 74–80, is a detailed comparative study of the lecture and book versions of two texts.

45   "The Paradox of T," *Scribner's Magazine*, 68 (1920), 335–42.

46   It should be noted that some writers feel that modern critics have gone too far in their analyses of the structure of *Walden*. Disregarding Shepard, who, in his comments on Sherman Paul's *The Shores of America* (University of Illinois, 1958), in "Approaching T through Modern Scholarship," *ESQ*, No. 18 (1960), p. 23–26, comes close to reaffirming his 1920 view, we still have the more moderate James McIntosh, who thinks the structure looser than has been argued, and Michael Moloney, who insists that, "in the manner of the great baroque masters, *Walden* is . . . rambling and discursive"; see his "Christian Malgré Lui," in Harold C. Gardiner, ed., *American Classics Reconsidered* (Scribners, 1958), reprinted in Lauriat Lane, Jr., *Approaches to Walden* (Wadsworth, 1961). On the other hand, L. E. Scanlon, "T's Parable of Baker Farm," *ESQ*, No. 47 (1967), pp. 19–21, argues the structural value of the Baker Farm chapter, which even Paul had regarded as merely transitional, and Kenneth Matthews, "Making the Earth Say Beans," *TSB*, No. 143 (1971), pp. 5–6, tests the unity of

the book by an analysis of "The Bean Field." Other discussions include Lauriat Lane, Jr., "On the Organic Structure of *Walden*," *CE*, 21 (1959–60), 195–202 (reprinted in his *Approaches to Walden*) and "*Walden*, the Second Year," *Studies in Romanticism*, 8 (1969), 183–92; Thomas Woodson, "The Two Beginnings of *Walden*: A Distinction of Styles," *ELH*, 35 (1968), 440–73; Raymond P. Tripp, Jr., "A Note on the Structure of *Walden*," *TSB*, No. 118 (1972), pp. 5–6; Jim Springer Borck and Herbert B. Rothschild, Jr., "Meditative Discoveries in T's 'The Pond in Winter,' " *TSLL*, 20 (1978), 93–106; Judy Schaaf Anhorn, "T in the Bean-Field: The Curious Language of *Walden*," *ESQ*, 24 (1978), 179–96. Charles Child Walcutt, "*Walden* as a Response to 'The American Scholar,' " *Arizona Quarterly*, 34 (1978), 5–30, argues that Thoreau "structured his *Walden* with the intention of implicitly refuting the argument of 'The American Scholar.' " See also "The Economics of *Walden*," in Mutlu Konuk Blasing, *The Art of Life: Studies in an Autobiographical Literature* (University of Texas Press, 1977), and Richard H. Dillman, "The Psychological Rhetoric of *Walden*," *ESQ*, 25 (1979), 79–91.

47 Paul, *The Shores of America*, especially pp. 197, 203, 210–11, 218; McIntosh, pp. 137–38, 140; Lynn, *Visions of America* (Greenwood Press, 1973). Among the articles which might be cited are Jonathan Bishop, "The Experience of the Sacred in T's *Week*," *ELH*, 33 (1966), 66–91; Joyce M. Holland, "Pattern and Meaning in T's *A Week*," *ESQ*, No. 50, Suppl. (1960), pp. 48–55; John Homan, Jr., "T, The Emblem, and the *Week*, *ATQ*, No. 1 (1969), pp. 104–08; Carl F. Hovde, "Literary Materials in T's *A Week*," *PMLA*, 80 (1965), 76–83; Paul David Johnson, "T's Redemptive *Week*," *AL*, 49 (1977), 22–33; Walter Hesford, " 'Incessant Tragedies': A Reading of *A Week* . . . ," *ELH*, 44 (1979), 515–25; Jamie H. Hutchinson, " 'The Life of the Current': T's Historical Vision in *A Week* . . . ," *ESQ*, 25 (1979), 211–23. Rosemary Whitaker, "*A Week* and *Walden*: The River vs. The Pond," *ATQ*, No. 17 (1973), pp. 9–13, compares and contrasts the two works, finding *Walden* "the more Transcendental, and hence more joyous, of the two works." The excellent account of the writing, publication, and reputation of the *Week* in the 1980 Princeton edition did not appear until after my book had been completed.

48 Walter Harding, *The Selected Works of T*, Cambridge Edition (Houghton Mifflin, 1975), pp. 533, 637; Garber, in W. B. Stein, ed., *New Approaches to T: A Symposium* (Transcendental Books, 1969) pp. 35–40; McIntosh, p. 211. Analyses of other works may be sampled in Leonard Pops, "An Analysis of T's *Cape Cod*," *BNYPL*, 67 (1963), 419–28; Robert C. Cosbey, "T at Work: The Writing of 'Ktaadn,' " *BNYPL*, 65 (1961), 21–30; Vesta M. Parsons, "T's *The Maine Woods*: An Essay in Appreciation," *Husson Review*, 1 (1967–68), 17–27; Joseph Laurence Basile, "T's Uncommon Cold: *A Yankee in Canada* Revisited," *CS*, 13, Spring 1978, pp. 7–11; Stephen Adams, "T Catching Cold: *A Yankee in Canada*," *ESQ*, 25 (1979), 224–34.

CHAPTER TWO. OTHERS

1 See *TSB*, No. 69 (1959), p. 270.

2 Nothing Thoreau ever wrote shows better his capacity to understand the values of

hospitality and warm human feeling than his essay "The Landlord," with its obvious echoes of *The Canterbury Tales*. See Sherman Paul's charming study, "T's 'The Landlord': Sublimely Trivial for the Good of Men," *JEGP*, 54 (1955), 587–90; cf. also Howard Mumford Jones, "T and Human Nature," *AM*, 210 (1962), 58–61, reprinted in Walter Harding, *The T Centennial: Papers Marking the Observance in New York City of the One Hundredth Anniversary of the Death of HDT* (State University of New York, 1964), and two articles in *TSB*: Raymond Adams, "T and his Neighbors," No. 44 (1953), pp. 1–4; Ruth R. Wheeler, "T's Village Background," No. 100 (1967), pp. 1–6. But see also Rhoda B. Nathan, "This Delicious Solitude," *TJQ*, 10, July 1978, pp. 3–8.

3   See Alan Seaburg's paper on Edmund Hosmer, *TSB*, No. 102 (1968), pp. 1–4, and Francis H. Allen's compilation of journal materials in *Men of Concord* (Houghton Mifflin, 1936), with magnificent illustrations by N. C. Wyeth, the originals of three of which are in the Concord Public Libary and one in the Boston Athenaeum.

4   *Early Essays and Miscellanies* in the Princeton edition of Thoreau, p. 121.

5   Perry Miller, *Consciousness in Concord* (Houghton Mifflin, 1958), p. 188.

6   Robert W. Bradford, "T and Therien," *AL*, 34 (1962–63), 499–506.

7   The fullest study here is George Ryan, "Shanties and Shiftlessness," *Eire*, 13, Fall 1978, pp. 54–78, but see also Frank Buckley, "T and the Irish," *NEQ*, 13 (1940), 389–400.

8   For the letter, see Walter Harding, *The Days of HT* (Knopf, 1927), p. 259, and, for a fuller text, *CS*, 13, Summer 1978, pp. 1–2. The poem was published by K. W. Cameron, "A New T Poem—'To Edith,' "*ESQ*, No. 18 (1960), pp. 40–41. Thoreau seems to have been less successful as a tutor in William Emerson's family on Staten Island; can this be the reason he gave up the idea of tutoring Horace Greeley's children? Besides the references to Thoreau in Conway's autobiography, see his "Emerson, T, and the Transcendentalists," originally in *Fraser's Magazine* in 1864 and 1866, but now most readily accessible in *ATQ*, No. 16, Part I (1972), pp. 62–81.

9   Raymond D. Gozzi's *Tropes and Figures: A Psychological Study of HDT*, a doctoral dissertation for New York University (1957), has been printed only as extracted in Walter Harding's *HDT: A Profile* (Hill and Wang, 1971), though it may be had from University Microfilms. See Gozzi's personal word in *TSB*, No. 150 (1980), pp. 3–5. Carl Bode also takes the Freudian view in "The Half-Hidden T," *Massachusetts Review*, 4 (1962), 68–80.

10   See especially the anonymous " 'In Virtue of Noble Living,' " *Outlook*, 63 (1899), 815–21, reprinted in Harding's *Profile*.

11   It does not seem to have occurred to any of the Thoreaus nor to anybody else in Concord that tuberculosis was contagious, nor is there any record of Thoreau having infected anybody. The only writer who has raised this question in any connection is Louise Hall Tharp, who wonders, in her book about the Manns, *Until Victory* (Little, Brown, 1953), whether the disease which killed young Horace Mann, Jr., was contracted when he accompanied Thoreau on his Minnesota journey.

12   Miller, pp. 101–02.

13   See S. Zisook and R. A. De Vaul, "Grief-Related Facsimile illnesses," *International Journal of Psychiatry in Medicine*, 7 (1977), 329–36, for an analysis of ten cases similar to Thoreau's. Thomas Blanding prints "Passages from John Thoreau's Journal," *TSB*, No. 136 (1976), pp. 4–6. Brief as these extracts are, they show that, in both frankness and temperament, John was a match for his brother, but they do not support the legend of his superior balance and equability. See especially the entry for July 2, 1850.

14   The shock of Waldo's passing was no doubt cushioned for Thoreau by the slightly earlier and much greater sorrow which had in a measure numbed him, and it is somewhat chilling to find him writing Mrs. Emerson's sister, Lucy Brown, that Waldo had "died as the mist rises from the brook, which the sun will soon shoot her rays through. . . . He had not taken root here. I was not startled to hear that he was dead. . . . His fine organization demanded it. . . . It would have been strange if he had lived." But this is the kind of thing one must expect from the transcendentalists, even Emerson himself. As Thoreau adds, "You must not blame me if I do *talk to the clouds.*"

15   See Perry Miller's discussion of the general phenomenon in *Consciousness in Concord*, pp. 88 ff., which, unsympathetic though it is, still exhibits valuable insights.

16   See Gail Baker, "Friendship in T's *Week*," *TJQ*, 7, Apr. 1975, pp. 3–15; "Thoreau exhibits a fine sensitivity to human relationships, rising from casual to intimate, familial to national, solitary . . . to convivial, from neighborly to loving."

17   Joel Porte's article, "T on Love: A Lexicon of Hate," *University of Kansas City Review*, 31 (1964–65), 111–16, 191–94, is important, as is Joseph J. Moldenhauer's "Textual Supplement to T's Essay on 'Love,' " *TSB*, No. 149 (1979), pp. 6–7.

18   There is no question that it was Thoreau who suggested to Hawthorne the *Septimius Felton* story; see Randall Stewart, *Nathaniel Hawthorne* (Yale University Press, 1948). But the persistent legend that Thoreau was Hawthorne's model for Donatello in *The Marble Faun* is supported by no real evidence; see Edward C. Peple, Jr., "T and Donatello," *TJQ*, 5, Oct. 1973, pp. 22–25, and Richard Fleck, "Hawthorne's Possible Use of T in *The Marble Faun*," *TJQ*, 6, Apr. 1974, pp. 8–12. More reasonable suggestions have been made concerning Thoreau's possible influence on *Mosses from an Old Manse*; see Frank Davidson, "T's Contribution to Hawthorne's *Mosses*," *NEQ*, 20 (1947), 535–42; Buford Jones, " 'The Hall of Fantasy' and the Early Hawthorne-T Relationship," *PMLA*, 83 (1968), 1429–39; G. Thomas Couser, " 'The Old Manse,' *Walden*, and the Hawthorne-T Relationship," *ESQ*, 21 (1975), 11–21. See also Raymond Adams, "Hawthorne and a Glimpse of *Walden*," *Essex Institute Historical Collections* 94 (1958), 191–93; David B. Kesterson, "Hawthorne and Nature: Thoreauvian Influence?" *ELN*, 4 (1967), 200–06, which denies that Hawthorne learned to observe nature through Thoreau or needed to; E. C. Peple, Jr., "Hawthorne on T: 1853–1857," *TSB*, No. 119 (1972), pp. 1–3; Raymond Hull, "Some Further Notes on Hawthorne and T," *TSB*, No. 121 (1972), p. 7–8.

19   The pioneering study of the estrangement between Emerson and Thoreau was

John Brooks Moore, "T Rejects Emerson," *AL*, 4 (1932–33), 241–56, a useful collection of data, though some of its conclusions now seem too sweeping. For a more recent study see Leonard Neufeldt, "The Severity of the Ideal: Emerson's 'T,' " *ESQ*, No. 58 (1970), pp. 77–84. William M. Moss, "So Many Promising Youth," *NEQ*, 49 (1976), 46–64, tries to show that Emerson's disappointment in Thoreau's development was paralleled in his relations with others. Much the fullest study, Joel Porte's *Emerson and T: Transcendentalists in Conflict* (Wesleyan University, 1966), is more concerned with philosophical than personal considerations. There is much more about personalities in Porte's later book, *Representative Man: Ralph Waldo Emerson in his Time* (Oxford University, 1979). See also Julia Wendell, "An Examination of the Emerson-T Friendship," *CS*, 14, Spring 1979, pp. 3–11, and Leonard Neufeldt, "Emerson, T, and Daniel Webster," *ESQ*, 26 (1980), 26–37, which contrasts Emerson's generally admiring attitude toward Daniel Webster with Thoreau's aversion, and concludes that " 'Uses of Great Men,' the opening essay of *Representative Men*, sums up Emerson's case for Webster and helps understanding of Thoreau's case against both Emerson and Webster."

20   There are two modern biographies of Channing, both of which involve consideration of his relations with Thoreau: Frederic T. McGill, Jr., *Channing of Concord: A Life of William Ellery Channing* (Rutgers University Press, 1967) and Richard N. Hudspeth, *Ellery Channing* (Twayne, 1973). See, further, Hudspeth's article, "A Perennial Springtime: Channing's Friendship with Emerson and T," *ESQ*, No. 54 (1969), pp. 30–36; Francis B. Dedmond, "William Ellery Channing on T: An Unpublished Satire," *MLN*, 67 (1952), 50–52, and " 'He Shone o'er mortal hearts,': Ellery Channing's Poetic Tributes to T," *CS*, 13, Spring 1978, pp. 1–4; Arthur G. Volkman, "Ellery Channing, A Tragicomic Poet," *CS*, 11, June 1976, pp. 10–12.

21   For Margaret Fuller, see Marie Urbanski, "HDT and Margaret Fuller," *TJQ*, 8, Oct. 1976, pp. 24–29. Richard Fuller's tribute to Thoreau may be read in *CS*, 9, Mar. 1974, p. 4.

22   See Earl J. Dias, "Daniel Ricketson and HT," *NEQ*, 26 (1953), 388–96; cf. Thomas Blanding, "Daniel Ricketson and Some More of his Friends," *CS*, 13, Winter 1978, pp. 1–17.
23   See John W. Clarkson, Jr., "F. B. Sanborn, 1831–1917," *CS*, 12, Summer 1977, pp. 1–8; also Harding, "F. B. Sanborn and T's Letters," *BPLQ*, 3 (1951), 288–93.

24   E. Harlow Russell's *A Bit of Unpublished Correspondence between HDT and Isaac T. Hecker* (Worcester, Press of Charles Hamilton, 1902), has been reprinted in *ATQ*, No. 14, Part 2 (1972), pp. 66–70. Before his conversion to Catholicism, Hecker had Brook Farm connections and at one time boarded with the Thoreaus. He became the founder of the Paulist order and editor of *The Catholic World*, in which capacity he was important in the literary career of Agnes Repplier.

25   Bradford Torrey, "T, Sensuous Transcendentalist," *TJQ*, 6, Apr. 1974, pp. 3–7.

26   Bradford Torrey, "T as a Diarist," *AM*, 95 (1905), 5–18. E. J. Rose, "The Wit and Wisdom of T's 'Higher Laws,' " *Queen's Quarterly*, 69 (1962), 555–67, writes, "In the

'Higher Laws,' Thoreau comes full circle. For although he desires that man must pass through what he must condemn in the end, he asserts that man must pass through it so that he can leave it behind." But John B. Pickard's interpretation, in "The Religion of 'Higher Laws,' " *ESQ*, No. 39 (1965), pp. 68–72, or at least his emphasis, is different: " 'Higher Laws' moves Thoreau more closely to a Puritan withdrawal from nature and distrust of the senses, where continence becomes the prime virtue and sexuality is sublimated to chastity. Rebirth occurs only if nature is overcome and the mind and spirit fully cultivated."

27 Anderson, *The Magic Circle of Walden* (Holt, Rinehart and Winston, 1968), pp. 164 ff.; Sanford, "Emerson, T, and the Hereditary Duality," *ESQ*, No. 54 (1968), pp. 36–43. See also David M. Holman's excellent article, "The Spiritual and the Wild: T's Middle Way," *TJQ*, 6, Jan. 1974, pp. 8–13.

28 Cf. Lawrence MacDonald, "HT, Liberal, Unconventional Nudist," *Sunshine and Health*, Jan. 1943.

29 "Scatology and Eschatology: The Heroic Dimensions of T's Wordplay," *PMLA*, 89 (1974), 1043–64. The title of West's other article, *"Walden's* Dirty Language: T and Walter Whiter's Geocentric Etymological Theories," *Harvard Library Bulletin*, 22 (1974), 117–28, is unduly sensational; the interest of the piece is linguistic.

30 Quoted, *TSB*, No. 138 (1977), p. 5, from Charles W. Wendte, *Thomas Starr King, Patriot and Preacher* (Beacon Press, 1921). See further on this theme Stephen Railton, "The Resurrection of Virtue," *AQ*, 24 (1972), 210–27; Lewis Leary, " 'Now I Adventured': 1851 as a Watershed Year in T's Career," *ESQ*, 19 (1973), 141–48; Deborah Robbins, "The Ascetic Winter and Excremental Spring of *Walden*," *ESQ*, 24 (1978), 77–82.

31 The best general account of the Sewall-Thoreau matter is in Harding, *Days*, pp. 94–104. T. M. Raysor's "The Love Story of T," *SP*, 23 (1926), 457–63, was the pioneering account; see also Florence Becker Lennon, "The Voice of the Turtle," *TSB*, No. 15 (1948), pp. 1–2.

32 Miller, pp. 207–08; Lebeaux, *Young Man T* (University of Massachusetts, 1977), p. 233; cf. Adams, *AL*, 12 (1940–41), 112–15.

33 Joseph Slater, "Caroline Dall in Concord," *TSB*, No. 62 (1958), pp. 1–2.

34 George Hendrick, "William Sloane Kennedy Looks to Emerson and T," *ESQ*, No. 26 (1962), pp. 28–31.

35 See Harding, *Days*, pp. 104 ff., for the best statement of Thoreau's interest in Mary Russell. He kept in touch with her and her husband to the end of his life.

36 Walter Harding, "T and Kate Brady," *AL*, 36 (1964–65), 347–49.

37 See Walter Harding, "T's Feminine Foe," *PMLA*, 69 (1954), 110–16; also Anton Kovar, "Sophia Foord," *TJQ*, 3, Jan. 15, 1971, pp. 22–23; "HT and Sophia Foord," *CS*, 11, Fall 1976, pp. 14–15; *A Sprig of Andromeda from Louisa May Alcott on the Death of*

HDT, with an introductory note by John L. Cooley (The Pierpont Morgan Library, 1962).

38   See Jonathan Katz, *Gay American History: Lesbians and Gay Men in the U.S.A., A Documentary* (Crowell, 1976), pp. 481–94, and, for a more considered account, Harding's afterword to his *Profile,* pp. 247–48. See, further, Clayton Hoagland, "The Diary of T's 'Gentle Boy,' " *NEQ,* 28 (1955), 473–89. Ellen Sewall's daughter, Louise Osgood Koopman, says Edmund Sewall was "always ashamed" of T's poem about him but gives no reason why. Katz seeks to make himself impregnable by producing a "documentary" study, but he forgets that documents must be interpreted and that interpretations are rarely free from bias.

39   "T, Womankind, and Sexuality," *ESQ,* 22 (1976), 123–48, is the fullest study of all the evidence bearing on the general subject. Harding, *TSB,* No. 137 (1976), p. 6, corrects her on the dating of Thoreau's essay on love.

40   Miller, pp. 205, 215.

41   "Redskins and Transcendentalists: A Reading of *A Week.* . . ," *Research Studies State University of Washington,* 40 (1972), 274–84.

CHAPTER THREE. WIDER CIRCLES

1   Raymond Adams, "T's Mock-Heroics and the American Natural History Writers," *SP,* 52 (1955), 86–97, reprinted Wendell Glick, ed., *The Recognition of T* (University of Michigan, 1939). On God's culmination in the present moment, see Joel Porte, *TSB,* No. 144 (1978), pp. 1–4.

2   Donald G. Hoch, "Theory of History in *A Week:* Annuals and Perennials," *ESQ,* No. 56 (1969), pp. 32–39, connects Thoreau's conviction that "the gods are partial to no era" with his acceptance of a cyclical theory of history. Lawrence Willson's "T, Citizen of Concord," *ESQ,* No. 14 (1959), pp. 7–12, is excellent on his localism and universalism and his use of Concord's past and present. C. E. Pulos, "The Foreign Observer in *Walden,*" *ELH,* 7 (1969–70), 51–53, shows that he sometimes views Concord from a traveler's point of view, and Carol Kroh, "Columbus of Concord: *A Week* as a Voyage of Discovery," *ESQ,* 21 (1975), 215–21, connects his interest in Columbus with his account of the journey in the *Week* as "a Columbus-like voyage of discovery." See also William L. Howarth, "Traveling in Concord: The World of T's Journal," in his *Puritan Influences in American Literature* (University of Illinois Press, 1979). It is interesting that the photographer Ivan Massar should have recorded in *The Illustrated World of T* (Grosset and Dunlap, 1974) that, though he had himself journeyed round the world, Thoreau taught him "how far I can travel by enjoying what is underfoot. I have applied Thoreau's precepts in my photography by slowing down, taking a closer look, and learning to see."

3   Sanborn's 1917 book on Thoreau, Chapter 12, has a summary account of all his travels. On CANADA, see Lawrence Willson, "T's Canadian Notebook," *Huntington*

Library Quarterly, 22 (1958–59), 179–200, and Sidney T. Pogner, "T as Yankee in Canada," *ATQ*, No. 14, Part 3 (1972), pp. 174–77. On the MOUNTAIN journeys, see Frederick W. Kilbourne, "T and the White Mountains," *Appalachia*, 14 (1919), 356–67, and two articles in the same periodical by Christopher McKee, "T's First Visit to the White Mountains," 31 (1956–57), 199–209, and "T: A Week on Mount Washington and in Tuckermann Ravine," 30 (1954–55), 169–83, with which compare Jeannette E. Graustein's comment, 31 (1956–57), 414–17; also see Elliott S. Allison, "T of Monadnock," *TJQ*, 5, Oct. 1973, pp. 15–21, and Thomas Woodson, "T's Excursion to the Berkshires and the Catskills," *ESQ*, 21 (1975), 82–92. Much has been written about the MINNESOTA journey. John T. Flanagan, "T in Minnesota," *MinnH*, 16 (1933), 35–46, made a good beginning. Evadne Burris Swanson, "The Manuscript-Journal of T's *Last Journey*," *MinnH*, 20 (1939), 169–73, corrects Sanborn's text in his *First and Last Journeys*. Walter Harding prints Horace Mann, Jr.'s letter to his mother, describing part of the journey, in "T and Mann on the Minnesota River, June 1861," *MinnH*, 37 (1960–61), 225–28, and more material in *T's Minnesota Journey: Two Documents: Two Notes on the Journey West and the Letters of Horace Mann, Jr.*, Thoreau Society Booklet, No. 16, 1962. But the fullest account of the whole journey is Harriet Sweetland, "The Significance of T's Trip to the Upper Mississippi in 1861, *TWASAS*, 51 (1962), 267–86.

4   "The Transcendental View of the West," *WHR*, 14 (1960), 183–91. See also C. A. Tillinghast, "The West of T's Imagination: The Development of a Symbol," *Thoth*, 6 (1965), 42–50; and, for an interest in Finland which Thoreau shared with Emerson, Ernest J. Moyne in *Neophilologische Mitteilungen*, 70 (1969), 738–50.

5   See Walter Harding, "In Defense of T," *Yankee*, 11, Mar. 1947, pp. 26–27.

6   See "Walden Pond as a Symbol," *PMLA*, 82 (1967), 289–300; also Francis B. Dedmond, "Economic Protest in T's Journal," *Studia Neophilologica*, 26 (1953–54), 65–76; Thomas Woodson, "T on Poverty and Magnanimity," *PMLA*, 85 (1970), 21–34; Kenneth Stikkers, "Living the Poetic Life: HDT's Experiment at Walden Pond," *CS*, 11, Fall 1976, pp. 1–9; Richard H. Dillman, "T's Humane Economics: A Reflection of Jean-Baptiste Say's Economic Philosophy," *ESQ*, 25 (1979), 20–25; Harold Hillenbrand, " 'A True Integrity Day by Day': T's Organic Economy in *Walden*," *ESQ*, 25 (1979), 71–78. Judith P. Saunders has an incisive study of Thoreau's use of economic terms and of the echoes of the New Testament involved in "Economic Metaphor Redefined: The Transcendentalist Capitalist at Walden," *ATQ*, No. 36, Fall 1977, pp. 4–7.

7   Richard C. Cook, "T and his Imagery: The Anatomy of an Imagination," *TSB*, No. 70 (1960), pp. 1–3.

8   See Paul Schwaber, "T's Development in *Walden*," *Criticism*, 5 (1963), 64–77, for an interesting argument to the effect that Thoreau had mellowed during his stay at Walden, so that he left it "a wiser, stronger, and shrewder man than he had been" and one "more at peace with himself because more in tune with his aspirations and, therefore, more amiably disposed toward the men and women with whom he will be living again."

9   Besides Leo Stoller's *After Walden* (Stanford University, 1957), see Isadore H. Becker, "T's 'Princely Leisure,' " *Husson Review*, 3 (1970), 161–67, and Herbert F. Smith, "T among the Classical Economists," *ESQ*, 23 (1977), 114–22.

10   Charles H. Nichols, Jr., "T on the Citizen and his Government," *Phylon*, 13 (1952), 19–24. Taylor Stoehr, *Nay-saying in Concord: Emerson, Alcott, and T* (Archon, 1978), considers the writers' awareness of evil and their interest in reform.

11   D. Gordon Rohman, "T's Transcendental Stewardship," *ESQ*, No. 44 (1966), pp. 72–77, views some of these issues against the background of American thinking clear back to the Puritans and defends Thoreau against the charge of indifference toward his obligations to society.

12   John C. Broderick, "T's Proposals for Legislation," *AQ*, 7 (1955), 285–90. Thoreau has little to say about crime, but a college essay lays down the principle that "the end of all punishment is the welfare of the state,—the good of the community at large, —not the suffering of the individual," and in 1849 he was one of the forty-eight Concord signers of a protest against the hanging in Boston of the Negro Washington Goode, whose conviction for killing Thomas Harding would seem to have rested upon doubtful evidence. See Ruth R. Wheeler, "T and Capital Punishment," *TSB*, No. 86 (1964), p. 1.

13   Michael J. Hoffman, *The Subversive Vision: American Romanticism in Literature* (Kennikat Press, 1972).

14   See Robert C. Albrecht, "Conflict and Resolution: 'Slavery in Massachusetts,' " *ESQ*, 19 (1973), 179–88; Francis B. Dedmond, "Burning the Root of the Hydra's Head: T and the Abolition Movement," *CS*, 11 Winter 1976, pp. 1–8; Nick Aaron Ford, "HDT, Abolitionist," *NEQ*, 19 (1946), 359–71; Wendell P. Glick, "T and the *Herald of Freedom*," *NEQ*, 22 (1949), 193–204; Walter Harding, "T and the Negro," *Negro History Bulletin*, 10 (1946), 12, 22–23.

15   John C. Broderick, "T, Alcott, and the Poll Tax," *SP*, 53 (1956), 612–26; H. H. Hoeltje, "Misconceptions in T Criticism," *PQ*, 47 (1968), 563–70; Walter Harding, "T in Jail: Was It Legal?" *American Heritage*, 26, Aug. 1975, pp. 36–37. Longfellow's approval of Thoreau's action is reported in Edward Wagenknecht, *Henry Wadsworth Longfellow: Portrait of an American Humanist* (Oxford University, 1966), pp. 55, 81.

16   Berel Lang, "T and the Body Politic," *Colorado Quarterly*, 18 (1969–70), 51–57. Among many other articles on the subject of the foregoing paragraphs, C. Carroll Hollis, "T and the State," *Commonweal*, 50 (1949), 530–33, Lawrence Bowling, "T's Social Criticism as Poetry," *YR*, 55 (1965–66), 255–64, and Thomas R. Carper, "The Whole History of T's 'My Prisons,' " *ESQ*, No. 50, Suppl. (1968), pp. 35–38, heavily stress Thoreau's individualism. Heinz Eulau, "Wayside Challenger: Some Remarks on the Politics of T," *Antioch Review*, 9 (1949), 311–22, and John Aldrich Christie, "T on Civil Resistance," *ESQ*, No. 54 (1969), pp. 5–12, include interesting consideration of developments in his thinking. C. E. B. Combellack, "Two Critics of

Society," *Pacific Spectator*, 3 (1949), 440–45, and John P. Diggins, "T, Marx, and the 'Riddle' of Alienation," *Social Research*, 39 (1972), 571–98, compare and contrast Thoreau and Marx. Combellack finds Thoreau the more radical of the two: "For whereas Marx accepted the current values of society and aimed primarily at a rearrangement, at some tinkerings and shufflings really, Thoreau called for a new set of values, a new moral order." John Haynes Holmes, "T's 'Civil Disobedience,' " *Christian Century*, 66 (1949), 787–89, and Eleanor Woods, "Cost What It May," *Humanist*, 21 (1961), 77–86, are both concerned with the application of Thoreauvian principles and techniques to the problems of today, and Jacob Schiffman, in W. B. Stein's *New Approaches to T: A Symposium* (Transcendental Books, 1969), considers the dangers of civil disobedience as now being practiced and its departure from Thoreauvian principles. See further Wendell Glick, " 'Civil Disobedience': T's Attack upon Relativism," *WHR*, 7 (1952–53), 35–42; Francis B. Dedmond, "T and the Ethical Concept of Government," *Personalist*, 36 (1955), 36–46; Robert Palmer Saalbach, "T and Civil Disobedience," *Ball State University Forum*, 13, Autumn 1972, pp. 18–24; Raymond Tatalovich, "T on Civil Disobedience: In Defense of Morality or Anarchy?" *Southern Quarterly*, 11 (1972–73), 107–13; Michael Ehrlich, "T's 'Civil Disobedience': Strategy for Reform," *Connecticut Review*, 7, Oct. 1973, pp. 100–10.

17 In 1841 Thoreau and his brother debated against Bronson Alcott on whether it was ever lawful to use forcible resistance, Alcott maintaining the negative. It is interesting to compare Thoreau's relatively objective account in the *Week* of Hannah Duston, the Indian killer, with that of Hawthorne, who bluntly called her "a bloody old hag." See Robert D. Arner, "The Story of Hannah Duston: Cotton Mather to T," *ATQ*, No. 18 (1973), pp. 19–23, but cf. Robert F. Sayre's comments on the matter in *T and the American Indian* (Princeton University, 1979), pp. 47, 52–53. On the general matter under consideration here, see also Max Cosman, "T Faced War," *Personalist*, 25 (1944), 73–76.

18 See Kenneth E. Harris, "T's 'The Service,'—A Review of the Scholarship," *ATQ*, No. 11 (1971), pp. 60–63.

19 See also *CS*, 12, Fall 1977, pp. 21–22.

20 The Pottawatomie Massacre "stands out, even in those turbulent times, as a fiendish atrocity." See Gilman M. Ostrander, "Emerson, T, and John Brown," *Mississippi Valley Historical Review*, 39 (1952–53), 713–26. Emerson has often been reported to have said that when Brown was hanged, he would make the gallows as holy as the cross, a saying which is supposed to have prompted Hawthorne's rejoinder that no man ever deserved hanging more. But in the new edition of Emerson's *Journals and Miscellaneous Notebooks*, xiv, 33 (Harvard University, 1978), he himself attributes this saying to one Mattie Griffith. In any event, Emerson's attack of Brown fever seems to have been milder and less protracted than Thoreau's.

21 "A Plea for Captain John Brown," "Martyrdom of John Brown," and "The Last Days of John Brown" are all included in the *Reform Papers* (Princeton University). For

further comment on Thoreau's attitude toward Brown, see the article by Heinz Eulau cited in note 16 above and Truman Nelson "T and the Paralysis of Individualism," *Ramparts*, 4, Mar. 1966, pp. 16–26; Gerald J. Galgan, "T on the 'Political,' " *TJQ*, 6, July 1974, pp. 19–22; Kerry Ahearn, "T and John Brown: What To Do about Evil," *TJQ*, 6, July 1974, pp. 24–28; James Goodwin, "T and John Brown: Transcendental Politics," *ESQ*, 25 (1979), 156–68; Michael Meyer, "Discord in Concord on the Day of John Brown's Hanging," *TSB*, No. 146 (1979), pp. 1–3.

CHAPTER FOUR. THE SEEN

1   See Paul O. Williams, "The Influence of T on the American Nature Essay," *TSB*, No. 145 (1978), pp. 1–5.

2   See Victor Angelescu, "HT's 'Night and Moonlight,' " *ESQ*, No. 22 (1961), pp. 64–67, also David Lyttle, "T's 'Diamond Body,' " *TJQ*, 7, Apr. 1975, pp. 18–29.

3   Willard G. Bonner is the writer who has gone into this aspect most carefully: see "Mariners and Terreners: Some Aspects of Nautical Imagery in T," *AL*, 34 (1962–63), 507–19, which shows that Thoreau used nautical imagery even when not writing about the sea, but does not deny his basic conviction that "man's proper place was on the shore"; "Captain T: Gubernator to a Piece of Wood," *NEQ*, 39 (1966), 26–46; and "T's River and T's Sea," *CS*, 8, Mar. 1974, pp. 2–4, which dissents from Sherman Paul's interpretation of the differences between Thoreau's use of the two symbols. See also R. K. Gupta, "T's Water Privileges in Walden," *TJQ*, 8, Oct. 1976, pp. 3–16, and Thoreau's letter to Charles Wyatt Rice, Aug. 5, 1836, printed in *TSB*, No. 145 (1978), pp. 5–6.

4   Various considerations of these matters will be found in E. J. Ross, "The Wit and Wisdom of T's 'Higher Laws,' " *Queen's Quarterly*, 69 (1963), 555–67; Charles R. Anderson, "T Takes a Pot Shot at *Carolina Sports*," *Georgia Review*, 22 (1968), 289–99; and Laurence Stapleton, *The Elected Circle* (Princeton University, 1973). On agriculture, see also John Paul Pritchard, "Cato in Concord," *CW*, 36 (1942), 3–4, and James S. Tillman, "The Transcendental Georgic in *Walden*," *ESQ*, 21 (1975), 137–41.

5   Robert Henry Walker, *Birds and Men: American Birds in Science, Art, Literature, and Conservation* (Harvard University Press, 1955).

6   See Joseph Wade, "Some Insects of T's Writings," *Journal of the New York Entomological Society*, 35 (1927), 1–21. Donald M. Murray, "T and the Example of the Muskrat," *TJQ*, 10, Oct. 1978, pp. 3–12, collects and interprets Thoreau's references to that animal, and James S. Hedges has an article on "The Cricket in the Journals," *TJQ*, 11, Apr. 1979, pp. 11–16.

7   Alan Seaburg, "Min Thoreau," *TSB*, No. 101 (1967), pp. 7–8, has assembled much of the lore about Thoreau's particular feline darling. Christabel Aberconway's book was published by Michael Joseph in 1949.

8   Yet Sayre himself calls Joe Polis "the most fully developed person (after the author

himself) to appear anywhere in Thoreau's writing. As Jim in *Huckleberry Finn* is the most realistic black portrait by a white writer in nineteenth-century American literature, Joe Polis is the most realistic and attractive native American." See also *TJQ*, 10, July 1978, pp. 10–13.

9 *Harper's Magazine*, 25 (1862), 270–71. In view of current developments, there can hardly be a more prescient passage in all Thoreau than his reference to the appearance at Eastham of an Indian calling himself Lieutenant Anthony who claimed to be the owner of land that had been preempted: "Who knows but a Lieutenant Anthony may be knocking at the door of the White House some day? At any rate, I know that if you hold a thing unjustly, there will surely be the devil to pay at the last."

10   Robert B. Sayre's book is *T and the American Indian* (Princeton University, 1977). Fussell's article, "The Red Face of Man," is in Sherman Paul's anthology, *T: A Collection of Critical Essays* (Prentice-Hall, 1962). See also Albert Keiser, *The Indian in American Literature* (Oxford University, 1933), and his article, "T's Manuscripts on the Indians," *JEGP*, 27 (1928), 183–99, which was the pioneering report on the 2800 pages of Indian manuscripts in the Morgan Library; Lawrence Willson, "T, Defender of the Savage," *ESQ*, No. 26 (1962), pp. 1–8; Mary P. Sherwood, "T's Penobscot Indians," *TJQ*, 1, Jan. 15, 1969, pp. 1–13; George W. Smith, Jr., "T and Bacon: The Idols of the Theatre," *ATQ*, No. 11 (1971), pp. 6–12; Bette S. Weidman, "T and Indians," *TJQ*, 5, Oct. 1973, pp. 4–10; Lauriat Lane, Jr., "T's Autumnal Indian," *Canadian Review of American Studies*, 6 (1975), 228–36; Jean Lantis, "The Place of the Indian in T's Vision," *CS*, 11, Winter 1976, pp. 9–15; Philip F. Gura, "T's Maine Woods Indians: More Representative Men," *AL*, 49 (1976–77), 366–84. Selections from the Indian notebooks have been published by Richard F. Fleck in *The Indians of T* (The Hummingbird Press, 1974); see also his "T's 'Indian Notebooks' and the Composition of *Walden*," *CS*, 7 June 1972, pp. 1–6; "Further Selections from the 'Indian Notebooks' " *TJQ*, 9 Jan. 1977, pp. 2–23; and "Some Unpublished Notes of T's on American Indian Practices," *CS*, 14, Spring 1974, p. 12–13.

11   For further useful and important comment upon some of the matters discussed above see Charles R. Metzger, "T on Science," *Annals of Science*, 12 (1956), 206–11; Albert F. McLean, Jr., "T's True Meridian: Natural Fact and Metaphor," *AQ*, 20 (1968), 567–79; and especially Eric R. Smith, "The Levels of Truth in T," *CS*, 11 June 1976, pp. 3–8.

12   On technology see further Leo Marx, *The Machine in the Garden: Technology and the Pastoral Ideal in America* (Oxford University, 1964) and the following: G. Ferris Cronkhite, "The Transcendental Railroad," *NEQ*, 24 (1951), 306–28; Lewis H. Miller, Jr., "T's Telegraphy," *ATQ*, No. 26, Suppl. (1975), pp. 14–18; Everett Carter, *The American Idea: The Literary Response to American Optimism* (University of North Carolina Press, 1977), especially pp. 106 ff.; Sam B. Girgus, "The Mechanical Mind: T and McLuhan on Freedom, Technology and the Media," *TJQ*, 9, Oct. 1977, pp. 3–9.

13   Representative discussions include Bradford Torrey, "T as a Diarist," *AM*, 95 (1905), 5–18; Fannie Hardy Eckstrom, "T's Maine Woods," *AM*, 102 (1908), 16–18, 242–50; John Burroughs, "Another Word on T," in *The Last Harvest* (Houghton

Mifflin, 1922); Charles D. Stewart, "A Word for T," *AM*, 156 (1935), 110–16.

14   Cf. in *Walden:* "I could always tell if visitors had called in my absence, either by the bended twigs or grass, or the print of their shoes, and generally what sex or age or quality they were by some slight trace left, as a flower dropped, or a bunch of grass plucked and thrown away, even as far off as the railroad, half a mile distant, or by the lingering odor of a cigar or pipe. I was frequently notified of the passage of a traveller along the highway sixty rods off by the scent of his pipe."

15   For further discussion of Thoreau's science, much more detailed and authoritative than can be given here, see Edward S. Deevey, Jr., "A Reexamination of T's *Walden*," *Quarterly Review of Biology*, 17 (1942), 1–11, and, with James S. Bishop, *Limnology*, Bulletin No. 63, Connecticut State Board of Game, reprinted in *TSB*, No. 33 (1950); Kathryn Whitford, "T and the Woodlots of Concord," *NEQ*, 23 (1950), 291–306, and, with Philip Whitford, "T, Pioneer Ecologist and Conservationist," *Scientific Monthly*, 73 (1951), 291–96, reprinted in Walter Harding, *T: A Century of Criticism* (Southern Methodist University, 1954). See also Raymond Adams, "T's Science,"*Scientific Monthly*, 60 (1943), 379–82; Alec Lucas, "T, Field Naturalist," *University of Toronto Quarterly*, 23 (1953–54), 227–32; Leo Stoller, "A Note on T's Place in the History of Phenology," *Isis*, 47 (1956), 172–81; Lawrence Willson, "T, Student of Anthropology," *American Anthropologist*, 61 (1959), 279–89; Donald G. Quick, "T as Limnologist," *TJQ*, 4, Apr. 15, 1972, pp. 13–20; Arthur G. Volkman, "HT, Physicist," *TSB*, No. 123 (1973), p. 4; Herbert Uhlig, "Improved Means to an Unimproved End," *TSB*, No. 128 (1974), pp. 1–3; Richard J. Schneider, "Reflections on Walden Pond: T's Optics," *ESQ*, 21 (1975), 65–75; Mary I. Kaiser, " 'Conversing with the Sky,' The Imagery of Celestial Bodies in T's Poetry," *TJQ*, 9, July 1977, pp. 15–20.

16   See, on this point, Nina Baym's important study, "T's View of Science," *JHI*, 26 (1965), 221–34. She finds "a pronounced anti-scientific bias as he becomes more obviously scientific"; his late journals "are at once more scientific in content and more opposed to science in comment." Cf. William W. Nichols, "Science and the Art of *Walden:* Experiment and Structure, " *ESQ*, No. 50, Suppl. (1960), pp. 77–84.

17   See Loren Eiseley, "T's Vision of the Natural World," in Ivan Massar, *The Illustrated World of T* (Grosset and Dunlap, 1974), pp. 165 ff., on his relationship to Darwinism and post-Darwinian developments. In the wake of Darwinism, "teleological direction" "was read out of the universe. It would reemerge later on in the twentieth century in more sophisticated guises that would have entranced Thoreau." Though granting that "it may be true enough that Thoreau in his last years never resolved his philosophical difficulties," Eiseley still thinks he forecast Alfred North Whitehead.

18   See Sherman Paul, *The Shores of America* (University of Illinois, 1958), pp. 378 ff.; James McIntosh, *T as Romantic Naturalist* (Cornell University, 1974), Chapter 6; also Mario L. D'Avanzo, "Fortitude and Nature in *Cape Cod*," *ESQ*, 20 (1974), 131–38. For Thoreau's adventure with the tides, see Walter Harding, *The Days of HT* (Knopf, 1927), pp. 382–83, and Ellen Watson, "T Visits Plymouth," *TSB*, No. 21 (1947), p. 1.

19   On the shipwreck, see Martin Leonard Pops, "An Analysis of T's *Cape Cod*,"

BNYPL, 67 (1963), 419–28; Lauriat Lane, Jr., "T's Response to the Maine Woods," *ESQ*, No. 47 (1967), pp. 37–41; Thomas Couser, "T's Cape Cod Pilgrimage," *ATQ*, No. 26, Suppl. (1975), pp. 31–36. On Ktaadn, see John G. Blair and Augustus Trowbridge, "T on Katahdin," *AQ*, 12 (1960), 508–17; John P. Jaques, " 'Ktaadn'—A Record of T's Youthful Crisis," *TJQ*, 1, Oct. 15, 1969, pp. 1–6; Jonathan Fairbanks, "T, Speaker for Wilderness," *SAQ*, 70 (1971), 487–506; Victor C. Friesen, "Alexander Heney and T's Climb of Mount Katahdin," *TSB*, No. 123 (1973), pp. 5–6; Lewis Leary, "Beyond the Brink of Fear: T's Wilderness," *Studies in the Literary Imagination*, 7, Spring 1974, pp. 67–76; Lewis H. Miller, Jr., "The Artist as Surveyor in *Walden* and *The Maine Woods*," *ESQ*, 21 (1975), 76–81. Charles W. Bassett, "Katahdin, Wachusett, and Kilimanjaro: The Symbolic Mountains of T and Hemingway," *TJQ*, 3, Apr. 15, 1971, pp. 1–10, concerns himself with both Thoreau's experiences. Friesen points out resemblances between Thoreau's ascent of Ktaadn and an incident recorded in Alexander Henry's *Travels and Adventures in Canada and the Indian Territories between the Years 1760 and 1776* (1809), which Thoreau knew, and suggests possible influence. Miller argues that Thoreau's most effective writing derives from a paradoxical tension arising from his secure awareness of limits and finds that where this is lacking, confusion and contradiction result. Walter Hesford, " 'Incessant Tragedies': A Reading of *A Week . . .* ," *ELH*, 44 (1977), 515–25, carries Thoreau's recognition of the hard side of nature and the tragic strain in human experience back to his earliest book.

20   In his *Emerson and T: Transcendentalists in Conflict* (Wesleyan University, 1966); also in "Emerson, T, and the Double Consciousness," *NEQ*, 41 (1968), 40–50.

21   B. R. Harding, "Swedenborgian Spirit and Thoreauvian Sense: Another Look at Correspondence," *Journal of American Studies*, 8 (1974), 65–79.

22   See, further, William Drake, "Spiritual Ideals and Scientific Fact: T's Search for Reality," *Utah State University Press Monograph Series*, Vol. 10, No. 1, Jan. 1, 1963; Tony Tanner, *The Reign of Wonder: Naivety and Reality in American Literature* (Cambridge University Press, 1965); Stuart Woodruff, "T as Water-Gazer," *ESQ*, No. 47 (1967), pp. 16–17; Carl Dennis, "Correspondence in T's Nature Poetry," *ESQ*, No. 58 (1968), pp. 101–09; William Reger, "Beyond Metaphor," *Criticism*, 4 (1970), 333–44; Larry R. Bowden, "Transcendence in *Walden*," *Religion in Life*, 46 (1977), 166–71.

CHAPTER FIVE. THE UNSEEN

1   See *TSB*, No. 129 (1972), p. 7.

2   See Robert and Betty Treat, "T and Institutional Christianity," *ATQ*, No. 1 (1969), pp. 44–47.

3   See Lawrence Willson, "T and Roman Catholicism," *Catholic Historical Review*, 42 (1956–57), 157–72.

4   See Theron E. Coffin, "HDT—Quaker?" *CS*, 10, Mar. 1975, pp. 4–9. Whatever may be thought of Thoreau's capacity, or lack of it, for being a good Quaker, there can

be no question that he did, in his own way, set up religious rites at Walden Pond, where everything from bathing to hoeing beans became a kind of religious exercise. This has been studied by Reginald L. Cook, "Ancient Rites at Walden," *ESQ*, No. 39 (1965), pp. 52–56, and by David E. Whishnant, "The Sacred and the Profane in *Walden*," *Centennial Review*, 14 (1970), 267–83. Leo Marx has an interesting suggestion on another phase of Thoreau's work in "T's Excursions," *YR*, 51 (1961–62), 363–69: "Adapting a conventional device of Christian writers, Thoreau uses the story of an excursion as a vehicle for a spiritual quest," but unlike Dante and Bunyan, he is more interested in the journey than the goal. William J. Wolf, who finds Thoreau's criticism of organized religion "justified . . . on nearly every count," still feels that "he fails to understand the corporate dimension in religious experience." He did not realize that to a large degree humanity's sacred books represent "the corporate response of individuals within their special historical traditions."

5   See, in this connection, Egbert S. Oliver, "T and the Puritan Tradition," *ESQ*, No. 44 (1966), pp. 79–86; Mason Lowance, Jr., "From Edwards to Emerson to T: A Revaluation," *ATQ*, No. 18 (1973), pp. 3–12; Alexander C. Kern, "Church, Scripture, Nature and Ethics in HT's Religious Thought," in Robert Falk, ed., *Literature and Ideas in America: Essays in Memory of Harry Hayden Clark* (Ohio University Press, 1975); John C. Hirsh, "HDT, Dewitt Miller, and Christian Bunsen's *Outlines of the Philosophy of Universal History*," *Papers of the Bibliographical Society of America*, 71 (1977), 351–56.

6   William J. Wolf, *T, Mystic, Prophet, Ecologist* (United Church Press, 1974), p. 163. Matthew leads with 116 references; Genesis comes next with 58. There are about 27 to the Psalter and many to the Wisdom Literature. Rupin W. Desai, "Biblical Light on T's Axe," *TSB*, No. 134 (1973), pp. 3–4, comments on an interesting echo of II Kings 6 in *Walden* and provides as good an illustration as can be found of the subtlety with which Thoreau used his literary references. Mario L. D'Avanzo, "T's Brick Pillow," *NEQ*, 50 (1977), 664–66, connects the brick pillow Thoreau speaks of in *Walden* with Jacob's pillow in Genesis and draws valid inferences concerning the religious implications of the Walden experiment. Edward and Karen Jacobs, "*Walden's* End and II Peter 1:19," *TJQ*, 10(1978), pp. 30–31, point out resemblances and probable indebtedness. See also Alison Ensor, "T and the Bible—Preliminary Considerations," *ESQ*, No. 33, Part 2 (1963), pp. 65–70; Larry R. Long, "T's Portmanteau Biblical Allusions," *TJQ*, 11, July–Oct. 1979, pp. 49–53.

7   Raymond Adams, "T and Immortality," *SP*, 27 (1929), 58–66; Mary Elkins Moller, " 'You Must First Have Lived': T and the Problem of Death," *ESQ*, 23 (1977), 226–39.

8   Thomas Blanding, "A Last Word from T," *CS*, 11, Winter 1976, pp. 16–17; Thomas Woodson, "Another Word on T's Last 'Good Sailing,' " *CS*, 12, Spring 1977, p. 17.

9   The pioneering study here was Helena A. Snyder's 1902 Heidelberg dissertation, *T's Philosophy of Life, with Special Consideration of the Influence of Hindu Philosophy*. Her method relies primarily on parallels between Thoreau and the Hindu writings, but she also considers music, love, and politics. See also Stephen D. Stracner, "*Walden*: T's *Vānaprasthya*," *TJQ*, 4, Jan. 1973, pp. 8–12.

10   Holbrook Jackson, *Dreamers of Dreams* (Farrar, Straus, n.d.), p. 222; Daniel Gregory Mason, "The Idealistic Basis of T's Genius," *Harvard Monthly*, 25 (1897), 82–93, reprinted in Walter Harding's *A T Profile* (Hill and Wang, 1971).

11   See my *Cavalcade of the English Novel* (Holt, 1943), pp. 464–65 n, and, more elaborately the introduction to Robert Nathan's *Portrait of Jennie*, in my anthology, *Six Novels of the Supernatural* (Viking Press, 1944).

12   Charles Calvin Kapp's Penn State dissertation (1963), "The Mysticism of HDT," found Thoreau a practising mystic and connected his "mystical beliefs and practices" with Jonathan Edwards and John Woolman. Walter Harding, *The Variorum Walden* (Twayne, 1962), p. 22, calls the second paragraph of the chapter on "Sounds" in *Walden* one of the most vivid descriptions of mystical experience in our literature, and I have quoted in Chapter 1 the poem "Inspiration," which, as Carl Bode points out, Thoreau "revised and refined" a number of times and quoted from half a dozen times in the *Week*. See Nils Bjorn Kvastad, "Mystical Influences in *Walden*," *TJQ*, 6, July 1974, pp. 3–10, and Roger C. Mueller, "T and the Art of Motorcycle Maintenance: Transcendentalism in Our Time," *TJQ*, 9, Oct. 1977, pp. 10–17. But the most careful and elaborate study of Thoreau's mystical experiences in their relationship to those of other mystics is in a very valuable article by Michael Keller, "HDT: A Transpersonal View," *Journal of Transpersonal Psychology*, 9 (1977), 43–82.

13   Joseph J. Kwiat, "T's Philosophical Apprenticeship," *NEQ*, 18 (1945), 51–69, stresses the influence of Dugald Steward and the "Scottish common-sense school," which Thoreau encountered at Harvard, "in preparing for the transition from the materialism of Locke and the utilitarianism of Paley, to the idealism of the Germans, Coleridge, and others." See also Nina Baym, "From Metaphysics to Metaphor: The Images of Water in Emerson and T," *Studies in Romanticism*, 5 (1965–66), 231–43; Gordon V. Boudreau, " 'Remember Thy Creator': T and St. Augustine," *ESQ*, 19 (1973), 149–60; Masayoshi Higashiyama, "A Japanese View of HDT," *TJQ*, 7, July 1975, pp. 25–29.

14   Wolf admits that the *Week* expresses reservations about the Divine Personality, but insists that most of Thoreau's names for God imply it; see Wolf's list on p. 72 of his book. Moreover, "the more picturesque titles are early; the more Biblical ones . . . become dominant in his later writings." There is an excellent brief discussion of Thoreau's religion from a somewhat different point of view than Wolf's in Charles A. Rogers, "God, Nature, and Personhood: T's Alternative to Inanity," *Religion in Life*, 48 (1979), 101–13.

15   Charles R. Metzger, "T on Science," *Annals of Science*, 12 (1956), 206–11.

SELECTED BIBLIOGRAPHY

I think it will be found
that he who speaks with most authority on a given subject
is not ignorant of what has been said by his predecessors.
He will take his place in a regular order,
and substantially add his own knowledge
to the knowledge of previous generations.
HDT, 1859

BIBLIOGRAPHICAL GUIDES

The basic bibliography is Francis H. Allen, *A Bibliography of HDT* (Houghton Mifflin, 1908), which has been several times supplemented by other writers. The best guide to Thoreauviana up to the date of its publication is Walter Harding, *A T Handbook* (New York University Press, 1959), of which a new edition, edited by Harding and Michael Meyer as *The New Thoreau Handbook* (New York University Press, 1980) has recently been published. Creative writing inspired by Thoreau or in which he figures is not covered in the following list, but see Harding, "A Bibliography of T in Poetry, Fiction, and Drama," *Bulletin of Bibliography*, 18 (1943), 15–18. Lewis Leary's review of Thoreau scholarship in Floyd Stovall, ed., *Eight American Authors* (Modern Language Association, 1956) is also important, as are the annual bibliographies in *PMLA* and the quarterly listings in *TSB*.

WRITINGS OF THOREAU

Since 1906 the standard edition of Thoreau's writings has been the Walden and Manuscript editions (twenty volumes, Houghton Mifflin), but this is now being superseded by the edition sponsored by the Modern Language Association and the National Endowment for the Humanities and published by Princeton University Press. Most of the editing of the fourteen volumes of the journal included in the Houghton Mifflin editions was done not by Bradford Torrey but by Francis H. Allen, who received no credit for it until the *Journal* was published separately in 1949. There is also a two-volume edition by Dover Publications. On omissions in the Walden-Manuscript edition of the journal and reprints thereof, see Harding, *Handbook*, pp. 82–84.

One volume of the journal was unavailable in 1906 and for long thereafter; this appeared in Perry Miller, *Consciousness in Concord: The Text of T's Hitherto "Lost Jour-*

nal" (1940–41), Together with Notes and a Commentary (Houghton Mifflin, 1958). Miller's commentary was very unsympathetic, and it is perhaps fortunate that his great reputation need not rest upon it, but surely nothing in it is so "frenetic," to use Odell Shepard's own word, as in the latter's savage review, "Unconsciousness in Cambridge: The Editing of T's Lost Journal," ESQ, No. 13 (1958), pp. 13–19.

For further writings by Thoreau, see Carl Bode, ed., Collected Poems of HT, Enlarged Edition (Johns Hopkins Press, 1964); The Moon (Houghton Mifflin, 1927); Leo Stoller, ed., Huckleberries (The Windhover Press of the University of Iowa and the New York Public Library, 1970). Thoreau's translation of The Transmigration of the Seven Brahmans, from the Harivansa of Langlois, has been edited by Arthur Christy (William Edwin Rudge, 1932) and that of The Seven Against Thebes by Leo Marx Kaiser, ESQ, No. 17 (1959).

F. B. Sanborn, ed., The First and Last Journeys of T, Lately Discovered among his Unpublished Journals and Manuscripts (two volumes, Boston: Bibliophile Society, 1905) contains some valuable materials, but, as with all Sanborn's work, the text is wholly unreliable. Harding, "Franklin B. Sanborn and T's Letters," BPLQ, 3 (1951), 288–93, demonstrates Sanborn's unreliability by specific examples.

Walter Harding has also published The Variorum Walden and The Variorum Civil Disobedience (Twayne, 1962 and 1967). Philip Van Doren Stern, ed., The Annotated Walden (Clarkson N. Potter, 1970) contains numerous passages not included in the final text. See also Harding's "Daniel Ricketson's Copy of Walden," Harvard Library Bulletin, 15 (1967), 401–11.

Richard F. Fleck has edited The Indians of T: Selections from the Indian Notebooks (Albuquerque, The Hummingbird Press, 1974); see also Carl Bode, "A New College Manuscript of T's," AL, 21 (1949–50), 311–20; Arthur Christy, "A T Fact-Book," Colophon, Part 16 (1934); Harding, "T and the Kalmucks: A Newly Discovered Manuscript," NEQ, 32 (1959), 91–92; Roger C. Mueller, "A Significant Buddhist Translation by T," TSB, No. 138 (1977), pp. 1–2.

Samuel Arthur Jones, ed., Some Unpublished Letters of Henry D. and Sophia E. Thoreau (Marion Press, 1899) was reprinted ESQ, No. 61 (1970), Part 2, but the definitive collection is Harding and Bode, eds., The Correspondence of HDT (New York University Press, 1958); see K. W. Cameron, "Annotations on T's Correspondence," ESQ, No. 24 (1961), 6–105; Companion to T's Correspondence, with Annotations, New Letters, and an Index of Principal Words, Phrases and Topics (Transcendental Books, 1964); Over T's Desk: New Correspondence, 1838–1861 (Transcendental Books, 1965). See, further, Albert F. McLean, Jr., "Addenda to the T Correspondence," BNYPL, 71 (1967), 265–67; also William White, "Three Unpublished T Letters," NEQ, 33 (1960), 372–74; Joseph J. Moldenhauer, "T to Blake; Four Letters Re-edited," TSLL, 8 (1966), 43–62.

The fullest volume of selections from T's writings is The Selected Works of T, Cambridge Edition, revised and with a new introduction by Walter Harding (Houghton Mifflin, 1975). The other two most important collections are Bartholow V. Crawford, ed., HDT: Representative Selections, with Introduction, Bibliography, and Notes (American Book Company, 1934) and Carl Bode, ed., The Portable T (Viking Press, 1947). Dudley C. Lunt's The River (Twayne, 1963) comprises selections from the journal, and The Living Thoughts of T (McKay, 1939) is interesting for the introduction by the editor, Theodore Dreiser. Howard Chapnick has edited *The Illustrated World of T: Words by HDT;* Photographs by Ivan Massar; with an afterword by Loren Eisely (Grosset and Dunlap, 1974). See also Charles R. Anderson, *T's World: Miniatures from his Journal* (Prentice-Hall, 1971).

ANTHOLOGIES OF THOREAU CRITICISM

Samuel Arthur Jones, ed., *Pertaining to T* (Edwin B. Hill, 1910), reprinted in *ESQ*, No. 62, Supplement (1971), was the earliest anthology of writing about T; the most extensive now is Wendell Glick, *The Recognition of T* (University of Michigan, 1939). Harding has edited three anthologies: *T: A Century of Criticism* (Southern Methodist University Press, 1954); *T, Man of Concord,* which comprises recollections and opinions of T's contemporaries (Holt, Rinehart and Winston, 1960); and *HDT: A Profile* (Hill and Wang, 1971). Others of value are Lauriat Lane, Jr., *Approaches to Walden* (Wadsworth, 1961); Sherman Paul, *T: A Collection of Critical Essays;* and Richard Ruland, *Twentieth Century Interpretations of Walden* (Prentice-Hall, 1962 and 1968).

Harding has also edited two valuable symposia: *The T Centennial: Papers Marking the Observance in New York City of the One Hundredth Anniversary of the Death of HDT* (State University of New York Press, 1964) and, with George Brenner and Paul A. Doyle, a collection of papers delivered at Nassau Community College: *HDT: Studies and Commentaries* (Fairleigh Dickinson University Press, 1972). See also John H. Hicks, ed., *T in Our Season* (University of Massachusetts Press, 1966), which is largely reprinted from *The Massachusetts Review,* Autumn 1962—"A Centenary Gathering for HDT" —and William Bysshe Stein, ed., *New Approaches to T: A Symposium* (1969), whose general subject is "the poetic of perception" but which also touches on other matters.

BOOKS ABOUT THOREAU

There follows a list of books about T, with a few pamphlets, arranged alphabetically by author:

Charles R. Anderson, *The Magic Circle of Walden* (Holt, Rinehart and Winston, 1968); J. Brooks Atkinson, *HT, The Cosmic Yankee* (Knopf, 1927); Leon Bazalgette, *HT, Bachelor of Nature,* translated by Van Wyck Brooks (Harcourt, 1924); Henry Seidel Canby, *T* (Houghton Mifflin, 1939); Stanley Cavell, *The Senses of Walden* (Viking, 1972); William Ellery Channing, *T, The Poet-Naturalist, with Memorial Verses,* New Edition, enlarged, ed. F. B. Sanborn (Charles E. Goodspeed, 1902); John Aldrich Christie, *T as World Traveler* (Columbia University Press, 1965); William Condry, *T* (Philosophical Library, 1924); Reginald L. Cook, *The Concord Saunterer . . .* (Middlebury College Press, 1940) and *Passage to Walden* (Houghton Mifflin, 1949).

August Derleth, *Concord Rebel: A Life of Henry D. Thoreau* (Chilton, 1962); Robert Dickens, *T, The Complete Individualist, His Relevance—and Lack of It—for our Time* (Exposition Press, 1974); Leon Edel, *Henry D. Thoreau* (University of Minnesota Press, 1970) and *The Mystery of Walden Pond* (University of Hawaii, 1971); Edward Waldo Emerson, *HT as Remembered by a Young Friend* (Houghton Mifflin, 1917), to which may be added the same writer's "Personal Recollections," [London] *Bookman,* 52 (1917),

81–84. Ralph Waldo Emerson's article on Thoreau's death, in the Boston *Advertiser*, May 9, 1862, has been reprinted in a pamphlet, *Henry D. Thoreau: Emerson's Obituary* (Ysleta, Edwin B. Hill, 1942).

Arthur L. Ford, *The Poetry of HDT* (Transcendental Books, 1970); Frederick Garber, *T's Redemptive Imagination* (Rutgers University Press, 1977); David Mason Greene, *The Frail Duration: A Key to Symbolic Structure in Walden* (San Diego College Press, 1966); Walter Harding, *The Days of HT* (Knopf, 1965), now the standard biography, also *T's Library* (University of Virginia Press, 1957), and, with Milton Meltzer, *A T Profile* (Crowell, 1962); George Hendrick, ed., *Remembrances of Concord and the Thoreaus: Letters of Horace Hosmer to Dr. S. A. Jones* (University of Illinois Press, 1977); Henry Beetle Hough, *T of Walden: The Man and his Eventful Life* (Simon and Schuster, 1956); Allen Beecher Hovey, *The Hidden T* (Beirut, N.p., 1966); William L. Howarth, *A T Gazeteer* (Princeton University Press, 1970) and *The Literary Manuscripts of HDT* (Ohio State University Press, 1974); Joseph Ishill, *T, The Cosmic Yankee* (The Oriole Press, 1954); Samuel A. Jones, *T: A Glimpse* (Concord: Albert Lane, The Erudite Press, 1903); Joseph Wood Krutch, *HDT* (William Sloane Associates, 1948) and *The Last Boswell Paper* (Printed for the Friends of Philip and Fanny Duschnes, 1951).

Annie Russell Marble, *T, His Home, Friends and Books* (Crowell, 1902); James McIntosh, *T as Romantic Naturalist* (Cornell University Press, 1974); Michael Meyer, *Several More Lives to Live: T's Political Reputation in America* (Greenwood Press, 1977); Charles R. Metzger, *T and Whitman: A Study of Their Esthetics* (University of Washington Press, 1968); Sterling North, *T of Walden Pond* (Houghton Mifflin, 1959); H. A. Page (pseud. A. H. Japp), *T, His Life and Aims* (James R. Osgood, 1877); Sherman Paul, *The Shores of America: T's Inward Exploration* (University of Illinois Press, 1958); Joel Porte, *Emerson and T: Transcendentalists in Conflict* (Wesleyan University Press, 1966); Bland Wells Robbins, *Discovery at Walden* (N.p., 1957), an account of the excavation of the site of T's cabin.

H. S. Salt, *The Life of HDT* (Richard Bentley and Son, 1890), the best early biography; F. B. Sanborn, *HDT* (Houghton Mifflin, 1882), *The Life of HDT, including Many Essays Hitherto Unpublished and Some Account of his Family and Friends* (Houghton Mifflin, 1917), and *The Personality of T* (first published in 1901, reprinted by The Folcroft Press, 1969); Robert P. Sayre, *T and the American Indians* (Princeton University Press, 1977); Nathaniel H. Seerfurth, *T: A View from Emeritus* (The Seerfurth Foundation, 1968), reprinted *ESQ*, No. 54, Supplement, 1968; Ethel Seybold, *T: The Quest and the Classics* (Yale University Press, 1951); J. Lyndon Shanley, *The Making of Walden, with the Text of the First Edition* (University of Chicago Press, 1957), the definitive study of the structure and development of the work.

Philip Van Doren Stern, *HDT, Writer and Rebel* (Crowell, 1972); Leo Stoller, *After Walden: T's Changing Views on Economic Man* (Stanford University Press, 1957); J. Golden Taylor, *Neighbor T's Critical Humor, Utah State University Monograph Series,* Vol. VI, No. 1 (1968); James Thorpe, *T's Walden* (The Huntington Library, 1977); Raymond P. Tripp, Jr., *With Pen of Truth* (The Society for New Language Study, 1972), an interpretation of *Walden* in terms of "Carl Jungian psychology, Owen Barfield in semantics, and Mircea Eliade in the history of religions"; Mark Van Doren, *HDT: A*

Critical Study (Houghton Mifflin, 1916); George F. Whicher, *Walden Revisited: A Centennial Tribute to HDT* (Packard and Company, 1945); William J. Wolf, *T, Mystic, Prophet, Ecologist* (United Church Press, 1974).

BOOKS CONTAINING SECTIONS ABOUT THOREAU

Among the many books containing sections on Thoreau or in which he figures prominently mention may be made here of the following, again in alphabetical order by author:

Carl Bode, *The Half World of American Culture* (Southern Illinois University Press, 1965); Mary Hosmer Brown, *Memories of Concord* (The Four Seas Company, 1926); Lawrence Buell, *Literary Transcendentalism: Style and Vision in the American Renaissance* (Cornell, 1973); Arthur Christy, *The Orient in American Transcendentalism: A Study of Emerson, T, and Alcott* (Columbia, 1932); George Willis Cooke, *Memorabilia of the Transcendentalists of New England,* which has been reprinted in *ATQ,* No. 27 (1975); Thomas Edward Crawley, ed., *Four Makers of the American Mind* (Duke University Press, 1976); Norman Foerster, *Nature in American Literature: Studies in the Modern View of Nature* (Macmillan, 1913); John Paul Pritchard, *Return to the Fountains* (Duke University Press, 1942); Robert D. Richardson, Jr., *Myth and Literature in the American Renaissance* (Indiana University Press, 1978); Anna and Walton Ricketson, eds. *Daniel Ricketson and his Friends: Letters, Poems, Sketches, etc.* (Houghton Mifflin, 1902); Eric J. Sundquist, *Home as Found: Authority and Genealogy in Nineteenth-Century American Literature* (Johns Hopkins University Press, 1979).

MATERIAL ON THOREAU AND OTHER TRANSCENDENTALISTS

Kenneth Walter Cameron has published through Transcendental Books, Hartford, an immense amount of important background material for the study of T. See *Emerson, T and Concord Early Newspapers* (1958); *The Transcendentalists and Minerva: Cultural Backgrounds of the American Renaissance with Fresh Discoveries in the Intellectual Climate of Emerson, Alcott, and T* (three volumes, 1958); *Transcendental Climate: New Resources for the Study of Emerson, T and their Contemporaries* (three volumes, 1963); *T's Literary Notebook in the Library of Congress* (1964); *T's Fact Book in the Harry Elkins Widener Collection in the Harvard College Library* (two volumes, 1968); *T's Canadian Notebook and Record of Surveys* (1967); *Transcendentalist Apprenticeship: Notes on Young HT's Reading: A Contexture with a Researcher's Index* (1976). See also Cameron's "T's Three Months Out of Harvard and his First Publication," *ESQ,* No. 5 (1956), pp. 2–10, and note #2 on "Biography" section.

PERIODICAL RESOURCES

Articles about Thoreau in periodicals are far too numerous to be listed here; those to which the writer is most indebted or to which he would like to refer his readers for further information are listed in the notes. Lewis Leary's *Articles on American Litera-*

ture, 1900–1950 and *Articles on American Literature, 1950–1967* (Duke University Press, 1954 and 1970) are immensely useful compilations for the periods covered. Three periodicals are exclusively devoted to Thoreau: *The Thoreau Society Bulletin, The Concord Saunterer,* and *The Thoreau Journal Quarterly.* The first hundred issues of *TSB* have been reprinted in a single volume by Johnson Reprint Corporation, 1970; there is also *A Bibliography of the TSB Bibliographies, 1941–1969: A Cumulation and an Index,* ed. Walter Harding (The Whitston Publishing Company, 1971). The Thoreau Society has also published a series of Thoreau Society Booklets.

INDEX

Library of Congress Cataloging in Publication Data
Wagenknecht, Edward Charles, 1900–
Henry David Thoreau: What manner of man?
(New England writers series)
Bibliography: p.
Includes index.
1. Thoreau, Henry David, 1817–1862—Biography—
Character.   2 Authors, American—19th century—
Biography.   I. Title.   II. Series.
PS3053.W26   818'.309 [B]   80–23542
ISBN 0–87023–136–7
ISBN 0–87023–137–5 (pbk.)